MW00809433

www.veloce.co.uk

First published in June 2022 by Veloce Publishing Limited, Veloce House, Parkway Farm Business Park, Middle Farm Way, Poundbury, Dorchester DT1 3AR, England. Tel +44 (0)1305 260068 / Fax 01305 250479 / e-mail info@veloce.co.uk / web www.veloce.co.uk or www.velocebooks.com.
ISBN: 978-1-787117-87-7; UPC: 6-36847-01787-3.

© 2022 Jack Barlow and Veloce Publishing. All rights reserved. With the exception of quoting brief passages for the purpose of review, no part of this publication may be recorded, reproduced or transmitted by any means, including photocopying, without the written permission of Veloce Publishing Ltd. Throughout this book logos, model names and designations, etc, have been used for the purposes of identification, illustration and decoration. Such names are the property of the trademark holder as this is not an official publication. Readers with ideas for automotive books, or books on other transport or related hobby subjects, are invited to write to the editorial director of Veloce Publishing at the above address. British Library Cataloguing in Publication Data – A catalogue record for this book is available from the British Library. Typesetting, design and page make-up all by Veloce Publishing Ltd on Apple Mac. Printed in India by Parksons Graphics.

THE LANCE MACKLIN STORY
A RACE WITH INFAMY

VELOCE PUBLISHING
THE PUBLISHER OF FINE AUTOMOTIVE BOOKS

Table of contents

Introduction & Acknowledgements

At the end of the Second World War Europe lay in ruins, its cities and towns destroyed. Millions were dead and millions more bore the scars of war. As a generation looked for an escape from the bleak, unremitting grind of daily existence, eyes increasingly turned to the race track.

Motorsport started gradually, through hillclimbs and on haphazardly converted aerodromes, the cars an unruly mix of pre-war behemoths and nimble backyard specials. For drivers and spectators it soon became a favourite outlet to avoid the harsh realities of postwar life, even if only for a few hours at a time. As racing's popularity grew it soon forged a new generation of stars – dashing young men who had either been in the war or, increasingly more often, had grown up surrounded by those who had. Moss, Fangio, Hawthorn, Collins, Ascari, Farina: they were semi-mythical figures, brave, charismatic, dazzling. The previous generation looked up to fighter pilots. The new one gazed in awe at racing drivers.

Cut to early 1947, Belgrave Square, London. The stillness of a cold, drizzly night is shattered as an ancient Invicta emerges out of the gloom. Its driver throws it sideways on the street's slippery wooden blocks, its engine revving, the crackling, snorting exhaust notes echoing around the surrounding buildings. Lance Macklin, 27 years old, is getting ready to join the new breed of heroes. Europe's race tracks beckon. He's ready.

Acknowledgements

The material in this book was sourced from a mix of first-hand interviews, historical interviews, and a rag-tag collection of books, magazine articles and internet sleuthing.

Two texts proved particularly indispensable: Peter Lewis' *Alf*

Francis, Racing Mechanic (Motoraces Book Club) – the entertaining memoir of hard-bitten HWM mechanic Alf Francis – was essential for understanding the exhausting tour of Europe's race tracks that the HWM team, and others, undertook. Francis obviously kept excellent notes.

Christopher Hilton's *Le Mans '55* (DB Publishing) shed much light on the Le Mans crash of that year. Containing a wealth of interviews with all the key players, it brought clarity to an event that was – on the day itself as well as subsequently – very complex. No mean feat.

Other texts I made use of include Mark Kahn's quote-rich *Death Race: Le Mans 1955* (Barrie & Jenkins); John Wyer and Chris Nixon's two *Racing With the David Brown Aston Martins* (Transport Bookman Publications) volumes; Chris Nixon's *Mon Ami, Mate* (Transport Bookman Publications); Mike Hawthorn's memoir *Challenge Me the Race* (William Kimber and Co); Donald Healey's *My World of Cars* (Patrick Stephens Ltd); Robert Edwards' *Stirling Moss: The Authorised Biography* (Orion): Stirling Moss' own *My Racing Life* (Evro Publishing); and Duncan Hamilton's autobiography *Touch Wood* (John Blake). Though the latter didn't mention Macklin specifically, it did give an excellent feel for the life lived by racing drivers of the time.

I'd like to thank the following for agreeing to be interviewed for the book, and/or for sending me their recollections: Shelagh Montague Browne; Perry Macklin; Michael Harrison; the late Sir Stirling Moss; the late Louise Collins; Allan Dick; Howden Ganley; Bob Constanduros; Ian Dove; Alastair Jones; Mike Harting; David Abecassis; George Huntoon. Also, thank you to the British Racing Drivers' Club, David Freestone, Screen Archive South East and Louis Galanos for digging out some late-in-the-day treasures. Apologies to anyone I may have missed, but rest assured your contributions were greatly appreciated.

Special thanks to the following: Gill Macklin, for providing an invaluable trove of precious letters and photographs, as well as illuminating phone conversations; Miranda Kelly and the Kelly family, for providing interviews, access to the family library, and letting me stay at Romden while writing and researching the book; Paddy Macklin, for the interviews, kind words and encouragement; Martin Buckley, for the run through of Facel history and tapes of Macklin's last interviews; Simon Taylor and the *Classic & Sports Car* team for the tips, contacts and help in getting the project started; Mark Hughes, for the encouragement when it was sorely needed; and the Veloce team, especially Rod Grainger, who saw fit to pick up the project when it was very nearly dead in the water.

On a final, personal, note I'd also like to thank everyone who put me up in the UK and Europe while working on the project: my mother and the rest of the Auckland family; my wife, Rachael, for the unwavering support while being dragged around the other side of the world with next to no money (we'd just started dating at the time!), and my dad, whose idea this was in the first place, and without whose support and belief this never would have happened.

Jack Barlow

Chapter 1

Noel

Appropriately enough, given what was to come later, the earliest memories of young Lancelot Noel Macklin centred on great tales of adventure. Perched on his grandmother Ada Macklin's knee, he would listen, enraptured, while Ada rolled off stories about wild oceans, windswept deserts, and arduous hikes through strange lands. His favourite, he would later write, was Ada's terrifying account of a turbulent journey across the Pacific Ocean in late 1896. With the ship rolling around in the throes of a massive storm, Ada looked out to see a gigantic wave bearing down on the small ship. "My grandmother rushed up to [the captain] and frantically asked 'are we sinking?'" Macklin recounted. "The captain replied, in a voice of the utmost calm, 'Lady, I can assure you that you are safer here than you would be in Piccadilly Circus.'" It was just the sort of thing that would make a young, impressionable boy squeal in delight.

– – – – –

Lance Macklin came from a remarkable family. In later life, during a rare period of application, he picked up a pen and wrote up an adventure-filled family history, drawing largely on the thrilling tales he'd been told by his parents and grandparents. It's an interesting read, written in a very matter-of-fact tone, with special emphasis on the scoundrels, explorers and ne'er-do-wells that most appealed to Macklin. There's the pioneer of modern acting Charles McLaughlin, "a rather irascible fellow" who, at the height of his fame, killed a man in a fight over a wig by poking out his eye with a cane. There's John Macklin, a roamer, writer and part-time soldier who mysteriously squandered the family fortune. Then there's a gap – "it's probably not very difficult to ... have this lineage traced," Macklin wrote, although he evidently didn't bother doing so – that ends with the birth of Lance's grandfather, Charles Campbell Macklin, in 1866. But the vast majority of the book, a good three-quarters or so, centres around one man whose life loomed largest over Lance Macklin's own. It was his father, Sir Albert Noel Campbell Macklin.

Noel Macklin was a great man by any measure. Handsome, with blue captivating eyes and an exceptionally inventive mind, he had an almost unrivalled work ethic that made so many of his projects great successes. Born in Australia to English parents – the adventurous Ada and her husband Charles – in 1886, Noel grew up in the distinctly un-English environment of Perth, Western Australia. The relatively carefree existence suited him, and he quickly showed impressive sporting prowess and flashes of the application that would later serve him so well.

In his late teens he underwent a drastic shift, hauled over to England by his parents to attend the prestigious Eton College. The change from outback roustabout to member of English high society must have come as a shock, although he seems to have acquitted himself rather well. Sporting prowess, after all, is easily translatable. Still, his academic career at Eton, rather like his son's in years to come, was not quite so impressive. "Noel seems to have been a fairly average pupil at Eton," his son wrote, "and while he was good at most games he does not seem to have excelled in anything in particular."

Noel quickly grew into an adventurous and capable young man. He also developed a penchant for raising hell in typically inventive ways, from the innocuous – heating copper coins and leaving them on the ground for passers-by to pick up – to the downright dangerous – getting hold of a pet lion, then shepherding it around the streets of London trying to get rid of it. His sporting prowess continued to develop, and he soon became known as a talented jockey, skier and, briefly, a big game hunter. A troublemaker and an exceptionally talented sportsman: qualities, again, that his son would later take to extremes.

Then there were the cars. Noel was captivated at an early age by the roaring, fire-snorting beasts, at that stage in their infancy. After leaving Eton without any great distinction, he promptly went out and bought an early Fiat that he called Mephistopheles. It was a fittingly mythical name for such a brutal car. Large, powerful, and with an almost complete lack of safety equipment – this was around 1910, after all – Noel learned to handle it by bravely flying round the famous banks of the Brooklands race track. True to form, he then took what he learned from the race track to the street, roaring around London at speeds far in excess of the 20 miles an hour speed limit then strictly imposed on the open road.

Naturally enough, it quickly got him into trouble with the law. At one point he even made it into the local press, with a 1911 edition of the *News Chronicle* penning a piece entitled "A Motorist's Wedding Present" after one particularly noteworthy scrape with local police. "Mr Montague Sharp KC and other magistrates sitting at the Middlesex Sessions this morning heard the appeal of Noel Campbell Macklin of Elm Park Gardens, Chelsea, a law student, against a sentence of one month's imprisonment, inflicted by the Feltham Justices on February 27th, for driving a motor car without a licence," it said. "Mr Laurie appeared in support of the conviction and stated that the sentence was passed (after Macklin) had on previous occasions been fined, once for dangerous driving, and five times for exceeding the speed limit. On December 7th he was fined in his absence and his licence was withdrawn."

The headline concerned Noel's wedding to Esme Stewart, his first wife. The incident had apparently occurred just before the couple's wedding day. Although Stewart was adventurously minded like her husband, even taking Mephistopheles out herself on regular occasions, their marriage didn't last long. Its failure was quickly swept under the rug, hidden out of sight and never talked about. Indeed, so serious was the taboo of a failed marriage that Lance didn't find out about it until he reached the age of 12, and even then only by ruffling through old newspapers with his sisters. Unbeknownst to almost everyone, Macklin and Stewart's divorce hadn't been finalised by the time Lance was born to Noel's second wife, Leslie Cordery, on September 2, 1919. Technically speaking, he was a bastard child. It remained a secret for years. When Lance's first wife found out, long after his death, she howled with laughter.

Noel led a privileged life as a member of the English landed gentry: skiing in St Moritz, travelling the world, and driving fast cars. This good life was brought to an abrupt halt on 28 July, 1914, when the First World War broke out and Europe was plunged into chaos. It was to prove a rough war for Noel. Sent into the Royal Field Artillery in 1914, he was lucky enough to survive the war's early bloodbaths, but was badly wounded in France in 1915 and sent home to recover. Later, after a couple of years spent recuperating, he was directed towards the Royal Naval Volunteer Reserve on the grounds that it was probably an easier wartime career for someone who'd suffered from a serious injury. It was, but the wounds he sustained on that muddy battlefield in France – both physical and psychological – never entirely healed. Haunted by shell-shock, and with a leg wound that spelled the end of his racing career, he kept a physician near him at all times for the rest of his life. Near the end of the war he remarried and his love-struck second wife, Leslie, completely devoted herself to his welfare. It was an arrangement that would last the rest of Noel's life.

It was partly because of Noel's constant need for care that his three children, Lance and his sisters Mia and Nada, grew up in an environment of material excess but emotional unavailability. "They wanted for nothing, those children," Shelagh Montague Browne, Lance Macklin's first wife, said. "In a way Noel did this to compensate for the fact that he was a very sick man. If they wanted to go skiing, they'd be sent skiing. If Lance wanted polo ponies, he got polo ponies.

"Leslie's whole life was spent looking after Noel. Nursing him was all she dedicated herself to, and she did it very, very well. But it meant that these children were so spoilt and had everything they wanted, except their parents. And that doesn't always work."

As an adult, when Lance talked about Noel, as he would from time to time, it tended to be with a mixture of pride and admiration. Yet underneath it all, invisible to most but those who knew him best, was just the slightest touch of hurt. "My father was a charming, though self-centred, man," he told journalist Mark Kahn in the book *Death Race*. "My mother had very little to do with her children. We were brought up almost entirely by governesses and nannies, and we hardly ever saw our parents." Growing up in the beautiful family home in Cobham, with family portraits proudly hanging on the walls and mementoes of Noel's exotic journeys scattered around, proved an oddly lonely existence. "We would be brought down on a Sunday, be presented to the family, if you can imagine it, sing a little song, recite a little piece of verse, and then be whisked back to the nursery," he later remembered. It was, he said, a "curiously Victorian atmosphere."

Noel's three children were all born within a relatively short period of time. Nada came first, in November 1917, followed by Lance in September 1919 and Mia in 1920. They were born just as Noel began his first foray into the motoring business, deciding to have a go as a manufacturer after the premature end of his driving career. Beginning with the Eric-Campbell marque in 1919, before moving onto the equally short-lived Silver Hawk, Macklin's ambitions were fully realised with the 1925 creation of the Invicta. Funded mostly by Oliver Lyle, an enthusiastic sugar magnate, the ambitious Invicta combined style, luxury and reliability in a tidy, if pricey, package. It was exactly what Noel wanted. Unable to perform the driving duties himself, Noel enlisted his sister-in-law Violette Cordery to prove the car's mettle, which she did with gusto. Beginning with a half-mile sprint victory at Brooklands in 1925, her and Noel's ambitions for the car grew as they began hopping around Europe, knocking over record after record.

In March 1926, Cordery travelled to the famous Monza track in Italy where she broke several long distance records, covering 10,000 miles at 56.47mph, and 15,000 miles at 55.76mph. Several months later, at the Autodrome de Montlhéry outside Paris, she and her team of co-drivers covered 5000 miles at 70.7mph over the course of 70 hours. In 1929 she was awarded the Dewar Trophy for logging 30,000 miles in 30,000 minutes at Brooklands. She was a press favourite, a symbol of the golden age of adventure. Her talent, gutsy nature and good looks were the stuff of many a glowing headline.

In 1927 she took the Invicta on its most famous voyage, a 'round the world' trip that began in France and wound its way through North Africa, Egypt, India, Australia, the United States and Canada. Such an undertaking would be difficult enough now, but in 1927, during the early years of motoring and in countries where proper roads hadn't even been thought of, it was ambitious almost to the point of delusion.

True to form, though, Cordery was unperturbed. In February 1927 she set off with a nurse, a mechanic and an apprehensive Royal Automobile Club observer in tow. Footage of the trip still exists: grainy, shaky shots of staring locals, shacks, herds of cows fleeing in fright. "In many parts of the world that they passed through the local populations had seldom seen a car, let alone one driven by an attractive fair-haired young girl," Lance noted. After five months and 10,266 miles, she returned home to a rapturous reception. Her fame, as well as that of the Invicta marque, was assured.

Popular though Invicta proved to be, the company's success didn't exactly send rivers of money flooding the Macklin family's way. Though they lived a life of comfort, shifting between various beautiful houses with a retinue of servants, they weren't quite as rich as they seemed. "They had money, but not that much money," Montague Browne said. "They always lived as if they had pots of it, with maids and butlers, cooks and chauffeurs. Leslie wasn't born into that at all, although she took to it like a duck to water." It's interesting to note that, of the three Macklin siblings, the two who ended up wealthy married into old, moneyed families. Lance never did. Still, while they may not have been as wealthy as the others they were surrounded by, they were still flush enough to go on regular expeditions to Switzerland and Monaco. Through their storied history as well as Noel's exploits the family also acquired a great amount of prestige in the right circles, something that counted for a lot in the stratified, class-conscious society of early 20th century England. To put it bluntly, being a Macklin in the 1920s and 1930s was no bad thing.

Young Lance's early years were fraught with conflicting emotions, especially when it came to his parents. He looked up to Noel with a great amount of pride, but he was always deeply hurt that his father didn't pay him much attention. The same applied to his mother, leading to a resentment he carried towards her for the rest of his life. Even though he would regularly visit her at her home in Monaco in later years, the two would frequently end up in fiery arguments. Never a hothead, Lance's visits would nevertheless often end with him storming out in a fury. "She's impossible," he once told his then-wife after another heated exchange. "She sacrificed everything and never did anything with us because she was always looking after (Noel)." Being Lance's wife and Leslie's beloved daughter-in-law, Shelagh Montague Browne got to hear from both sides afterwards. "Leslie always said 'I don't understand my children, they don't really seem to care about me at all,'" she said. "Of course, I couldn't actually say 'well, they say you don't really care about them either.'"

Though Lance spent his time constantly surrounded by people and with all the material goods he wanted, he was often lonely. It was a period that would have long-lasting implications, its effects reverberating long into adulthood.

– – – – –

Noel's inquisitive mind and determined nature occasionally led him and his family into some extraordinary scenarios. During a brief period around 1921, between the end of Silver Hawk and the beginning of Invicta, Noel found himself at a loose end. In idle moments he thought back to a theory that he had been working on for a few years concerning, as he called it, "the law of chance and probability." It was something that had come to him while on his semi-frequent trips to Monte Carlo and its famous, luxurious casino. Could there be, he wondered to himself, a way to predict patterns in supposedly unpredictable sequences? In other words: was there a way to break the bank?

He wasn't, of course, the first person in history to ponder this. However, he was likely one of the most determined. He immediately threw all his considerable intellectual power into finding an answer. He bought every book on the matter that he could, spending hours in his study reading long into the night. He spoke to every suitable person he could think of. Casinos would often publish pamphlets detailing every throw made on a particular table throughout the day, and Noel made a special trip to the Monte Carlo casino to buy up the last 100 issues of these small pamphlets, taking them back to England. Once back home he would get a friend to dismantle their mass of numbers into colours, combinations and sequences. These were drawn out as lines on massive graphs, forming a bewildering array of different frequencies and shapes.

Noel took over a room in the family home that must have ended up looking like the product of mad professor – which, in a way, it was – and spent hours poring over the charts, searching for the patterns that he was sure lay among the jumble of lines and numbers. Sure enough, as he'd suspected, little sequences began to emerge. There were long runs of red or black that would keep going – the trick, which Noel suspected he'd figured out, was knowing when to back out before the run ended. He was delighted. Still, he knew the difference between proving something on a series of graphs in a room and actually seeing if it worked in reality. There was only one thing for it. In mid-1921, not long after the dissolution of Silver Hawk, he dragged the ever-obedient Leslie and Lance, Nada and Mia to Monte Carlo. It was time, he decided, to give it a go.

The timing was convenient. Just before the Macklin family left England Noel sold the family home, a gothic mansion they nicknamed Glengariff, and bought a new place a few miles down the road in Cobham. A relatively humble – by their standards, at least – country cottage, Noel decided to christen the new home Fairmile. It was a name that would later become famous around the world. For now, though, the family's focus lay elsewhere, across the channel and in the exquisitely exotic, palm tree-lined streets of Monaco.

The entourage immediately moved into a villa Noel rented in the hills just outside Monte Carlo. While Leslie looked after their young family Noel immediately set to work, requisitioning one of the rooms as an "operations room" that bustled with a frenetic energy. The walls were papered with charts, telephones were set up – one with a direct line to the Monte Carlo casino – while a sizable team of friends and family were constantly taking calls, making notes and shouting out the latest casino plays. Someone was chosen as the team's "professional player," heading to the casino every day with detailed notes on what bets to place and when. Word about Noel's obsession spread throughout the town, the intrigued locals greeting it as the workings of another eccentric, wealthy Englishman.

Things quickly settled down into a routine. The results gradually began to unfold and, as Noel had suspected, it turned out that there was a way to pick and time your runs and to come out on top if you played often enough. Making masses of money was never the object of the exercise but, nonetheless, Noel consistently made enough to pay off the rather large expenses of renting the villa and maintaining the operations team. Of course, the casino noticed, too. One morning Noel took the inquisitive casino director up to the villa, figuring it would be best if he could see what was going on for himself. Amiable enough, the director was shocked when he walked into the communications room. He looked around at the charts, the women on the phones, the people rushing to and fro, the desks with pencils, pens and rulers scattered haphazardly. He started to sweat.

"Mr. Macklin," he said when he'd gathered himself. "First of all I would like to thank you for showing me all this and I have to say that I am very impressed." He muttered about the casino not being overly worried about their losses, which were relatively small by their standards. Then he cleared his throat. "There is one thing that worries me, though." Noel, revelling in having worried the director of the Monte Carlo casino, suppressed his glee and asked the director what the problem was. "Mr Macklin, would you mind telling me exactly what your intentions are with regard to your system. I mean, how do you intend to exploit it in the future? Are you intending to publish a book showing people how it works?" Noel, who had been stifling so much as a smile, laughed. "Good heavens no," he exclaimed. He explained he was doing if out of his own curiosity and that, once the six-month lease on the villa was up, the family would be on their way back to England. "By the end of that time I should have reached a fairly conclusive result one way or the other," he added, thoughtfully. The casino director, no doubt staggered by the bounds of Noel's curiosity, was also thoroughly relieved. Four months later, just as he said, Noel wrapped everything up and the family headed back over to England.

Lance didn't have any real memories of the Monte Carlo expedition, being all of two years old when the family headed there. Still, he would talk about it in later years as an example of his father's tenacity and single-mindedness. The two even discussed it shortly before Noel died. "The law of chance is rather like perpetual motion," Noel told his son. "A lot of brilliant minds have been occupied trying to find solutions to both, but although many people have got close no one has ever, or probably ever will, solve either problem completely." Lance took note, although his father's words didn't stop him turning his own mind to similar problems in later years. Again, like father, like son.

Chapter 2

Mischief-maker

Lance Macklin's life until the age of eight was relatively sedate, with occasional trips to the continent offsetting the odd emotional vacuum that existed at home. At the age of eight, he was unceremoniously uprooted from his stable life at home and sent to a prep school in Camberley, a small town in Surrey. It was a seismic shift from the sheltered life he'd been leading up to that point, and one that he immediately resented. "I was snatched from a pleasant country house into a world of horrible, screaming, nasty little boys," he later recalled. His first few days passed in a nightmarish blur of sleepless nights as he became the subject of some typical boarding school hostility. The other boys took great delight in teasing him about his first name – "Lancelot? Gosh! We've got a Sir Lancelot here!" – his background, and, in possibly the most hurtful episode of all, his belief in Father Christmas. It was a thoroughly unpleasant introduction into the wider world.

He proved early he was made of strong stuff. Once he weathered the initial storm he began to enjoy boarding school life, even if he never entirely fitted in to its brutish, testosterone-fuelled culture. He began to establish a pattern that he would continue to use in the coming years when dealing with formal groups or institutions. He would get along, take notes, charm the right people, and use what he'd picked up for his own ends. That he never entirely went with the crowd wasn't because he was unable to do so, but more down to an individualistic streak that he developed in his early years. "Maybe it's a French side to my character," he later mused.

His trips home during school holidays, initially full of relief at being away from school, soon became infused with a certain swagger. He showed the first signs of becoming style-conscious, something many would remark on in years to come, when he developed a way of turning up his cuffs that he thought was particularly fashionable. He also began to develop a taste for speed and danger, tearing around the streets of Cobham on his bike with close friend Oliver Tate in tow. The two would ride around at high speed and even developed a taste for jumping their bikes off buildings, which everyone in the family regarded as complete madness. He was beginning to come into his own.

In the early 1930s Lance also began to accompany Noel to Brooklands. After returning from the Monte Carlo expedition Noel had returned to the automobile world with Invicta, which, around the time Lance began visiting Brooklands, was at the height of its competition glory. This wasn't just through the speed and reliability runs of Violette Cordery. The famous Raymond Mays set class records at Brooklands in 1931 and 1932 while, further afield, Donald Healey won the 1931 Monte Carlo rally in an S Type Invicta, having scored a class victory the previous year. The sight of his father's cars flying around the track, and him getting to meet the daredevils who drove them, stirred something inside the younger Macklin. "My feeling for motor racing grew," he later put it mildly. Really, he was beginning to fall in love.

His family didn't particularly care for his interest in cars, speed or style. They were more focused on grooming him for an expected life in British high society. In 1933 he was sent to the breeding ground of future prime ministers and members of the aristocracy, the prestigious Eton College. Macklin was the third successive member of his family to be sent there, following in the footsteps of his father and grandfather. Unlike them, though, he hated it. His rebellious streak first glimpsed around Cobham and in the stuffy buildings at Camberley, fully exerted itself. "I wish I hadn't gone," he later said. "I wasn't really cut out for it." In later years he wouldn't talk about his time at Eton too often, and it's not hard to get the sense it was a dark chapter he'd rather have forgotten. On the rare occasions he did mention it he did so in almost warlike terms, him as a resistance fighter surrounded by Eton's all-encompassing, soul-destroying conformity. "It was more like a pitched battle with the authorities," he said. "It's a matter of having to subjugate yourself to that sort of discipline, the weight of tradition. I found it very difficult." By this stage, it's likely his parents were beginning to realise they weren't going to end up with the tradition-following, compliant son they were hoping for.

His time at Eton, miserable though it may have been, wasn't entirely without value. The school's focus on preparing its students for life in society's upper echelons taught Macklin important social skills, ones that would later prove useful in occasionally unexpected situations. He was also beginning to show a clear aptitude for sports, particularly skiing and polo, and Eton's focus on sporting prowess played neatly into his hands. With the exception of French, in which he had been fluent from an early age, his academic grades remained distinctly average. His sporting ability, on the other hand, grew more and more impressive. Along with skiing and polo, he dabbled in football, squash and cricket. To his surprise he found himself enjoying boxing, where his quick reactions made up for his lack of stature. He soon realised that the skills he developed inside the ring proved to be very handy outside it, too. Bullies learned to stay away.

Interestingly, his time spent boxing at Eton gave rise to a useful idea a few years later. Looking to wear something more nimble than the standard shoes he'd so far been driving in, he decided to try on his boxing boots while racing. Comfortable, breathable and responsive, they worked a charm. Quizzed by other curious drivers, the idea of wearing boxing boots took off and, with slight modifications, soon became standard issue racing driver footwear. The result of Macklin's brain flash can be found in every Formula One cockpit to this day.

Throughout this period, and even with his enjoyment of other sports, it was still motor racing that captured his attention most of all. At Eton he spent pleasant afternoons sitting by the roadside with his friend, future Grand Prix driver Tony Rolt, patiently waiting for interesting cars to pass by, dreaming that someday he'd be the one behind the wheel tearing down the narrow English roads. Still, for all his enthusiasm, Noel proved to be unusually reluctant to help his son. It even went beyond gentle discouragement, as there were times he tried everything, it seemed, to steer Lance in other directions. Even now it's hard to say exactly why this was the case. Noel had been a driver himself, had employed Violette Cordery for years, and was friends with the likes of Donald Healey and many other leading drivers of the 1930s. Despite the distance he kept from his son and his workaholic self-involvement, he couldn't have failed to notice his son's intense interest in the race track, especially given their frequent trips to Brooklands together. Perhaps it was recognition of, and disapproval at, his son's rebellious streak. More likely, though, he was trying to shield Lance from what he'd seen out on the track. Though he may have been a distant father he wasn't, it seems, an uncaring one.

Early motor racing was extremely dangerous. Cars were quick, and were getting progressively quicker, but safety wasn't keeping up. Crashes were frequent, and fatalities equally as common. Noel was on hand when one of his Invictas, a 4½-litre driven by the talented Sammy Davis, went skidding off the track at Brooklands and hit a telephone pole. Although Davis survived, he was laid up in hospital for months. It was one of many incidents that no doubt ran across Noel's worried mind every time his son pestered him about racing.

He did cave in on one small point. He agreed, with much reluctance and, no doubt, plenty of sighing, to buy his son a car for his 17th birthday. Lance was overjoyed. Still, there were conditions. Not only was it not going to be anything flash – certainly nothing like an Invicta – if Lance really wanted it he had to promise not to smoke or drink until he was 21. It was an extraordinary request on the face of it. Yet it was something that Lance stuck to. Even when he was well away from his father and his family's prying eyes and could easily have gone out for wild, boozy nights on the town, he never gave in. Years later he discussed it with his daughter Miranda. "I said 'but daddy, how did your father know you weren't smoking or drinking before you were 21?'" she recalled. "And he looked at me with those beady eyes and said, 'because I gave him my word.'" It was clear: if he made a promise, he took it seriously.

He didn't get much time to enjoy his new car. As his underwhelming time at Eton wound up it was obvious to all that he probably shouldn't follow his former classmates to Oxford or Cambridge. Noel stepped in. Looking further afield, he settled on a college in Villars-sur-Ollon, a small skiing village high in the Swiss Alps. Lance was to study business and languages, of which he was to prove adept at the latter and utterly inept at the former. It's likely he was sent so far away with the idea of instilling some sort of discipline and removing him from the prospect of mischief-making, which everyone saw coming after his struggles conforming at Eton. If that was in the intention, it failed spectacularly.

It was in Switzerland that he first came in close contact with girls. Years spent in boys-only boarding schools had fostered a deep curiosity about the opposite sex, and being away from home and any sort of extensive supervision proved to be intoxicating. His obsession with women began in Switzerland and kept up for the rest of his life, often to the detriment of his future endeavours. "Knowledgeable observers, such as John Wyer and George Abecassis, were convinced that had he put half as much effort into racing cars as he did chasing girls, he would have been a truly great driver," Chris Nixon wrote more than half a century later. "Macklin was always more interested in the chase than the race." Noel's attempt to keep his son out of trouble backfired more than he would ever know.

Bustling during ski season, Villars proved to be nearly dead when Macklin turned up in October 1936. He did occasionally get to indulge his passion for skiing – something that he was beginning to show outstanding talent in – but he quickly grew bored. His aptitude for French no doubt made the language courses too easy, while he was never business-minded and didn't have the drive to become so. At night, looking out over the village's scattering of chalets, its winding streets and the jagged peaks of the surrounding mountains, his thoughts wandered. "What the hell am I going to do now?" he said to himself, quietly.

The answer presented itself a couple of weeks later. Hanging about outside the college with a bunch of friends, he turned around to the sight of a couple of very pretty young women strolling past. "Good heavens, where did they come from?" he asked, surprised. Informed that they had come from a finishing school up the road, and confronted with even more making their way from the same direction, his interest was well and truly piqued. "Tell me more," he said, the hint of a smile forming as he watched them pass by.

The finishing school, of the sort then popular among wealthy European families, turned out to be only minutes down the road from the college. Showing an application that had so far been lacking in his studies, Macklin used his charm (and fluent French) to schedule a dance between the two schools. Things went off without a hitch. During the course of the dance he managed to charm a young French girl enough to convince her to meet him the next day, which was, of course, entirely against the finishing school's rules. It was all very surreptitious, the two meeting in secret in a backstreet café well away from the college and any prying eyes. They managed to make their secret tryst work, and soon the daring young Englishman was spending evenings cuddled up in his girlfriend's dormitory room. Getting there was quite a process. Without making a sound he had to squeeze out of his own window as soon as the building's lights were turned off, then shimmy down an apple tree, run through some woods – in the pitch black – and, when the coast was clear, dive in through his girlfriend's ground storey window.

Everything came unstuck courtesy of a sudden, six-inch snowfall.

Walking to her office one day, the school's headmistress noticed a suspicious trail of footprints heading from one of her students' windows in the direction of the college up the road. Infuriated, she threatened collective punishment and the teary-eyed girl quickly caved. Word was passed to the college, and a sheepish Macklin was summoned to the principal's office, where he was promptly expelled. Horrified that the principal planned to phone Noel with the news, Lance raced through the village and called his resolutely unimpressed father from a phone box in town. Noel was furious. "He didn't say anything very much," Lance later said. "No reproaches. He didn't laugh."

Luckily for both of them, Lance's older sister Nada happened to be in Switzerland, so an embarrassed Lance was sent to stay with her and act as her chaperone. Nada had just finished her débutante season in London, and had grown into a talented ice-skater with an almost classical beauty. Yet, although she could have done with a helping hand, Lance was having none of it. He instead had the time of his life, spending his days skiing and his nights in swanky Swiss clubs. Although he still wasn't drinking alcohol, his bills soared and he soon ran out of the money his father had given him after his expulsion (money which was no doubt supposed to go to his care of Nada, not to buying young women drinks in bars). He sent a cheeky telegram to his father, "No mon. No fun. Your Son," to which an exasperated Noel replied: "Too Bad. How Sad. Your Dad." "He did come across with some a little later," Lance noted.

It was at Villars, and under Lance's supposed protection, that Nada met the French Count Jean de Caraman. To Noel's continued distress – he had a view of French men as philanderers, the aristocracy especially so – the two fell deeply in love and married soon afterwards. At least some of the Macklins, Lance's parents hinted to him, were behaving appropriately.

After his short-lived Swiss escapade, Lance briefly moved back to England where he pondered his next move. He had obviously picked up some style tips during his time in Europe. Years later, others would remember him pulling up to a girl's school in his car during lunchtime with an air of sophistication that instantly caught the young women's eyes. It was, of course, exactly what he wanted.

Just months after touching down on English soil he was off again. This time, to his parents' undoubted relief, he was headed much further afield than a chalet in the Swiss Alps. It wasn't a bad time to leave. By the time he left, around December 1938, Europe was becoming an increasingly tense place to be, even for privileged members of the upper classes. Lance never talked about it later – his focus in Europe was fixed firmly on women – but a trip to the other side of the world would have been a breath of fresh air, in more ways than one.

There are conflicting accounts of exactly why he ended up on the other side of the world. Lance later said it was partly to escape a girl who had taken rather too keen a liking of him – " ... she started talking about marriage ... I found the answer to my problem" – and, after becoming friendly with a few Argentinians during a polo match, decided it was as good a place as any. There's a good chance, though, that it was more by Noel's command than anything else. "My father ... thought it would be good for me to get some world-wide experience before settling down in the family business," Lance later admitted. If Noel still thought his son would be prepared to settle down in the business world, it was almost certainly more down to wishful thinking than anything else.

He worked his passage across the Atlantic on a rusty steamer, surrounded by rough Argentine seamen. It must have come as quite a shock given the level of company he was used to, but he soon worked his charm and, with the help of his well-honed athleticism, blended in well enough. Even at this early stage it was clear he didn't enjoy hard work but could do it if he had to.

He didn't spend much time in Buenos Aires. He was soon whisked off into the mountains where, in a complete change of scene, he spent most of his time working with local roughnecks as a gaucho. It was hard work, and while he loved the animals he didn't like the rough and ready locals at all. The romanticism of living in the open fields of a beautiful country quickly soured. "I hated it," he told Shelagh Montague Browne later. "I loathed it. I was stuck in this place, herding cattle, spending months with really cruel and horrible men. There was nothing romantic about it at all." He did get the odd moment of respite. Back in Buenos Aires was an expat polo club, one that played host primarily to British business owners and entrepreneurs, and where a young Englishman from an upper-class family was more than welcome. There he finally got to occasionally indulge his passion for polo, which he'd come expecting in the first place. On the back of his horse under the bright blue South American sky, his polo mallet swinging backwards and forwards, and with the rattling streetcars and charming centre of Buenos Aires in the distance behind him, things didn't seem quite so bad.

For better or worse, though, things weren't set to last. On September

3 the simmering tension that had been felt through continental Europe for so long finally gave way as war broke out. Despite the slowness of communications in the mid-20th century, the news travelled quickly. As soon as he heard, Lance dropped everything – with, ironically, a feeling of relief – and jumped on-board the first steamer headed back to England. He was off to war.

Chapter 3

War

England proved to be a very different place from the one Lance had left over a year earlier. After a tense crossing of the Atlantic, always mindful of the threat of U-boats, he returned to a country that had been at war for several months. Many of his friends had been sent away to fight, some had already been killed, and the entire UK was a bustling hive of nervous energy. As ever, his family was right in the thick of things. While Lance was away in Buenos Aires, Noel had been captivated by an article in *The Seagoer* magazine about submarines and the shift away from big battleships in naval warfare. Left with time to think after winding up his various car concerns, he came up with the idea of mass producing 120-foot long, fast, heavily armed boats that would patrol the waters around the UK. Ever-patriotic, his latest idea, it was hoped, would offer a huge helping hand to Britain in a time of desperate need.

Using his brilliant imagination, Noel decided to take a novel approach to producing his latest creation. Avoiding huge expense and offering unheard of levels of flexibility, the boats were to be prefabricated, using existing factories that produced commonplace items (such as, say, furniture) to knock-out easily-put-together plywood pieces. Despite the obvious selling point of his idea he was initially frustrated in his approaches to a stuffy and wary Admiralty. It was only after a great amount of persistence, charm and, most of all, a promise to finance a prototype, that he was given a reluctant go-ahead. His plan worked, of course, and Fairmile Marine ended up producing over 1300 Motor Torpedo Boats (MTBs), Motor Gun Boats (MGBs) and Motor Launches (MLs) before the war ended. They served all over the world, too, and were produced in countries as far away as Canada and New Zealand. Ironically, the roaring success of his boats proved to be Noel's undoing.

Unable to finance such a large undertaking himself, he was forced to hand over control of the company to the Admiralty, and was given a lump sum payment and a small salary as payoff. It wasn't enough to cover his initial costs and, although he attempted to gain compensation after the war, his pleas fell on deaf ears. "He found himself far worse off than when the war began," Lance later wrote, with a palpable sense of disgust. "His health was broken, he was in continual pain, and when the Admiralty refused to support him ... it broke his heart."

While Noel was hard at work with Fairmile Marine, Lance headed straight into the Navy. On 15 April, 1940, he turned up in Hampshire to join HMS Collingwood for training. It was the first time that he'd really been among the English working classes, which turned out to be an eye-opening experience. "Naturally I got my leg pulled a lot because of my lah-de-dah voice," he said. "Some of the chaps automatically assumed that the way I spoke meant I was effeminate." They soon learned, via a well-timed uppercut, that this wasn't the case. Macklin's Eton boxing skills proved to be very handy indeed.

Despite the war and all the hardships it created, life in British high society still had to go on. There was an early break in military life when Lance, going through rigorous training, headed back to the family home for his sister Mia's wedding. Like her older sister Nada, Mia had grown into a dazzling and talented young woman. Like all her siblings she had shown a particular interest in winter sports, although she preferred ice skating to the much more dangerous world of skiing. She, like all the Macklins, displayed outstanding natural talent. Mia was even good enough to join the British woman's ice skating team, and, in 1936, competed in both the European championships in Berlin and the World Championships in Paris, with respectable results. In 1938, halfway between the busy 1936 ski season and her marriage, she posed for a series of portraits that now belong to Britain's National Portrait Gallery. Shot in striking black and white, they show a young, almost cherubic woman with puffy hair and a measured smile. The family resemblance is obvious.

Like Nada, Mia also married into wealth. Her husband was Peter Hodge, a tall, dark and handsome man who was the son of millionaire shipbuilder Sir Rowland Hodge. Their wedding was an impressive social event, important enough to make the society pages as far afield as New Zealand, and temporarily restoring some semblance of normality during days where life in war-torn England was being turned on its head. Some colour footage of the wedding still exists. It's full of important-looking older men wearing bow-ties and top hats, elegantly dressed young women, and young men in immaculately pressed armed forces uniforms. Nada, resplendent in a pink dress, accompanies the slightly stooped Duc de Caraman as they walk behind a dashing-looking Hodge and his new wife. The camera catches little snapshots, light-hearted moments of the sisters clowning for the camera, playing with dogs, taking silly photos of each other. Lance, wearing his dashing new Coastal Forces uniform, makes a couple of appearances. In one he stands with his sisters and Noel, while in another, less guarded moment he eats cake as Noel happily chats away to him. He looks slightly awkward, a little less at ease than the other confident children of society he was surrounded by. Years later his son would say that while Lance was sociable he didn't like big groups. Moreover, there's also a sense that, to put it bluntly, this just wasn't his crowd. He was born into high society, but maybe, even this early, he was beginning to reject it.

– – – – –

After heading back from the wedding he carried out some additional training before being sent down to the southern English coastal town of Portsmouth. There he was pushed into action just after his 21st birthday, September 24, 1940, on one of his father's boats, ML 112. The family connection soon proved useful. His ability to acquire desperately needed engines, via a quick phone call to Noel, made him exceedingly popular with the base engineers. It also inspired a bit of jealousy, although not, interestingly, among the ordinary seamen he was surrounded by. It tended to be his immediate superiors who gave him trouble. One unnamed petty officer on ML 112, in particular, "bitterly resented the fact that my father was a VIP (and) spent his life trying to catch me out and make things tough." In a particularly egregious case, he turned up to his River Hamble base 45 minutes late after spending most of the preceding evening stuck in Portsmouth during a Luftwaffe raid. Despite staying up all night to rescue a local hotel, then being slowed by debris strewn across local roads, his excuses cut no ice and he was confined to his ship for a few weeks.

The ML's fighting activities were shrouded in secrecy. Lightly armed yet nimble, Coastal Forces MLs tended to spend their time zipping quietly around the British coastline. They were mostly tasked with chasing submarines, laying mines and escorting convoys through the English Channel, though they would go out of their way to cause German ships trouble whenever the opportunity arose. Often working through the night, sailing on any of the small Coastal Forces ships could be a numbing, surreal experience. Soaked through by the rough English waters, surrounded by pitch blackness, and accompanied by nothing more than the constant throb of the boat's engines, crewmen were well aware that they were never far away from one catastrophe or another. Like so many others, ML112 wasn't destined to last the distance.

In late May, 1941, ML 112 was returning from an uneventful escort trip through the Straits of Dover. As the boat headed closer to home, the sense of tension on-board – present from the moment the ship left its berth – began to ease. A relatively relaxed Macklin headed up to the bridge. Then, out of nowhere, came a withering explosion. "One moment the top of the funnel had been over my head," he remembered. "The next, I was looking down into it." The boat had hit a mine, sending Macklin high into the air and nearly tearing off the back of the boat. Somehow, despite the severe damage, ML112 managed to stay afloat just long enough to be towed into nearby Sheerness. Ethereal groans coming from the depths of the mangled engine room let Macklin know that he'd been very, very lucky to make it through without injury. As he went to hop off the ship in Sheerness, he slipped. He looked down. Beneath him, glistening in the moonlight, the boat's wooden decks were covered in blood.

After this traumatic incident, Macklin and the other surviving crew-members were transferred to another boat and sent up the coast to Fort William in Scotland. The more leisurely lifestyle suited him perhaps a little too well and he was about to be charged with "some other offence," as he put it vaguely, when he was unexpectedly sent down to Hove, Sussex, to be trained as an officer. On May 15, 1941, he was promoted to sub-lieutenant. Despite his troublemaking he had excelled at sea, a quality that was partly down to sailing on his father's yachts before the war. He impressed other officers with his boat handling, although not everyone was quite so charmed by his work ethic. "Of small stature, quiet, but rather blasé for his age," one otherwise encouraging report noted. "Requires supervision."

After more training, followed by another year spent on motor torpedo boats and motor launches, he eventually wound up in Felixstowe on the North Sea coast. He had clearly impressed, for he suddenly found himself in the most ferocious MGB flotilla of the lot, the ferocious 6th MGB Flotilla commanded by devil-may-care commander Robert Peverell

Hichens. The MGBs were a different kind of beast from the MLs Macklin had previously served on. Heavily armed, their job was not to escort friendly convoys but to go flat-out and attack enemy ones. His job had shifted from defence to offense, and the MGBs often found themselves on dangerous marauding missions off the Dutch, French and Belgian coastline. Hichens had demonstrated what MGBs were capable of in late 1941, in one celebrated incident taking on a numerically superior pack of E-boats off the Dutch coast and forcing them to flee with heavy damage. Not one for blind admiration towards his superiors, Macklin always looked up to Hichens. After the war he would refer to him as a "fabulous man," something that, coming from him, was high praise indeed.

By late 1941, Macklin had been promoted to First Lieutenant and had made a name for himself as an expert seaman while on-board MGB 331. Reports from this time tend to paint a similar picture, that of a young man who was reliable, pleasant, almost shy, yet highly skilled. His maverick streak, on full display before the war, was certainly still there. Parts of his progress reports make for almost comical reading, his superiors often unable to get a handle on his mixture of charm, laziness and striking ability.

The most revealing report was penned by motor gun boat commander Derek Sidebottom, himself no slouch when it came to fighting. Sidebottom's most heroic moment came in August 1942 when he was patrolling the straits of Dover in MGB 330. Spying a line of German R-boats, he moved in for the attack. With shells flying all around he headed straight towards the rear of the German line where he rammed the nearest R-boat. A burst of return fire knocked out both him and the four other men on the ship's bridge but, recovering quickly, he groggily seized the ship's wheel and promptly silenced the offending German ship by ramming it.

As good a judge of character as any, Sidebottom's report on Macklin makes for interesting reading. "A rather unusual type," he wrote, "who is apt to make rather a poor first impression which has to be changed on closer acquaintance with his work and character. He has a definitely warlike attitude, is keen on his work, especially on the more offensive respects, is a sound navigator, handles a ship competently and has more than the usual measure of self-confidence. His worst fault is his somewhat 'bored' manner which is apt to irritate those who do not realise that it is only on the surface.

"It is felt that he is the type that will show better advantage as he gets more responsibility as he has ample initiative, but," Sidebottom underlined, "(he) is apt to lose keenness if too closely directed or supervised."

He finished by recommending he take charge of an MGB. "The responsibilities and authority of command would be good for him and ... he would make a good CO."

After finishing up in Felixstowe, Macklin briefly joined another MGB in Yarmouth then, in what he later described as an "exciting spell," headed up the coast to the battle-ravaged port of Dover. By now he had developed a well-polished routine with women – being a handsome young sailor would hardly have hurt his cause – and he was delighted to find scores of young ladies ready, for a weekend at a time, to find an excuse to forget about the war. Though his dalliances never lasted long, it was a way to relax, to get away from the traumas he faced while out on the water. It made everything just a little more tolerable.

After several long, weary months at Dover he was again shifted, this time to Shoreham, Sussex. Mystified about the move at first, he was delighted to find out the reason: Sidebottom's recommendation had been taken to heart and he was to be given command of his own ship. Still only 24, he was delighted. A week after setting foot on his brand new ML, his first crew was assembled. "You can imagine how proud I was," he recalled. His first day in charge, however, didn't go entirely as planned.

Tasked with interviewing his new crew, the delighted captain ordered his Cox'n to bring them to his office individually. His excitement only grew as he heard them trample down the stairs and begin to line-up in the cramped passageway outside his office, chatting guardedly with each other. With a cheery "come in," the door swung open and in wandered a tall, gruff Able Seaman. "He was weather-beaten, with a red face, and his formidable bulk seemed to fill the small room," Macklin remembered. "I had been a ten-year-old at prep school when he had joined the Navy. It was incongruous, but I didn't realise it at that moment." Unaware that his youth and refined, public schoolboy accent wasn't acting to his advantage, a fully confident Macklin chatted away with the gruff deckhand happily enough. "Have you been on small boats before?" he asked. The sailor, who had doubtless spent hundreds of hours on-board the Royal Navy's mighty battleships, replied that he hadn't. "Well," said Macklin with what he thought was a sage look, "you may find this a bit different."

A few minutes later the interview concluded. After the seaman left Macklin eased back in his chair, looked around his office and then congratulated himself on his new-found interviewing skills. Then he heard talk from beyond his cabin door. "What's he like?" someone excitedly asked the first interviewee. There was a pause. "Fuckin' schoolboy," came the terse reply. Macklin was mortified. "My ego fell to the deck," he recalled.

The animosity soon faded away. As he would prove time and again he had none of the toff-nosed snobbishness his accent suggested. He quickly became good friends with his crew, and his tremendous ability reassured them that he wasn't, indeed, just a typical public schoolboy. "In the end, being a fuckin' schoolboy didn't matter much," he later said. On occasion, the crew would even try and rein him in. "Now listen, skipper," he was told earnestly after one mission. "If you want your name on the Cobham War Memorial, that's up to you. But we don't want ours. We don't want any medals. All we want is leave."

His time at the helm appears to have been relatively uneventful. At night his ship would slip out under the cover of darkness and head to the European coastline, patrolling up and down and looking for easy targets where they could. Occasionally Macklin would slip out and light up a buoy, then quickly paddle back to his ship and wait for other boats, their curiosity piqued, to approach. It was like watching moths drawn to a flame. Anyone who got too close would be racked with gunfire.

His navigational skills proved useful on these night-time forays, operating as they were without lights or many high-tech navigational aids. Heading back from the Dutch coastline one night, his boat became slightly lost on the approach to the treacherous Thames Estuary. Not wanting to alarm the crew, he used his nous and a bit more guesswork than he liked to admit, and confidently predicted they were about to pass a marker on the left side of the boat. Moments later, to his relief, his guesswork proved correct and the marker passed by the bow of the ship. Everyone, except himself, was amazed. "The luck of the damned," he self-deprecatingly called it.

The last 18 months of Macklin's war remain a bit of a mystery. After being granted his watch-keeping certificate he was sent, in mid-1944, to the Royal Navy's base in Reykjavik, Iceland. Quite what he did there is unclear, although a somewhat cryptic report from the time suggested that he was still taking part in operations, at least to some degree. "He suffered from sea sickness and appeared recently to have let this get the better of him, probably because of the knowledge of an impending operation," the report noted, adding that he was "quiet and retiring." He spent nearly a year there, before heading back to England to see out the last few months of the war. After war was declared over in Europe on May 8, 1945, he spent time at the HMS Victory, a naval base in Portsmouth. On March 15, 1946, he was dispersed. His eventful naval career was over.

Shortly after his discharge from the Navy, Macklin, enjoying his new-found freedom, sat in a bar discussing the future with his friend and crewmate Donald Gosling. "Oy, skip," Gosling said, between beers. "I'm going to buy bomb sites in London and turn them into car parks, you can put 100 quid in with me if you want." Macklin, though, already had his attention fixed firmly back on the race track. "No thanks, Gosling," he said. "I've got my own plans." "Suit yourself," Gosling replied. It was a fateful conversation. In October 1948, Gosling formed Central Car Parks with Ronald Hobson, someone who had wisely seen the promise in Gosling's scheme. Beginning by purchasing a site in Holborn for all of £200, the two began making the most of London's bombed out state and started buying up large. In 1959 the two took over National Car Parks, the UK's biggest car park operator, and turned it into a giant. By the mid-1990s, National Car Parks was one of the most successful businesses in the UK. Not for the last time, Macklin's lack of business acumen had cost him dearly.

In later years he rarely talked about the war. Although he was quietly proud of his accomplishments, he saw his time in the Navy as something that he'd done out of necessity and not something to brag about. "It was a rough war," he said. "I hated it." Later in life, when his son Paddy came to stay, he'd sit in his Spanish home and sink bottle after bottle of red wine. Sometimes, after the third or fourth bottle, the stories would come out, memories flooding back of lost friends, explosions, blood soaked floors, the infinite darkness of nights on the North Sea. He may not have talked about the war, but he certainly remembered it.

Chapter 4

The race track beckons

In 1946, Noel Macklin died. Long a sick man, his hard work throughout the war had quickly worn him down and stretched him more than he could handle. Despite the Navy's initial opposition to his ideas, he'd gained huge respect among the British military elite, who later came to realise he'd been right all along. Even Winston Churchill came to visit him from time to time, having, on at least one occasion, to sneak in his own brandy. Noel had been a strict teetotaller his entire life, and not even the great British Prime Minister could get around it.

Noel's death came as a shock to his son. Despite Noel's distant parenting style Lance had always looked up to him, watching with admiration as his various businesses unfolded with success, and important people showered him with praise. He was very similar to his father, inheriting Noel's dashing charm, skills and intelligence, although he never picked up his father's endless capacity for hard work. Where Noel would become fixated on something, determined to see it through, Lance was the complete opposite. Lance would proudly talk about Noel's inventiveness and tenacity, yet, deep inside, he always felt overshadowed by him. "I think he was overwhelmed by his father," his son Paddy said. "He felt like he'd failed him somehow. He could never ever come up to his standards. He held him in great esteem and never really felt he could achieve what Noel had."

Noel's death, distressing as it was, did at least open the door for Lance to go racing without parental disapproval. Noel had been the reason Lance hadn't driven a racing car in anger before the war, putting a halt to Lance's plan to enter a 750cc Austin in a Brooklands meeting shortly before he left for Argentina. After spotting Lance's name on an entry list, an inquisitive Clerk of the Course at Brooklands, Percy Bradley, rang up Noel to ask if his son was about to follow in his footsteps. Noel was having none of it. "We'll see about that," Noel said, and when Lance went to pick up his car on the big day he was distraught to discover that it had disappeared. After a bit of frantic searching, Lance tracked its disappearance back to Noel. Despite the young man's repeated protests that he was good enough to race, Noel cut Lance short. "Not with your allowance from me," he told him, sternly. "If you want to go motor racing, fine, but you make your own money and pay for your own car. I'm not going to support you ... either you cancel your entry and you may have your car back, or you go ahead and make your own way." Noel knew full well Lance couldn't afford to pay for it on his own. The matter, and Lance's racing career, was dropped for the time being.

Now the race track beckoned, although there was to be a brief business interlude first. Looking to get settled upon his return from the war, Macklin found a flat for £2 a month in London's Kensington, with several rooms and a remarkably large garage. Macklin was taken off guard when, not long after moving in, his friend Peter Hodge dropped by and mentioned he wanted to start a car dealership. Although it hadn't been in his plans Macklin figured he'd give it a crack, and it wasn't long before the flat had been reconfigured, with his bedroom now an office and the garage packed with cars. The two decided to focus solely on high end sports cars, hundreds of which had been hidden away throughout the English countryside during the war. Macklin and Hodge spent hours poring through classified ads. When they stumbled upon something interesting, they'd head out into the countryside in a banged-up ex-Army Jeep they'd bought for the cause.

The two joyously embraced the dubious spirit of used car salesmen everywhere. Often the cars they found hadn't been started for years, a state of affairs they would turn to their advantage. "Sometimes it would be standing on blocks and we'd have to pump the tyres up," Macklin told Mark Kahn, gleefully. "We would say to the owner, 'obviously it isn't going to start, so we'll have to tow it away. How much will you accept for it?' We never said that we'd try to start the thing." The two would then talk the owner down after stressing the costs of getting the long disused car running. After making a show of hooking it to the Jeep's tow rope they would thank the seller and set off down the road, but, as soon as they were out of sight, they'd pull over. "Then we'd put a drop of petrol in the car and try to start it on the button," he said, with an almost discernible chuckle. "Nine times out of ten it would start right away." With one of them in the now fully functional sports car and the other in the Jeep, the two would then roar off back to London with grins a mile wide.

Chipstead Motors, as they decided to call their enterprise, became another of Macklin's great lost causes. Deciding not to retain a share in the company when he left to pursue his racing career, his bad financial luck – or, more appropriately, bad planning – struck again. The company developed a sterling reputation and went from strength to strength, ending up as the main Alfa Romeo distributor in London by the late 1960s. It was another golden opportunity missed.

While his main focus, for the time being at least, was on his business, motor racing was always at the back of Macklin's mind. In an idle moment, his mind wandering, he recalled meeting the well-travelled and ever-entertaining Robert Waddy in Dover during the war. A contemporary of Noel's, Waddy had enjoyed an endlessly exciting existence prior to the war, working as a welder and a train driver in the United States; then a lifeguard, professional dancer and flying instructor upon his return to the UK. Above all, he was keenly interested in motorsport. It was surprising Waddy and Macklin hadn't met before the war. Waddy was a regular at Brooklands, instantly recognisable, as a *Motor Sport* magazine scribe later recalled, as a "thin, wiry character with longish windblown locks, usually wearing a broad grin, a pair of shorts, and nothing else."

Mechanically minded, Waddy had spent a great deal of his time at Brooklands working on his most famous creation, the fabulously bizarre Fuzzi. Taking his cues from the fuselage of an Avro Avian aircraft – Fuzzi being short for fuselage – Waddy had designed what was possibly the first space-frame racing car. It was certainly unusual, looking something like a downsized and squashed version of the famous Auto Union Type D. It was even stranger underneath, powered as it was by two JAP engines, and with an accelerator pedal that could provide throttle to either engine individually or both at once. Quite a handful, Waddy nevertheless achieved success with it in hillclimbs before war forced it under wraps.

On the search for a racing car, Macklin gave him a call. It turned out that the Fuzzi was in a state of considerable disrepair. During the war Waddy had sold the two engines and other bits and pieces during a spell of financial hardship, leaving little but a now-dusty frame. After returning from the war he'd decided against getting back into racing and so, after a pretty straightforward haggle, Macklin was the proud owner of his first race car. It was in pieces, but that didn't matter. Excited, he set to work immediately.

After everyone else at Chipstead Motors had gone home for the day he would get to work, hammering away long into the night as he painstakingly put the Fuzzi back together. He decided to abandon the effective, yet tricky, two-engine arrangement and stuck a big Mercury V8 in it instead. Because of its complexity, reassembling the Fuzzi took longer than he had anticipated. Deciding that if he couldn't join them, he'd watch them, Macklin began heading to every motorsport event he could. He quickly began to take notes.

– – – – –

In early 1947 he made another addition to his personal car collection. Driving through the countryside on one of his Chipstead Motors excursions he came across a barn find that instantly brought back a flood of memories. There, under a thick layer of dust, but perfectly intact, was a 1932 Invicta. The family connection was too good to ignore, so, instead of putting it up for sale, he snapped it up and used it as his runabout car. While its good looks aided his burgeoning man-about-town image, it was the old car's sporting side that came in handy the most. While the Fuzzi slowly came together in the corner of the Chipstead Motors garage, Macklin practiced his driving skills by roaring around the streets of London in the Invicta. He thought back to the races he'd seen before the war, not so much Brooklands but the bigger races at Donington and the fast, flowing road courses in Europe. There he'd perched in the stands, his eyes glued to the track, watching the loud, impossibly fast Auto Unions and Mercedes as they roared past and threw themselves sideways into bends. He watched Nuvolari, Varzi, Caracciola and all the other prewar greats, saw the way they tugged the wheel, their faces covered in grime, and knew he wanted to be like them. It was them he thought of when he gripped the wheel of his Invicta during late night runs through the heart of London, hurtling past the city's empty lots and its bedraggled façade, kicking the back end out and throwing it sideways through every corner he could. On rainy nights he would head to Belgrave Square in the middle of London. Surfaced with wooden blocks, the square would become, he said, "so slippery it wasn't true." He'd throw the Invicta sideways and keep it there, going round in circles in a constant four-wheel drift, steering with the throttle. Sometimes he'd reach sixty miles an hour, the whine of the engine bouncing off the stately Belgrave Square apartments, through the pouring rain and into the night.

During this period he began hanging about with fellow troublemaker Jon Pertwee. The two had met during the war, becoming fast friends when they'd discovered each other's passion for motorsport and fast cars. Pertwee, a talented actor who later became famous for playing *Doctor Who* in the early 1970s, had a mischievous streak that aligned perfectly with Macklin's own. The two would sneak into sprint events dressed as marshals, wearing overalls they'd borrowed from Chipstead Motors and carrying brooms over their shoulders. Nobody ever questioned them. Once inside they'd find the best viewing spot and set up camp, leaping up and pretending to sweep gravel on the rare occasions when an official would wander past.

Occasionally the two would jump in Pertwee's little Frazer Nash and head across the channel to France. Europe, despite sustaining heavy and widespread damage during the war, was the place to go if you wanted to watch motor racing. Full scale racing resumed relatively quickly postwar, the mighty prewar Mercedes, Alfa Romeos and Fiats being dragged out of their hiding places in an attempt to quickly resume at least some semblance of normality. The British, on the other hand, had to be content with hillclimbs. It wasn't quite the same.

In July 1948, Pertwee and Macklin took the Frazer Nash to the lightning quick Reims track for the French Grand Prix. The entry list was an interesting mix of prewar legends, including Louis Chiron and Nuvolari, plus up-and-comers like future champions Alberto Ascari and Juan Manuel Fangio. Though there were new postwar racing cars, it was the old prewar Alfa Romeo 158s that were still quickest. Racing car development, understandably, hadn't quite taken off just yet.

Arriving in Calais and setting off south-east, the two passed through the golden French countryside under bright blue skies and in a sweltering heat. Despite the wonderful weather and the natural beauty they were surrounded by there were constant reminders of what the area had gone through only recently. They passed through ghostly, empty villages, and past burnt out farmhouses and rusting military trucks abandoned on the side of the road. They were sights people sought to block out, and motorsport, even if only for a few hours, helped.

The two turned up four days early, long before anyone else was around, and parked the Frazer Nash, with a caravan in tow, in a prime spot to watch the race. Nicely set up for the weekend they now had time to kill. After chatting amongst themselves they decided to head for Paris and hunt for the enigmatically-named Whizzo Davies, a character who, a friend had assured them, would be delighted to host them on-board his yacht on the Seine. Always keen for an adventure, and undeterred (and probably a little excited) by word that French Customs officers were looking to seize Davies' boat, they set off.

A couple of hours later they arrived. It didn't take long to find Davies, and after a friendly hello they dropped their bags on board and wandered into the nearest classy nightclub they could find. They stayed out on the town for hours, having a riotously good time, and didn't stumble back to the boat until the early hours of the morning. They didn't get to rest long. After only a few hours they were woken by the ominous thump of boots trampling the deck above their heads. A minute later, their cabin door flew open. A young, immaculately dressed gendarme looked at the two startled Englishmen. "Monsieur Davies?" he asked, his eyes narrowing. Macklin, his mind still clouded by the previous night's boozing, shook his head. "Alors," the gendarme said, turning his attention to Pertwee. "You are Monsieur Davies?" Pertwee shook his head and groggily pointed down the hallway. Shortly after the Frenchman ran out the sound of a heated argument began to echo down the hallway as the gendarme found his man. While the real Monsieur Davies and the gendarme moved upstairs, the Englishmen planned their escape. "I'll have a look around upstairs," Macklin whispered. "If there's nobody about I'll get off and into the car. You bring the case up, and if I make a sign that it's all right, come across and we'll drive off." Pertwee agreed.

At first everything went smoothly. Popping his head through the yacht's hatch, Macklin swivelled his head from side to side. Realising that the coast was clear he hauled himself onto the deck and casually strolled off the boat and over to the waiting Frazer Nash. A minute later Pertwee's head emerged. Everything was going smoothly, but as soon as Macklin gave Pertwee the 'all clear' signal things began to go horribly wrong. "Jon is a natural comedian," Macklin said, no doubt shaking his head. "He thought the whole situation was terrible (sic) funny." Instead of walking to safety, Pertwee decided to act like the vaudeville comedian he was and started to creep around in exaggerated movements, peering over his shoulder in a faux-clumsy escape attempt. The French police didn't see the humour, and moments later the air was filled with the sound of whistles. The two were arrested.

Cleared of any part in the yacht's legal troubles, the two nonetheless failed to produce their passports – which were in the caravan in Reims – and were promptly thrown in jail. Pertwee spent the time writing out postcards he'd bought the day before, thinking it would be hilarious to write to his friends from a French jail cell. After a few hungry hours, the two eventually kicked up a fuss and were released. "Perhaps this will teach you not to leave your passports behind," their French jailer said, sternly.

Chapter 5

Heroics at Chimay: from Invicta to Aston Martin

Work on the Fuzzi continued. Late one afternoon, after yet another hard day of tinkering, Macklin hopped into his little race car and crossed his fingers. Turning the ignition key, the Chipstead Motors garage became filled with an ear-splitting roar as the Fuzzi, in all its dysfunctional glory, showed it was ready to go. After so many obstacles, so, too, was Macklin's racing career.

He entered the first event he could find. This turned out to be the Brighton and Hove Motor Club's grandly titled Brighton International Hillclimb, held on the main road between Brighton and the small town of Lewes. The Fuzzi joined an eclectic field of cars, ranging from small Austins and MGs to prewar behemoths, including mighty Lagondas, and even a famous 4½-litre Bentley. The drivers comprised a similarly motley crew, some prewar enthusiasts, the others young, postwar hopefuls. Among the latter was the diminutive, shy and startlingly quick Stirling Moss, in his tiny Cooper-JAP. It was the first time Macklin became aware of the precociously talented young driver. A few years later, their paths would cross again.

Revelling in the riotous atmosphere, and overjoyed to finally turn a wheel in anger, Macklin was in his element. Even though it was only a hillclimb, he went for broke, using every trick he'd learned from his time on the sidelines, and, of course, his late night runs on London's streets. After a nearly-flawless run around the narrow, twisty course, he hopped out of the Fuzzi to find that he'd set the fastest time in his category. As the hours ticked by nobody else beat it, and, by the end of the day, Lance Macklin had his first racing victory. It wasn't much, but he was over the moon.

As chuffed as he was by his early taste of success, Macklin quickly figured out that hillclimbing wasn't what he wanted to do. Racing up a hill in the Fuzzi was fun, and he was certainly learning more every time he went out, but it lacked the wheel-to-wheel action and high speeds that he'd seen on the continent and in his youth at Brooklands. He wanted to get on a proper racing track. Unfortunately for him – and other ambitious young British racing drivers – there was a profound lack of British circuits to race at. The British postwar racing scene was dominated by hillclimbs and sprints simply because they were easy to get going in Britain's shattered economy. Even though the war had been over for several years the British still had to live as if it were going on, in a sense: not having to worry about bombs but still dealing with harsh wartime rationing. Essential items were in short supply. The country was broke. It was a gloomy age of austerity, and, of the many things to sort out, motor racing was not high on the priority list.

The great old British racing circuits hadn't had a good war. Donington Park, which had been requisitioned by the Ministry of Defence and turned into a military vehicle depot, didn't reopen until 1977. Macklin's beloved Brooklands, which had been the scene of so many family victories and brought back hundreds of memories, fared even worse. Used for RAF aircraft production during the war, the track had been cut up and left to decay. Bought by Vickers-Armstrongs in 1946, it never reopened.

Still, there were signs of progress. During the war a host of aerodromes had been hastily built for the RAF, most of them in southern England, only to be left abandoned once hostilities ceased. Usually shaped like triangles, it was only a matter of time before their long straights and natural hairpin bends caught the attention of ambitious motor racing fans. In 1947, young Maurice Geoghegan and a bunch of friends took to the disused Silverstone aerodrome on the Northamptonshire/Buckinghamshire border for a short, wild race. Despite the affair ending with Geoghegan driving into an unfortunate sheep that had wandered onto the tarmac, the idea of Silverstone as a race track stuck. The following year, the venerable Royal Automobile Club placed a lease on the airfield and turned it into a full-blown, if somewhat rough and ready, race track. Others, like the Thruxton circuit in Hampshire, soon followed. For eager young racers like Macklin, there was a light at the end of the tunnel.

– – – – –

Desmond Scannell was sitting calmly at his desk at the British Racing Drivers' Club in London when his office door flew open. In stormed a dishevelled and furious Lance Macklin. Unperturbed, Scannell looked up. "Ah, Mr Macklin," he said, calmly. "Please sit down."

Scannell had been expecting him. For weeks the two had been involved in a back and forth about Macklin's attempt to ditch hillclimbs and enter his first proper race. In the course of the wheeling and dealing he had become adept at, Macklin had bought a beautiful Maserati 6CM racing car that he shared with his friend John Gordon. In need of some repair, he had piled a whopping – for 1948 – £800 into the car, nearly all the money he had at the time, in order to get it race-ready. By the time all was said and done he finally had something powerful and modern enough to go racing. The first event he decided to enter the Maserati in was a BRDC event at the Isle of Man. Thrilled, he sent his entry form off to the BRDC office with the £5 entry fee and waited.

He was set to be disappointed. Although official competition licences didn't exist at the time, race organisers did occasionally demand to see some evidence of ability if they weren't sure about who they were dealing with. Entering the Maserati, which was basically a Formula One car, raised eyebrows. Scannell quickly sent a letter asking to see proof of his experience. Macklin, crestfallen, was forced to reply that he didn't really have any. His entry was declined.

His sadness soon gave way to frustration, which then gave way to anger. Not long after receiving the letter he picked up the phone, curtly informed the BRDC that he was on his way to see them, and furiously headed out the door.

His anger quickly dissipated when he sat down in front of Scannell. "I'm sorry," Scannell said, looking him in the eye. "I really sympathise with you, but you must see it from our point of view. You are inexperienced. If we authorise you to drive in a race and you cause an accident which kills twenty people, we are going to be blamed for letting you loose."

Macklin knew he was right. Still, he found himself in a bit of a catch-22: he couldn't get experience unless he raced, yet he couldn't race unless he had experience. "Well, how the hell am I supposed to start racing?" he asked Scannell, exasperation creeping into his voice. "The bloody war has been on for the past five or six years. I couldn't race before the war. I've got to start somewhere, sometime." Scannell leaned back in his chair, thinking.

"Do you have a sports car you can drive?" he asked.

"Only an old Invicta," Macklin replied.

"Does it go all right?"

"Yes"

"Very well." Scannell looked across his table. "Would you be willing to race it?"

"Certainly," a guarded Macklin replied, "if anyone's prepared to accept a 1932 motor car in their event."

"I'll see what I can do."

Macklin left dejected, although his gloomy mood proved to be short-lived. A week later the phone rang. On the other end, to Macklin's surprise, was Desmond Scannell. He'd done some looking around, he said, and found a race in the small Belgian town of Chimay. The race was set for a month's time, and the organisers were on the lookout for British entries. Macklin would have to get himself and his Invicta over there, Scannell cautioned, although any transport fees would probably be offset by the £50 he'd receive for just starting the race. "Would you be interested?" he asked. There was only one answer. In May 1948, Lance Macklin and his ageing Invicta found themselves on a ferry to Belgium.

He arrived at Chimay for the grandly titled Grand Prix des Frontières full of excitement. Although there were several old-time cars, including a lovely Bugatti Type 49, the field was mostly made up of new French racers, including low-slung, bright blue Delahayes, elegant Delages, and even a rare Talbot Special. Doubtless thinking how nice it would have been to have the Maserati on hand, he nonetheless hopped into the old Invicta and began lapping the circuit quicker and quicker. He already had a feel for the car and he soon had a grip on the circuit, too. With every lap he grew more confident. Something very good could happen here, he thought to himself.

"Chimay was run by a man named, if I remember, Buisseret," Macklin recalled. "He ran it independently, in his own way, virtually a law unto himself. There was no sophisticated nonsense about practice times determining your start position ... I think he did it on the basis of personal distinction." As an undistinguished first-timer, unknown to the all-powerful race director, and in an antiquated car to boot, Macklin was unsurprisingly sent straight to the back of the grid.

Race day rolled around. That afternoon he found himself sitting in his Invicta, staring up ahead at the neat rows of French grand prix cars in front of him, wearing nothing but a short-sleeved shirt, some trousers and a pair of plimsolls. He sweated, his stomach turning. The cars ahead of him began to rev their engines. He firmly shifted into first gear. He continued to look ahead, waiting ...

The flag dropped. He'd moved forward barely an inch when he was almost blinded by an explosion right in front of him. French driver Marc Versini's beautiful Delage had hardly turned a wheel an inch when it inexplicably burst into flames, sending its panicked driver running for the stands. Macklin slammed on his brakes and jammed the car into reverse, but as he was about to swerve around the blaze in front of him he found his path blocked by an army of marshals brandishing fire extinguishers. The seconds ticked by as he frantically gestured for the marshals to move out of his way, the track too narrow for him to power around them, but they were too preoccupied with the fire to pay him any attention. Finally, after 30 long seconds, they noticed and moved aside. He was now miles behind.

When he eventually came round the first corner he caught a glimpse of the crowd. They were laughing at him. Of course, they didn't know about the disaster at the start. All they knew was what they saw in front of them, which was an ancient-looking Invicta, hopelessly out of place anyway, 30 seconds behind the car in front and not even halfway through the first lap. It was comical.

Macklin saw the laughter and felt like an idiot. "Oh Christ," he said through gritted teeth. "I don't want to drive this bloody stupid motor car in this race anyway." His thoughts travelled back to the Maserati, the BRDC and Desmond Scannell, and he cursed them. "I'm only here because of their bloody ridiculous attitude," he thought. In his fury he went for broke, throwing the Invicta through corners and down-changing furiously, his anger pouring onto the track. 40 minutes later, still cursing the BRDC, he spotted a car in the distance as he crossed onto Chimay's main straight. His mood calmed, slightly. Two laps later he overtook it. Shortly afterwards he came up behind another car and rapidly passed it, then another, then another. Somehow, despite everything, he quickly found himself in fourth place. It was remarkable. He was full of confidence and rapidly gaining on third place when he heard an ominous rattle coming from the bottom of his car. Moments later, with a thud, the Invicta's battery fell out. His eventful race was over.

Though he'd been forced out his impressive run hadn't gone unnoticed. Despite the Grand Prix des Frontières' relative obscurity, there was still a small press contingent on hand due to the paucity of motor races at the time. Among the contingent was an English motoring writer who, thrilled to see his countryman's fantastic drive, wrote up a glowing report centring almost solely around this new, young star of the track. Back in Britain, word began to spread. Unaware of what Macklin had been thinking as he angrily powered around the track, Scannell read the report with a smile.

– – – – –

Macklin's social life began to boom. He was especially taken by the Steering Wheel Club, a bar exclusively for those involved in motorsport, located in the middle of a maze of winding streets in London's very-exclusive Mayfair. Slightly dark and gloomy, its walls littered with signed photos and a rapidly expanding collection of racing memorabilia, it was a comfortable place for racing drivers and journalists to gather in their off-moments. Wandering in throughout the day you could easily find motoring writers hunkered down in its corners, writing race reports over a glass of beer, while the drivers they were writing about sat at the bar, animatedly discussing the race. It was a social centre that, especially in the years immediately ahead, proved to be a gathering spot for all kinds of hell-raisers.

A couple of weeks after Chimay, Macklin was sitting in the Steering Wheel Club when Ian Metcalfe walked in. Metcalfe was one of the old guard, having raced (without any great success) before the war, and was instantly recognisable due to his mass of facial hair and his jovial demeanour. He was known around the Steering Wheel Club as the 'laughing lavatory brush' ("He had a beard, you see," Macklin explained. "He laughed a lot. What else could we call him?"). While he wasn't the finest driver around, he was always up for a challenge, and he'd decided to tackle the upcoming 24-hour race at Belgium's intimidating Spa track in his special Barnato-Hassan Bentley. Still, with the race only a month away, he was nervous. His attempts at recruiting co-drivers had so far proved fruitless, primarily because nobody was willing and/or foolish enough to try and drag a prewar car around one of the most dangerous circuits in Europe for 24 hours. "You must be mad," was a common response. "A bloody 8-litre track car at Spa?" His laugh, normally ever-present, was beginning to fade.

Like everyone else he had read about Macklin's heroics at Chimay, but, when someone suggested his younger colleague as a co-driver, he was less than enthusiastic. After all, by this stage Macklin did only have a bunch of hillclimbs and one unfinished race under his belt. For all his doubts time kept ticking, and after a while Metcalfe realised he didn't really have a choice. Reluctantly sauntering over to Macklin in the Steering Wheel Club, he put the question to him. Macklin was delighted. "In those days, anyone who mentioned the possibility of a drive to me was fabulous," he said later. Relived that he'd found a co-driver, although not especially happy about who the co-driver was, Metcalfe admitted that he could only pay expenses and a share of the prize money. That'll work perfectly, Macklin said.

Three weeks later he was back in Belgium. He drove through wide flat fields and little stone towns, then climbed higher and higher into the imposing Ardennes forest. Spa was a serious race track, long, unforgiving and intimidating, with a history that stretched back long before the war. Its long straights mixed with tight corners, twisty sections and, most famously, the uphill right-hand bend called Eau Rouge. It was enough to make even experienced drivers nervous, and for someone about to take part in their second ever race it was terrifying.

When Macklin turned up Spa was already a hive of activity. Unlike Chimay, with its entry list full of French amateurs, Spa attracted many of the top teams and drivers throughout Europe. It was a whole other level. This time there was also more of a British presence, David Brown's newly-resurrected Aston Martin team proving to be the one to beat.

One person who wasn't there was Ian Metcalfe. He had insisted on driving the Bentley down to the track, a practice that was common enough in the days of amateur racers with their own cars, but come Friday's practice session he was nowhere to be seen. Macklin's concern grew when he still hadn't arrived a day later, and it was only on the evening before the race that a call from Metcalfe reached the circuit. It turned out that disaster had struck. Just as Metcalfe had hit Brussels the Bentley's clutch had disintegrated. Rushing around, he'd organised a new one to be sent out to Spa, although he warned Macklin that the two of them would have to fit it themselves. After a brief chat Macklin hung up, dejected. The race organisers, who knew that neither Metcalfe nor Macklin had so much as driven around Spa before, were dubious. "This does present a bit of a problem," one of them said. "I'm not sure we can allow you to start unless you practice." Macklin knew they weren't being unreasonable.

That afternoon the clutch arrived, followed shortly afterwards by the stricken Bentley. The two immediately set to work. Though neither were trained mechanics they were both familiar with Bentleys, Metcalfe since before the war and Macklin having dealt with a constant stream of them at Chipstead Motors. They worked on the massive bulk of the Bentley as the sun set, continuing through the night and well into the next morning. Sweating, going on little food and no sleep, they hammered away until the last possible minute before towing it to the track. Perhaps out of pity, the organisers decided to go easy on the two unfortunate Englishmen and let them race, despite their lack of experience, a call that was lenient even by lax 1948 standards.

It started to rain as the grid formed. The Bentley wasn't among them, sitting in its pit garage as the two exhausted drivers frantically screwed in the last few bolts. The flag dropped and the field roared up towards Eau Rouge for the first time, jostling and sliding in a sea of spray. Five minutes later the Bentley, with a sleep-deprived Metcalfe at the wheel, set off in hot pursuit. Macklin slumped back against the pit wall, exhausted.

Cumbersome through the corners, the Bentley had a high top speed that suited Spa's long straights. After three hours Metcalfe was, amazingly, running 16th, despite his five-minute delay. While standing on the pit counter and getting ready for his first stint, Macklin had run into Aston Martin driver Dick Stallebrass. An experienced driver, Stallebrass nonetheless cut an uneasy figure. "Oh Christ," he said to Macklin, "I'm scared stiff about this bloody motor race." "But why?" Macklin asked, trying to calm him. "Take it easy." Stallebrass didn't listen. When Jack Fairman pulled in for their Aston's first driver change, Stallebrass was still a bundle of nerves. Macklin anxiously watched as he roared off onto the wet track and disappeared out of sight.

It was the last time anyone saw him alive. Coming up to the Malmédy corner part-way through his first lap, the Aston Martin ran out of control. It went off the track and into a field, pieces shearing off as it travelled end over end. Stallebrass was killed instantly. The incident was relayed by a horrified announcer over the circuit's loudspeakers. 30 seconds later, Metcalfe came in. Shaken by what he'd just heard, Macklin had no choice but to jump in. "Take it easy, Lance," Metcalfe said as the two swapped over. "It's slippery out there. Bloody slippery." Macklin's confidence sank even further.

He spent the first few laps tiptoeing around gingerly. Slowly but surely he began to get a feel for the car and the circuit, and when the rain stopped he decided to put his foot down. "I'm in a motor race," he said to himself. "Let's get cracking, for god's sake." His early nervousness vanished. At one point he kept up with a leader who'd lapped him, using the Bentley's mighty engine to power away on the straights before being rapidly caught up on the corners. "It was like driving a battleship," he recalled. "Everything it did was ladylike. When you went fast into a corner it just slowly and majestically came round. The power was fantastic. Put your foot down in second coming out of a hairpin bend and the thing took off." He started to lap faster, easing the Bentley sideways into corners, his foot to the floor on straights. People in the pits began to notice. John Eason Gibson, the Aston Martin team manager, watched every time the ridiculously outdated prewar relic roared past the pits, its young driver manhandling it round the track. He was impressed. Inside the cockpit, Macklin was having the time of his life. "Christ," he said to himself. "This is tremendous fun." As a racing driver, in only his second race, he was coming into his own.

After a few hours Macklin pulled in and handed over to Metcalfe, hopping out drenched in sweat and wearing a massive grin. For his part, Metcalfe soldiered on for another few hours before the duo's luck deserted them and the clutch they'd worked so hard to put together packed up, sending them out of the race. It didn't really matter. As far as Macklin was concerned, it had been a great success. After their premature exit the two decided to stick around and wait for the race to finish, grabbing a bit of much-needed sleep before making the long trek back to the UK. Later, while hanging around the paddock and taking in the festive post-race atmosphere, Macklin was surprised to look up and see Aston Martin team manager John Eason Gibson striding towards him. Eason Gibson, whose drivers Jock Horsfall and Leslie Johnson had won the race, cut straight to the point.

"Both our drivers saw you out on the circuit in that enormous Bentley," he said. "They say you are very fast."

He paused. Macklin looked at him, intrigued.

"We are going to start a team next year," he continued. "Would you be interested in being considered as one of the drivers?"

Macklin's heart leapt. He could hardly believe what he was hearing.

"Of course I would," he replied, doing his best to disguise just how excited he really was.

Eason Gibson nodded. "We'll contact you at the beginning of the spring," he said. "We'll be trying out new drivers, and we'll see if you're any good."

Macklin was ecstatic. Reflecting while on his drive back to England, he found it hard to believe what had just happened. 48 hours earlier he'd been a relative unknown, reluctantly dragged along in an ancient car to make up the numbers. Now he was about to test for the latest, most exciting British racing team in years. Things, he thought happily, couldn't have gone much better at all.

Chapter 6

On the rise

On a cold, blustery morning in October 1948, Lance Macklin joined the
Aston Martin brains trust at the newly reconfigured Silverstone circuit.
Alongside him was regular driver Charles Brackenbury, there to help him
get to grips with the Spa-winning DB1, while watching from the sidelines
were Eason Gibson and Aston Martin owner David Brown. Macklin
knew he needed to impress. Photos from the session show a distinct
difference between him inside the car and outside it. Outside, standing
around the DB1 with the Aston crew, he appears considerably more
laid back than the people he's surrounded by, his unkempt shock of hair
and ragged coat a sharp contrast to the others' tidy short hair and suits.
Nevertheless, there's also a touch of apprehension in his body language,
the sort of mild uneasiness that comes with a first day on the job. It's a
completely different story behind the wheel, summed up best by one shot
where his dark sunglasses and impish grin stand in sharp contrast to the
intense concentration on Brackenbury's face as the two negotiate one of
Silverstone's bends. It's clear: in the car, he was in his element. Although he
clearly wasn't a suit and tie man, the team was impressed and, by the end
of the day, he was officially an Aston Martin works driver.

Though he was overjoyed there was still something nagging him. Even
at this moment, having achieved something he'd dreamed about for years,
his mind travelled back to his father. Noel, he knew, wouldn't have been
happy. "I thought of ... how disapproving he would have been if he had
known that I was signed up to race, even for a famous marque," he recalled.
His dad's long shadow still followed him.

He now had time to kill. His first assignment for Aston was Le Mans
on June 25, 1949, which seemed to be an age away. He spent his time
doing the things he loved best, and at which he was, by now, very capable:

skiing, racing cars, and chasing women. His skiing, in particular, was coming along strongly. As children he and his sisters had loved winter sports, and his adventures in Switzerland before the war had helped polish his early promise on the slopes. He had reportedly trained with the French ski team in 1937, and nine years later, following the war, joined the British ski team for trials in the run-up to the 1948 Winter Olympics in St Moritz. His progress came to a halt when he suffered an injury, putting him out of the team and blowing his shot at Olympic glory. Later on he would say he was too small in stature to ski competitively anyway, something that, fortunately, wasn't a problem inside the cockpit of a racing car.

Since selling his share of Chipstead Motors he had been living a relatively itinerant lifestyle. He regularly shifted between England and France, although after a while he began spending more time in the latter, his love of the culture, the language, and the continent's vastly superior opportunities for motor racing capturing his attention. His family connections there also came in handy. In France he would spend days in the countryside at the holiday château of his brother-in-law, the Duc de Caraman, while he soon stumbled into an even better deal courtesy of his other brother-in-law, Jack Vietor.

Mia Macklin's marriage to Peter Hodge hadn't lasted, and just six months after the two divorced she married Vietor in an exquisitely opulent wedding in New York. An American native, Vietor seemed to have it all. He was charming, intelligent, well-connected, and, as the heir to the Jello family fortune, stupendously wealthy. In the late 1940s he maintained a suite at the prestigious George V hotel, just off the Champs-Élysées in the heart of Paris, where he and Mia often stayed. In their little enclave, Vietor and his new wife enjoyed all the benefits of French high society. They had the finest food and wine, travelled in style, conversed with the rich and powerful, had maids tend to their every need. It was unsurpassable luxury, making for a sobering contrast to the poverty that ravaged most of France at the time.

On one of his frequent trips through Paris, Lance stumbled upon Mia, who was in town briefly with Vietor. When Lance mentioned that he was living in a cheap and beaten up little room on the outskirts of Paris, Mia had an idea. It turned out the Vietors kept a special maid's room at the top of the George V, even though, at that moment, they didn't actually have their own personal maid. "Do you think," Mia asked Lance, "You'd like to live there? It wasn't much," she added, "but it was all his free of charge if he wanted it." Lance gleefully accepted. A maid's room at the George V was, after all, still a room at the George V. Every morning Lance would wake up and look out the window and scan the rooftops of downtown Paris, before heading through the hotel's plush corridors and out onto the wide, flowing Champs-Élysees. "I used to stroll in and out of the George V with the air of a man who regularly broke the bank at Monte Carlo," he recalled, "and there I was, staying in the maid's room."

He still had the Maserati, which he now had no problems entering in races, storing it in the garage of French racing driver Henri Louveau between events. He also bought an ex-American Army GMC truck that he used to drive around the countryside, and which he kept behind the Duc de Caraman's country house, about 30 miles outside Paris, while he was in Paris leading his slightly watered-down version of the high life. His time in the city was a colourful whirl, of races, of beautiful women, evenings spent strolling down the Seine, stumbling out of jazz clubs in the early hours. For the moment, until he needed to report to Aston Martin in a few months, he had no responsibilities and no commitments to anyone but himself. It was a world away from the confines of his childhood and the strict regimentation of the Navy. It was, he often thought to himself, just the way he liked it.

His first race in the new year, the Grand Prix de Paris at the fearsomely quick Montlhéry circuit on April 24, was a bust, with the Maserati falling victim to a faulty magneto after just seven laps. At Montlhéry he was up against some faces that would later become familiar, members of the new motor racing fraternity that was quickly coming together after the war. There were the rising stars of French motorsport like Maurice Trintignant and Robert Manzon, plus British jazz trumpeter and gentleman driver Johnny Claes, the older, yet dazzlingly quick, Louis Rosier, and future British star Roy Salvadori. Also driving that day, his Talbot Lago finishing in fifth and, effectively, last place, was the enigmatic Frenchman Pierre Levegh.

Macklin had more success in a much more eventful race two weeks later. Back at Chimay for the Grand Prix des Frontières, he returned more like a conquering hero instead of the nervous beginner he'd been a year earlier. It was a remarkable turnaround.

Though the race itself was one thing, getting there was quite another. He'd reached an arrangement with Louveau, a fellow privateer without any sort of factory backing, where the two would load their cars onto Louveau's big truck and ferry them to and from races together, splitting the expenses and the driving. The night before they were due to head out to Chimay, though, disaster struck. The phone in Lance's little room at the top of the George V rang. It was Louveau. "Lance, I'm sorry," he said. "When we started my Maserati up this afternoon for a final test the throttle jammed wide open, and the engine went straight up to ten thousand revs and flew apart." Macklin could already tell the following day was going to be more difficult than he'd planned. "I'm afraid I won't be going," Louveau continued, "and you'll have to make your own arrangements to get to the race." Macklin said he was sorry, sighed, and hung up.

He quickly concocted a plan. Minutes after hanging up the phone he was out the door and on the way to the Duc de Caraman's country house. When he arrived he immediately swapped over to his mighty GMC truck, which he drove at a considerably slower pace back to Paris. After arriving he headed straight for the George V, parking the "ugly great American brute," as he liked to call it, outside the hotel. The sight of the beaten up, tatty army truck outside the most luxurious hotel in Paris raised a few eyebrows. With a bit of a chuckle, a weary Macklin wandered back up the stairs and fell into a deep sleep.

In the morning Lance drove around to Louveau's garage where, after casting a sad glance at Louveau's stricken Maserati, he loaded his own car onto his truck and headed north to Chimay. Not wanting to push the old truck too hard he was making slow progress, and just as he was beginning to wonder if he would make it in time for scrutineering the truck gave a couple of alarming little coughs. A minute later he was standing on the side of the road in the middle of the French countryside, cursing both his luck and the GMC, and wondering what on earth he was going to do next. Scanning the countryside, he noticed he wasn't too far away from a quaint looking farmhouse. He sprinted towards it, arriving at the door panting and drenched in sweat. After quickly gathering himself, he knocked. A withered, severe-looking peasant opened the door. Macklin's heart sank.

"Could somebody come and give me a hand to get a racing car out of the truck that has broken down over there?" he asked, in French, turning and pointing to the stricken GMC that lay down the road.

The farmer's eyes followed Macklin's finger without changing. He looked back at the frantic driver and a bemused smile began forming on his face.

"Un moment, monsieur," he said, before disappearing back inside the farmhouse. Macklin waited nervously. Minutes later the farmer reappeared with three farmhands and the little crew set off for the truck. When they arrived they opened the back, set down the ramp and rolled the Maserati gently onto the road. Macklin grabbed his toolbox and put it on the floor of the Maserati, his carnet de passage wedged firmly underneath, before locking the truck and hopping back into the Maserati. "I'll be back," he told the peasant and his farmhands gathered around the Maserati. "Could you give me a push?" Minutes later he was on his way, tearing through the gears, the Maserati's throaty roar reverberating throughout the countryside. Farmers and their animals stared as he flew past, Macklin going hell for leather in a car entirely unsuited to the road. He gritted his teeth. He was determined to make the start of his race.

At the Belgian border the guards, who had so far been enjoying a pleasantly relaxing afternoon, heard a whine in the distance. Intrigued, they were startled when they realised a racing car was coming their way in a hurry. When Macklin arrived he thrust out his papers like, he later recalled, "a man with hell at my heels." "Quick, quick," he shouted at the astonished group. "I've got to get to Chimay for a race." Caught off guard, a flustered inspector handed Macklin his papers, and before he realised what had happened the little Maserati was gone, its exhaust blaring deep into the Belgian countryside.

He arrived with moments to spare. The hassle in getting there turned out to be worth it. Unlike the previous year he now had some serious machinery under him, and he used it to full effect, finishing second behind Guy Mairesse in the much newer Talbot Lago T26C. After the post-race celebrations he hopped back in the Maserati – which was having quite an eventful weekend – and headed back the way he came. This time, the border guards were ready for him. Curious, they'd found a broadcast of the race and listened as the Englishman who had disturbed their peaceful afternoon wound up on the podium. They were delighted, and waved him through with smiles on their faces as he made his way back to France. He was in for an even nicer surprise when he returned to the broken-down truck, for it transpired that the locals there, too, had listened to the race and were overjoyed. When he turned up, the GMC was covered by a mass of freshly picked flowers.

– – – – –

On June 25, 1949, Le Mans was alive. Europe's premier motor race since 1923, it hadn't seen a racing car in action since the dark days just before war in 1939, and now, finally, everything was back on. People were delighted, arriving in their tens of thousands and lending the normally sleepy little French town a vibrant and noisy carnival atmosphere. The French president, Vincent Auriol, even made an appearance, doing a lap of honour before the race, at a rather more sedate pace than what was to follow.

It was also Macklin's first time there, and he took it all in with interest. He had joined the Aston Martin team for what would possibly be his first race but, although he had a few practice laps in the team's beautiful new DB2 saloon, it was decided to keep him on the sidelines as a reserve. He wasn't overly disappointed, settling down in the pits and savouring the atmosphere. He was still in the thick of it, he reminded himself, even if he wasn't on the track.

Tragically, it wasn't to be a happy race for Aston Martin. While most of the drivers took things relatively easily, Pierre Maréchal, a 33-year-old Frenchman, had no such intention. Driving the wheels off his DB2 he was up to seventh place, fourth on the index of performance, when a brake line fractured, leading to a trail of brake fluid slowly seeping out from the bottom of the Aston. Maréchal noticed, but in his determination he decided to continue. It was to be a fatal call. His furious pace continued as he took fourth place, and he was closing in on third when, just three hours from the finish, his luck ran out. Coming into Maison Blanche corner he suddenly found he had no brakes. His desperate attempts to stop came to nothing as he plunged off the track and overturned, the engine somehow managing to tear itself loose and flatten the car's roof. Maréchal was alive but only just, and although he was quickly rushed to a hospital nearby he died the next day. It was an inauspicious start to Aston Martin's racing season.

The team parted, Macklin heading back to Paris in a cloud of gloom. He had been friendly with Maréchal, a daredevil child of the French aristocracy, and his friend's death hurt deeply. On his first visit to Le Mans he had learned that it wasn't a place to be trifled with. Noel's words about the dangers of motorsport were beginning to ring true.

Maréchal's death opened up a place in the team for a full-time driver, and it was Macklin, already in the reserves, who duly slotted in. On July 10, just two weeks after the tragedy at Le Mans, he returned to Spa, the scene of the drive that led to him being picked for Aston in the first place a year earlier. Naturally enough everything went much more smoothly this time. Instead of the old Bentley he had a state of the art four-cylinder DB2 at his disposal, teaming up with Aston regular Nick Haines. This time he wasn't fighting the elements either. In contrast to last year's cold and rain, this year was calm and bright. It was the perfect atmosphere for his Aston debut.

It turned out to be a relatively uneventful, yet successful, outing. The cars were set up with large, long-range fuel tanks, and after a few driver swaps it was decided that Macklin would handle the last stint, from 11am until the finish at four in the afternoon. Although on-the-track-action was scarce, inside the DB2's cockpit Macklin was becoming quietly desperate. The lovely weather was getting to him for, with a lack of water on-board, he was quickly becoming dangerously dehydrated.

A few laps into his stint he'd caught a glimpse of his friend Charles Lewis. Lewis was among a group sitting outside a roadside café on the Masta straight, lazily watching the race unfold with a tall glass of beer underneath the hot Belgian sun. He recognised Macklin, and began holding up his glass in encouragement every time the Aston came streaking past. After a few laps Macklin, sweating and with his mouth completely dry, furiously gesticulated at Lewis' glass the next time he came past the café. Lewis got the idea. One lap later the green number 30 Aston hauled on its brakes and stopped, for the briefest instant, on the side of the road as Lewis thrust a beer through Macklin's side window. At that moment photographer Louis Klemantaski just happened to be wandering by and, with a laugh, took a quick picture of the handover. Months later, around Christmas time, Macklin received a copy from Klemantaski. "What's it worth not to send a copy to Astons?" he wrote, cheekily.

Aston Martin, which evidently wasn't timing every lap, never found out. The Macklin and Haines DB2 finished fifth overall, behind the Astons of Leslie Johnson and Charles Brackenbury in third, and Charles Horsfall and Paul Frère in fourth. The top two spots were decided in dramatic fashion. Macklin's good friend Henri Louveau looked to have second place locked down in his Delage when his car developed an oil leak, forcing him to drive the last lap of the race almost at walking pace. Meanwhile, the leading Ferrari 166 of Le Mans winner Luigi Chinetti was happily minding its own business when it hit the oil slick Louveau had left behind, causing it to spin off the track, knock down a spectator and crash into the corner of a house. Chinetti hopped out, administered first aid to the woman he'd hit, jumped back in his ailing car and somehow managed to drag it around two more laps for the win. That year's podium was filled with some very relieved men.

After the race Macklin was asked if he wanted to drive one of the Astons back to England. He agreed, although matters were delayed when, in the Spa paddock after the race, he ran into a Belgian girl he'd known from his skiing days. With little persuasion he gladly accepted her offer to stay with her at her parent's place, and the next day the Aston took a slight detour up to the north of Belgium. What followed was like something, as Macklin later put it, out of a French farce. Because of the girl's parents' the two were forbidden to sleep in the same room, although his friend nonetheless sneaked out and tiptoed into Macklin's guest room in the middle of the night. His delight quickly turned to horror when he heard the stairs outside the bedroom creak, causing his companion to jump out of bed and hide behind the nearest curtain while the dashing racing driver turned over and covered himself in blankets. The light clicked on. The girl's mother cast a glance around the room and quickly headed for the now-bulging, quivering curtains. "Go back to your bed, my girl," she bellowed as she pulled the curtain aside, revealing her quivering daughter who promptly ran down the corridor to the safety of her bedroom. She said nothing to Macklin, who was probably relieved it wasn't the girl's father with a shotgun in his hand. "Next morning I decided this was probably no longer a good place to be," he said, with an air of understatement. After a quick and embarrassed thank you, he hopped in the Aston and high-tailed it back to England as quickly as possible.

He hadn't raced much in 1949, but his work with Aston and his fine performances in the Maserati were beginning to carve a reputation as one of Britain's quickest young prospects. Off the track he was still having the time of his life, leading a cash-strapped yet exhilarating existence from the maid's quarters at the George V. His star was on the rise. Exciting things were on the horizon, but even he wouldn't have realised just how busy 1950 would turn out to be.

Chapter 7

Drama at the Targa Florio; success with Aston Martin

Much like the previous year, Macklin had another long, lazy off-season that he happily filled by driving around the continent, sailing, and continuing his eternal pursuit of women at bars throughout Europe. His mother, Leslie, had also moved to the continent, buying a tidy villa, which she had staffed with maids and assistants year-round, overlooking great expanses of the Mediterranean in the idyllic village of Roquebrune-Cap-Martin, right next to Monaco. Leslie tended to spend her winters in southern California with Mia and her esteemed son-in-law, Jack Vietor, a situation that suited Lance perfectly. In her absence he took over the villa and its retinue of servants, hosting fabulous parties at night or, if he wanted a little peace and quiet, sitting on the porch, lost in thought, and looking out over the town's green, rolling hills, its weathered orange rooftops, and the light blue Mediterranean. It was the perfect place to spend some downtime.

His winter idyll finally came to an end. Although he didn't have anything on the official Aston Martin schedule until Le Mans in June he was itching to get back into the cockpit, and, after a few phone calls and a little persuasion, he managed to get hold of a DB2 for his own ends. Looking around to see what was going on, he decided to take on the jewel in the crown of Italian racing circuits: the long, fast, forest-lined Monza circuit north of Milan. On March 26 he found himself, for the first time, at a race track in Italy. It was an ambitious choice. Over the years Monza had developed a fearsome reputation, especially after an horrific crash in the 1928 Italian Grand Prix when Emilio Materassi's Talbot shot off the track and into a grandstand, killing its driver and 27 spectators. It was not a place to be taken lightly.

When Macklin turned up he found he was the only non-Italian in a field dominated by Fiats, with the odd Ferrari and Abarth thrown in to spice things up. It was a situation he'd often found himself in at meetings in France – almost as if he was intruding on a local get-together – but he fitted in well, finding the DB2 to be as quick and pleasant to drive as the others he'd experienced. It was also a bit of a test session for what was to come later. Although the DB2 he was driving was an original works development car, built a year earlier, he had decided it could do with a bit of hotting-up. Just before Monza he had driven it to the Weber factory in Bologna where it was fitted – remarkably, free of charge – with three twin-choke Weber carburettors. The difference in speed was astonishing. He drove the newly invigorated Aston out of the factory and over to Monza, grinning every time he put his foot to the floor.

The race was a success. While his DB2 still didn't have the outright pace of the race winner, Consalvo Sanesi's gorgeous, streamlined Alfa Romeo Sperimentale, nor the two Ferraris that followed it onto the podium, it was a good, solid start to the year. Taking the flag after two sweltering, yet mostly uneventful, hours, he found himself lying fifth. The Aston had held together and proved to be much quicker than the year before. It wasn't a bad start at all.

The next race was something entirely different. A daunting challenge for even the most hardened drivers in Europe, the Targa Florio was one of the world's great road races. Entering it hadn't been on Macklin's agenda until a chance meeting in Monte Carlo in early March. In town to watch the Monte Carlo rally, Macklin had been socialising in moneyed circles when he was introduced to a "very old" Italian prince called Raimundo Lanza. Lanza, it turned out, was a motor racing fan who had heard of Macklin's exploits behind the wheel and was familiar with his Aston Martin works deal. The prince cornered him. "Do you think", he asked, "you'd like to come down to Sicily?" Macklin raised an eyebrow. "You can come stay with me," the prince continued. "Don't worry, I'll pay you some starting money. Just see if you can get a car ready." With that, the prince ambled off. The more Macklin thought about it, the more excited he became. The Targa Florio, he thought. Why not?

A couple of weeks later Macklin hopped in the DB2, fired it up and drove down through Italy to Naples, where he sent it on a late night cargo ship across to Sicily. He followed early the next morning. Upon arrival in Palermo he headed straight down to the harbour, where he looked out over the tangle of cargo ships bobbing in the early morning tide in search of the one carrying his Aston Martin. After a few inquiries in broken Italian he discovered that his car wouldn't be unloaded until later in the day so, with nothing better to do, he decided to head to his friend Raimundo Lanza's house. He didn't have any directions. Back in Monte Carlo, Lanza had assured him that all he needed to do was hire a Drotchki – a local term for a horse drawn cart – and say "Villa Trabia, Palermo." Macklin did as he was told and soon found himself on the back of a cart trotting through the lush Sicilian countryside. When he arrived he was confronted with two enormous, intimidating wrought iron gates and a towering wall that spanned as far as he could see. The cart driver shook his head. "I can't take you any further," he said, apologetically. "The last time I went in there, about a week ago, I nearly got myself and my horse killed by all those lunatics driving racing cars about the place." Intrigued, Macklin hopped off the cart, thanked the driver and wandered through the gates, wondering just what he'd gotten himself into.

When he arrived at the villa he was greeted by the elderly prince and a distinguished crowd of racing drivers, including the age-defying Tazio Nuvolari and the young up-and-comer Alberto Ascari. It turned out that the prince had his own race track on the villa's grounds, and every morning, to the prince's delight, his guests would hop into their cars and conduct their own private races. In typically Sicilian fashion the prince was also rumoured to have deep connections to the local mafia. Apparently, when a mafia turf war threatened that year's race, he worked his well-practised diplomacy and the matter was resolved. There was the odd hiccup. When a yellow Belgian coupé came in from a practice session full of bullet holes, and two terrified drivers, Lanza stormed into the villa and made a few furious phone calls. There had been a mistake, he explained apologetically after getting off the phone, and there would be no more problems. So it proved.

Macklin's co-driver was John Gordon, the friend who co-owned his Maserati. Squeezing into the DB2 around 2am, the two Englishmen were set to head off directly behind Ascari's Ferrari. They knew they were in for a tough run. Not only were they starting in the middle of the night but the weather was dreadful, ice-cold and pouring with rain, making the long road ahead dangerously slippery. Waiting behind the wheel, Macklin ignored the lights and the bustling crowd surrounding the starting box, his eyes fixed on the road ahead. The flag dropped. Macklin floored the accelerator and they were off into the enveloping darkness, winding into

Sicily's treacherous hills with nothing accompanying them but the roar of the Aston's engine. For the moment, they were all alone.

After a couple of hours Macklin spotted a pair of tail lights in the distance. Assuming it was one of the slower drivers he was astonished when, catching up through a slow corner, he realised he was right on the tail of Ascari, the pre-race favourite. A realisation dawned on him. Stick with Ascari, he told himself, and you might win the Targa Florio. Dawn was beginning to break, creating a hazy, murky grey as the Aston and the Ferrari roared through the countryside in convoy. For about an hour the two cut through the lonely dawn until, suddenly, things went wrong. Coming upon a small, slow Fiat, a furious Macklin could only watch as its driver let the Ferrari sail by before slamming the door on the bright green Aston. Ascari disappeared off into the distance, and it wasn't until a long few minutes later that Macklin was able to finally barge past. By now he was descending through a particularly dangerous mountain pass, the Aston slipping on the wet tarmac as he set back off in hot pursuit of Ascari. Gordon nervously looked out his passenger window and down the side of the mountain, following its steep plunge until it levelled out in some fields far below. There were no barriers. He gripped his seat tightly.

The rain continued to hammer down. Macklin was gaining fast when he came up to what looked, in the early morning gloom, like a straight stretch of road. He floored it, but just as the Aston reached 90 miles an hour he realised that the road in fact doubled back on itself. It had been an optical illusion and beyond lay a straight drop down into a ravine. Quickly realising what was happening he slammed on the brakes but knew there was no way the car would stop in time. As he and Gordon braced themselves the Aston smashed through a flimsy barrier and soared into the air, hitting the ground a few seconds later with a dull thud. For the two of them, everything went black.

Macklin woke to something trickling down the back of his neck. Thinking it was blood, he felt around trying to find where it was coming from. Moments later a thick, pungent smell began to fill the car. His eyes widened. It was petrol. In a flash he unbuckled himself and crawled out the window of the Aston, which was lying upside down on the side of the mountain, then ran around and dragged out his semi-conscious co-driver. Looking around, he discovered the car had become caught in a four foot deep by six foot wide drainage ditch, carved out to stop boulders rolling onto a railway line far below. Behind them was a 100 foot drop. They cast their eyes over the drop and shuddered, realising just how lucky they'd been, then began clambering back up to the road.

A robed priest was waiting for them when they reached the top. He beckoned for them to follow. Exchanging glances and silently agreeing that things couldn't get much stranger, they wearily trudged along behind him. Entering a small country house the two Englishmen sat down at a dusty wooden table, the priest plunking two glasses in front of them and filling them to the top with an unknown liqueur. Downing it quickly, they instantly felt better. Soon they were on their way back to Palermo in the back of a truck, leaving behind a broken race car and thinking about their great escape in the haunting, lonely Sicilian dawn.

– – – – –

Although the Aston was a write-off, luckily, the loss of the car didn't derail Macklin's season, since his next engagement was with the works Aston Martin team. The coming race, at Le Mans two months later, was to prove one of the most important races of his career.

Originally paired with Aston Martin regular Dudley Folland, Macklin was thrown into a bind when Folland's family inexplicably barred him from taking to the track that year. Scratching his head, Aston's new team manager John Wyer asked Macklin if he could think of anyone he'd particularly like to drive with. One name immediately popped into his head. "Why," he said, "don't we ask George Abecassis?"

George Abecassis was someone Macklin had always looked up to. Fast, determined, and always up for a challenge, he was ideally suited to the increasingly lively postwar racing scene. Abecassis was no newcomer to motor racing. Six years older than Macklin, he had begun his career in 1934, although it wasn't until he jumped in an Alta in 1938 that he really began to make a name for himself on the British racing scene. By the time war halted proceedings he had become one of British racing's leading lights. Like many of the drivers he had an eventful war, signing up immediately for the RAF and forging an impressive reputation as a talented bomber pilot. He was rated so highly that he eventually went out on top secret missions flying stripped down bombers low over occupied Europe, although it was during one of these, in late 1944, that his luck came to an end when he was shot down by a night fighter. He spent the remainder of the war in a Nazi prison camp.

When he returned to England he wasted no time in getting down to business. Like Macklin, he decided that selling cars wouldn't be a bad bet and soon put a call through to his old friend, and fellow racing enthusiast, John Heath. Heath, tall, serious and occasionally cantankerous, already had a used car dealership in Walton-on-Thames that he'd named HW Motors. Abecassis bought in, and soon the two natural businessmen were doing a roaring trade. They soon decided that selling cars just wasn't enough, though. Taking things a step further they indulged their shared passion, and, at the beginning of 1948, HWM became a racing concern as well as a car dealership. They were delighted.

By the time Aston Martin began to consider using Abecassis for Le Mans, HWM had been competing with its attractive little HW-Alta racing cars for two years. During that time Abecassis – the team's designated lead driver – had shown tremendous application and no shortage of speed, and, given the team's frequent reliability issues, patience. He was a go-getter with a devil may care attitude about him, both personality traits that appealed to Macklin and the Aston Martin crew. A few enquiries were made, and a quick call later everything was settled. Abecassis would be partnering Macklin at Le Mans. Everyone was delighted.

Heading into Le Mans Macklin felt optimistic. He had a good car under him, a quick co-driver, and he was in an environment he knew. It was a set of circumstances that hadn't come together particularly often in his career thus far, and he was determined to make the most of it. At 4pm on the afternoon of June 24, 1950, Macklin found himself waiting alongside the other drivers in a line of nervous energy on the hot Le Mans track, all eyeing their gleaming racing cars on the other side of the pit straight. With the crack of a pistol they were off, sprinting across the tarmac and leaping into their cars before throwing them into gear and heading off towards the Dunlop Curve.

From the start Macklin was in complete control. The Aston immediately shot into second place in the Index of Performance – "the thing that carried the real prize money," he later said – and was cruising along comfortably. The driver was evidently more comfortable than the team, for every time his DB2 came past the pits Macklin would look out to see a "go slow" sign flash past. He ignored it.

The next morning, after an uneventful journey during the night, they were still lying in second on the Index of Performance and gaining on the tiny Monopole-Panhard that had the lead. Around 10am on Sunday, after a short stint from Abecassis, it was a weary Macklin who jumped into the

Aston for one last, long stint. John Wyer had looked at the times, worked out how much fuel the car could take, and decided that he was going to give his fastest driver one last shot at the Index win. It was a gamble. Macklin had been up all night – possibly, if rumours were anything to go by, with a girl he'd met in a nearby town as well as in the cockpit – and the car itself was in a sorry state. The shock absorbers were completely gone and the brakes were alarmingly soft, but he was game. In contrast to the day before, he was now confronted with "go faster" signs hanging from the pit wall. His eyelids drooping and every bump jarring him, he tried his best to knock down his lap times, but he was just too exhausted. When he crossed the line, banged-up and nearly delirious, he found himself fifth overall and first equal on the Index with the little Monopole. Swamped by his joyous team as he pulled into the pits, he slowly pulled himself out of the oil-smeared DB2 and wandered gingerly over to a satisfied John Wyer and George Abecassis to have a much-needed drink.

After the race, David Brown mentioned he'd like to drive the now thoroughly banged-up Aston back to the team's hotel to see how it felt after 24 hours of punishment. The drivers winced, knowing that it was a completely different beast to the delightful car he'd driven to the circuit a day earlier. Though they tried to dissuade him Brown was firm, and it came as a surprise to nobody that he found the return trip horrifying. "He was absolutely shattered," Macklin recalled later, laughing. "He couldn't believe that the lovely motor car ... had almost been reduced to a wreck on wheels."

Aston Martin's success at Le Mans also had longer-lasting implications. Macklin and Abecassis turned out to be kindred spirits and quickly formed a deep friendship that lasted the rest of their lives. They also shared a mutual admiration for each other's driving abilities, and after Le Mans Abecassis came to Macklin with a question. "Do you think," he asked, "you'd like to drive for HWM?" "Certainly," Macklin replied. It was the start of the busiest, and most adventurous, period of his racing career, and, arguably, of his life. He left Le Mans in a happy daze.

Chapter 8

Professional racing driver

If things had gone slightly differently, and George Abecassis had been a less patient man, Macklin's opportunity might not have come around at all. Throughout its short existence the HWM team had been beset by constant problems. After initially trying out an assortment of cars, Abecassis and Heath had become enamoured with the beautifully designed HW-Alta that designer Geoffrey Taylor had shown them in late 1947. However, while it looked quick on paper, and was certainly gorgeous in reality, the Alta turned out to be a problem child. Rolled out for the 1948 season it broke down in the first practice session it took part in, then in the first race, and then the next two races after that. 1949 wasn't much better, for while it did manage to make it through half of the six races it was entered in, it turned out to be painfully slow, usually finishing far down the leader-board. When it broke down, yet again, during the 1949 French Grand Prix, a disillusioned Abecassis wondered if it was all worth it. The Alta, left forlornly on the side of the track, never raced again.

Luckily for all involved, John Heath was having no such issues with his own HW-Alta. Though not a great natural talent, Heath was doing well, and his enthusiasm cheered his dejected business partner. Crawling back from the precipice of retirement, Abecassis did an about-turn and decided to join Heath in building a serious team for the 1950 season, this time running cars that Heath had designed. HWM had big ambitions. It knew that the UK was lagging far behind its European rivals when it came to racing teams, for even though Britain had Aston Martin and Jaguar in sports car racing, there was still a massive, glaring hole in Europe-dominated Formula Two and Formula One. Despite the constant series of disappointments they'd endured over the past two years, Heath and Abecassis decided to go all out and take it to the Europeans. These were days of patriotism, and the duo from Walton-on-Thames wanted to do their bit.

They assembled a crack team. At the heart of HWM was the cantankerous ex-Polish army veteran Alfons Kowaleski – better known as Alf Francis – who, despite not even having seen a racing car prior to joining HWM, had proved to be an extremely hard-working and brilliant mechanic. Francis' right-hand man was Rex Woodgate, and the two were joined by young mechanic Frank Nagel the same weekend Macklin turned up. While Abecassis had been the team's lead driver, things would change when Heath and Abecassis stumbled across one of the great talents of British postwar racing. Young Stirling Moss had finally made the transition to proper circuit racing and, despite his car's constant unreliability, he had blown everyone away. He was so quick that many watching – Alf Francis included – thought the precocious young talent was heading for a fall. "I must admit that at this time I saw Moss as a rather thrusting driver who tended to push his car and himself just a little too near the limit," Francis later wrote. "How wrong I was."

Despite the team's excitement going into the 1950 season, it quickly became clear that it wasn't going to be all smooth sailing. The HWMs, good looking as always, simply didn't have the speed to keep up with their lighter, more powerful continental rivals. Reliability was also a never-ending issue, and a look at Francis' notes from the season reveal an extraordinary amount of sleepless nights, the team's mechanics tearing apart and rebuilding the cars on a steady diet of cigarettes and Coca Cola. This would be followed by an inevitable rush to get to the next race – the same, exhausted mechanics had to drive the team's transporter – where the process would be repeated all over again. From an organisational standpoint it was madness.

It was a different story for the drivers, who led a comparatively easy life. Macklin knew he wouldn't have to worry about fixing broken magnetos – or driveshafts, or gearboxes – or driving massive transporters on little to no sleep. That was the mechanics' job. All he had to do was drive as fast as he could, then attend the inevitable post-race party and all the comforts that went with it. Naturally, he fitted right in.

Everything moved remarkably quickly. A week after stepping out of the Aston he was back in the cockpit, although this one was much airier, smaller and louder. Despite the HWM's relative lack of speed Macklin was overjoyed to finally be behind the wheel of a proper, modern, racing car. His first race was at Reims on July 2, joining Moss and Heath against a field that included some of the great talents of early 1950s racing: the ever-present French trio of Robert Manzon, Maurice Trintignant and André Simon; the rotund Froilán González; Ferrari's Luigi Villoresi; and his Targa Florio rival Alberto Ascari. He mingled with them all on the grid with a sense of disbelief. This, he thought, is what it's all about.

It turned out to be an uneventful first race. Despite being outclassed on Reims' long straights, Moss, Heath and Macklin still came in third, fourth and fifth, respectively. It was a solid first outing. After the race the team headed to the Hotel Welcome in the town of Reims, where they took full advantage of the generosity then afforded to visiting racing drivers. Macklin wisely decided not to get too carried away on his first day with the team and went to bed early, as did teetotaller Moss, which left John Heath, Frank Nagel and Rex Woodgate to represent the rest of the team at the bar. Wandering down for a quiet drink after finishing the team's accounts around two o'clock in the morning, Alf Francis was horrified to find the HWM trio leaning up against the bar surrounded by fans, all three completely plastered. Heath stumbled over. Gesturing towards his two drunken mechanics, he told Francis to get them moving. "Can you remind them that they have a long journey tomorrow?" he said, slurring over the din. Appalled by the lot of them but unable to chastise the team owner, Francis swiftly sent the two sheepish mechanics up to bed. The next day, Francis wrote, "they appeared so ill and tired I almost felt sorry for them."

The next race was five days and 1100 miles away at Bari, Italy. Francis and the two hungover mechanics immediately set off at a furious pace to try and make it in time for Friday practice, while Macklin, Moss and Heath enjoyed a much more comfortable and leisurely drive in Heath's roomy Citroën Traction Avant. It proved to be one of the mechanics' most adventurous journeys. Setting off in the afternoon, the two mechanics drove the transporter while Francis followed in the team's van, which he'd recently had to get out of pawn after temporarily running out of money. They were all supposed to drive through the night, although after they were out of sight the mechanics sneakily pulled into a quiet road and promptly fell asleep, causing an infuriated Francis, when he eventually found them, to say that he "felt like committing a double murder and then maybe shooting myself." Waking to their red-faced chief mechanic banging on their window, the two quickly got back on the road, fortified, like Francis, by the occasional swig of brandy. Around 10am the front axle became detached on the van, forcing a stopover in Aix-Les-Baines, followed by a rush to the treacherous, snow- and ice-covered Mt Cenis Pass. They descended slowly in tandem, creeping along and holding their breath, terrified they were going to lose concentration and tumble to the valley below. They made it through and, feeling like they'd come out the other side of an expedition across the Antarctic, the sleep-deprived convoy stopped in the town of Piacenza for a coffee. Sitting outside and enjoying the fresh air, barely keeping their heads off the table in front of them, the three were less than impressed when Heath's Citroën breezed past, Macklin giving a cheery wave and a thumbs up.

The £1000 guaranteed entry fee was the real reason they were heading to Bari, the team figuring they didn't really have a chance to mix it with a Formula One crowd that included the all-conquering Alfa Romeo team of Giuseppe Farina and Juan-Manuel Fangio. For a while it was beginning to look as if even the money might not have been worth it, with one of the mechanics getting lost on the way to the track and then, more seriously, the team's garage at Bari catching fire with all three HWMs inside. Luckily for all involved, and despite an almost-comical series of attempts to put out the fire with empty fire extinguishers, the blaze was doused before damaging the cars. It did, however, lead to oversights by the flustered mechanics that came back to haunt them in the race. Macklin's car, unscathed though it was, went to the grid without any fluid in the back axle. It was an oversight that turned out to have dramatic consequences.

On race day Macklin roared off the grid and quickly found, to his immense surprise, that he was actually keeping up with the big boys after all. Up ahead he could see Moss in close pursuit of Farina and Fangio, the little HWM flashing in-between the bright red Alfa Romeos, while he diced with a motley crew of Talbots and Maseratis. He was more than holding his own until, 11 furious laps in and surrounded by a jostling pack of cars, disaster struck. Before he knew what was happening his HWM was spinning down the middle of the track at 120 miles an hour, the other cars flashing past him in a multicoloured blur of noise, missing him by inches. Completely helpless, he gripped the steering wheel, his knuckles white. When he eventually came to a halt on the side of the track he leaped out and looked back up the track at a winding set of skid marks that covered half the length of the main straight. The back axle had seized solid, and Macklin trudged off back to the pits as Moss flew past. Despite being in the middle of a furious battle with the two Alfa Romeos, the younger driver nevertheless found time for a quick wave.

– – – – –

Moss would never forget the first time he saw Macklin. It was at one of the early HWM team meetings that Macklin strolled in with graceful ease, radiating a quiet confidence and with a sense of style that was subtle yet sophisticated. He lived in Paris. He'd been in the war. He'd driven at Le Mans. To an impressionable 20-year-old like Moss, it was thrilling. "The only word that sums him up is 'cool'," he recalled. "He was so cool. He would sort of turn his cuffs up and turn the collar up, and all these sort of things. He was very much a man of the world." Macklin was ten years older than Moss, and took on, if not a fatherly role, then that of a debonair older brother. The two would head into classy bars between races, order – in Moss' case, non-alcoholic – drinks, and the younger driver would watch while Macklin sidled up to the prettiest girl in the bar and effortlessly began chatting her up. They devised a particular term for it: 'slanting off.' "You'd go into a bar for a drink and Lance would have just slanted off to that pretty girl down the end of the bar, and you'd know he was chatting her up," Moss said. "It was a pretty sophisticated situation for me. I mean, I was only 17, 18 years old and here's a guy who's a sort of sophisticated man about town who also drives racing cars and things like that. He had a pretty good story there (for the women)." Moss, watching eagerly, took note.

It was quickly established that while Moss was certainly HWM's number one driver, Macklin was a very quick deputy. On individual laps there often wasn't much between the two, but it was Moss' intense power of concentration, and Macklin's distinct lack of it, that made the difference. Macklin admitted as much. "I could usually go as fast as he for some time, but then I'd start to think, 'Christ, there's nobody in front of you and there's nobody immediately behind you, what's the point of keeping up this crazy speed all the time?'" His mind would drift away, recalling the women he'd pulled prior to the race and the fun he was going to have at the party afterwards. He'd chuckle quietly to himself, in a dream, before suddenly realising that the car in front was now a speck in the distance. "You have to realize that Lance was so laid back," Moss said. "You're talking about a really pretty cool character." Being laid back may have helped off the track, but it was often a different matter on it.

After the all-round drama at Bari – during which Moss, remaining focused, drove one of his finest races to end up third – the HWM team now had a couple of weeks to kill. While the mechanics refused to do anything strenuous after their stressful two weeks, Moss and Macklin – now well and truly brothers in arms – were feeling a little more adventurous. At Bari they had met an astonishingly beautiful young woman who, to their delight, turned out to be Miss Italian Air Force. Despite their best efforts neither of them managed to sweep her off her feet but, undeterred, they kept in touch. When downtime came along, they decided to hop in John Heath's beloved Citroën and head to the island of Capri, off the coast of Naples, to track her down. They arrived at Capri to find an abundance of natural beauty but, to their dismay, no Miss Italian Air Force. It was also off-season and the island was more or less deserted. They were dejected. Wandering around, the two slumped down in one of the town's small cafes and ordered two sodas, Macklin looking out onto the road and Moss perusing a magazine he'd picked up. Flicking through, Moss came across a picture of Miss France.

"Look at that!" he exclaimed, pointing the picture out to Macklin. "What a fantastic girl. What I wouldn't give to go out with a girl like that." He shook his head in admiration.

Macklin began to grin. "I know her," he said.

"Really?"

"She's the daughter of a policeman in Monte Carlo."

Moss was incredulous. "Are you joking?" he asked, with a hint of suspicion.

Macklin shook his head. "Well," Moss said, cautiously, "would you introduce me to her?"

"Certainly. We could probably go up to Monte Carlo and find her there now."

The two looked at each other. Hours later they were on a ferry back to the mainland, and, after quickly making a beeline for Heath's Citroën, were off on the 900-odd kilometre trip to Monte Carlo. Taking it in turns they made the drive in one swoop, the two powering through the winding Italian mountain roads much more quickly than Heath would have been comfortable with. They arrived and, after a quick rest at the Macklin family villa outside Monte Carlo, the two immediately got on with the job of tracking down Miss France. It wasn't to be. It turned out that Miss France, to Moss' severe disappointment, was out of town. Macklin cheered him up. "I wasn't going to let him down if I could help it," he recalled proudly, and, using his considerable powers of charm as well as his local connections, he managed to introduce Moss to another pretty friend of his instead. Things worked out, as Macklin put it, and two days later the two were happily on their way back to Naples.

They parked the Citroën back in the garage and were trotting off to their hotel when Moss happened to turn around for one final glance. "Christ," he said, horrified. "Look at those bloody tyres." Macklin turned round and immediately saw the problem. The Citroën's front two tyres, only a few days old, were completely, utterly, bald. "Oh my god," he exclaimed. He then quickly jacked the car up and swapped the tyres around, putting the still-roadworthy rear ones on the front. Crossing their fingers and hoping Heath wouldn't notice, they scurried off. Heath did notice, of course, and when he found out he was furious. The cost of their Italian adventure amounted to an expensive new set of tyres and an extended period in their boss' bad books.

In an attempt to make up for their French misadventure the two put special effort into the next race, a Formula Two event in Naples on July 23. Early signs were promising. The HWMs were well suited to the twisty track, and proved to be quick in practice and qualifying, lightening Heath's dark mood. When the flag fell on race day Moss was immediately on the tail of Franco Cortese's Ferrari, while Macklin barged his way through the field to join the pursuit. Stuck behind Cortese, Moss and Macklin hatched a plan. Closing up behind Moss, Macklin swiftly pulled to the right. Cortese saw him, went to block the line, and could only watch as Moss went soaring past on the left. Moss' grin was still visible to the HWM pit crew a lap later.

Then, for Moss, it all went wrong. Worried about his HWM leaking water, he had decided to go flat-out to build up a lead in case he needed to make a late-race pit stop. Ignoring Francis' frantic go-slow signals from the pit lane, he was miles in the lead when he came to lap back-marker Berardo Taraschi for the second time. Waving Moss through, Taraschi then abruptly lost control and spun, clipping the rear of Moss' drifting HWM in the process. It wasn't much, just a touch, but enough to burst Moss' front tyre and send him off the track and straight into a tree. The impact smashed his front teeth and broke his kneecap, but he still had the foresight to leap from his stricken car and run a few yards before collapsing. In the days before flame-proof overalls and well-trained marshals he didn't want to take any chances on ending up trapped behind the wheel of his car, burning to death.

Macklin had by now taken the lead and was pulling away comfortably, but seeing his friend prone on the side of the road threw him. Cortese took advantage of Macklin's temporary lack of concentration and zipped by. That was how it stayed, Macklin relieved to discover later that Moss was alive and relatively well in a local hospital. It was a lucky escape.

While Moss was out of action it was up to Macklin, now the team's de facto lead driver, to make the most of the next couple of races. His luck appeared to have temporarily abandoned him, though, the situation not helped by a couple of oversights from his shaken team. At the next race, a Formula Two event in Geneva, he was hamstrung by an unsuitable gear ratio – which, to the annoyance of Alf Francis, had been passed off by John Heath – and had to slip the clutch to get around the corners on his way to sixth place. After Geneva came the king of all European race tracks, Germany's 14½-mile-long Nürburgring. To do well on the forbidding Nürburgring required a car with a lot of power and a driver with a lot of track knowledge. Macklin had neither. Still, he ended up sixth and probably would have done even better if his team hadn't accidentally brought him in a lap early.

After a brief trip back to England for an uneventful outing at the BRDC International Trophy race, by September 2 the HWMs were again back on the continent for a Formula Two race in the small Belgian town of Mettet. Moss was back in action, and, up against an assortment of Gordinis and Ferraris, the two HWMs finished fourth and fifth in the first heat and then demolished everybody in the second. To the delight of the HWM crew, Alberto Ascari and two other Ferraris blew up their motors in a vain effort to keep up. Moss and Macklin finished the weekend second and third on aggregate. The travelling road-show that was HWM was beginning to get worn out but only had a few more races to go. There was Périgeux, where the cars raced through an ancient market square in the tiny town, and where Macklin retired, then Lago de Gardi in Italy, where the HWM pit was crowded with women screeching either "Stirleeng" or "Mackleen." Moss and Macklin's reputation had evidently preceded them, much to their shared delight and the disapproval of Alf Francis. Their happiness wasn't to last long. The next day, while putting in a fast lap on the beautiful lakeside circuit, Macklin had his first real accident in a racing car. Failing to take a corner he hit a wall near the town's gasworks, merely denting the wall but completely twisting the HWM's chassis. Looking even sorrier was Macklin, severely bruised and sporting a huge black eye. It's possible that his thoughts had been on how to charm the Italian women waiting back at the pits rather than on the race. "Italians are difficult girls to get into bed with," he once said. Francis suspected Macklin's thoughts were elsewhere, too. "(It) was going to put him out of the running in more ways than one," he said, knowingly.

He didn't have long to lick his wounds. While the HWM roller-coaster was over for the moment – John Heath fervently plotting exciting things for the following year – it was time to get back to sports cars. He had one final Aston Martin race, the Tourist Trophy sports car event at the hilly Dundrod circuit in Northern Ireland. Excited to be back behind the wheel of a DB2, he promptly posted the fastest times in practice, ahead of both Abecassis and the venerable Reg Parnell, but he quickly came unstuck on race day. Getting under way in torrential weather, he fluffed the start and wound up halfway down the field, surrounded by thick walls of spray and a slithering, sliding pack of drivers. He did his best to work his way back up, and quickly glued himself to the back of the other Astons, but his concentration again let him down. Going for one over-ambitious pass too many, he ended up heading off the circuit and down an escape road. He held it together and made it back on-track, but finished only third in class.

Further up ahead, history was being made. That day, Moss was simply in a class of his own, manhandling his Jaguar XK120 around the track in a way that captured the attention of everyone watching. Ignoring the pouring rain, he made driving look easy, and, by the end of the day his name was on everyone's lips. Jaguar's William Lyons offered him a contract shortly afterwards. It was the beginning, not that he knew it at the time, of the super-stardom that was soon to follow.

Watching from the banks and sheltering under her brother's umbrella was a young racing fan who would later get to know Macklin better than nearly anybody. Shelagh Mulligan had come to Dundrod simply to take a look around and hang-out with her brother and his friends. Despite the treacherous weather she'd been enjoying herself, the little group wandering over to the soaking-wet cars before the race, admiring their sleek curves and smelling the distinctive, almost earthy smell of hot racing car engines ticking over. Tall, vivacious and beautiful, she didn't have any trouble meeting the drivers, one of whom was a short, charming man with a cheeky smile. It wasn't a particularly memorable first meeting. "Dundrod was the first time I spoke to him," she recalled, years later. "I didn't think anything more of it. You know, it was 'Lance Macklin, a driver.' Just like 'S Moss, a driver,' and so on. What do I remember? Not much." The group wandered off to watch the race. For Macklin, whether it was a smile, her looks, or a glint in her eye, there was something about the young woman that lingered in his mind long after she'd gone. He'd get to know her later, he said to himself.

After Dundrod there was one last date with the official Aston Martin team for the year. Flipping through the record books in a quest to drum up some publicity, John Wyer had stumbled upon a record he figured the Aston team could handle with ease. He'd learned that the 24-hour record for three-litre cars was relatively slow, around 90mph, which seemed entirely doable. A few months later Macklin found himself anxiously standing on the side of the track at Montlhéry with Eric Thompson, Charles Brackenbury and the Aston Martin brains trust in anticipation of making history. They were aiming to average 105mph, something Wyer figured wouldn't be much of a stretch for the sturdy DB2s.

Although things started off fairly well, it quickly became apparent that they had all underestimated what they were in for. Montlhéry proved bumpier than anyone had realised, and, as the night wore on, the DB2 began to shake itself, slowly but noticeably, to pieces. That wasn't the only problem. In the evening, ominously, a thin mist began creeping onto the circuit. Macklin, behind the wheel, nervously told himself that if his hero Bernd Rosemeyer could tackle the Nürburgring in the fog, driving round an oval shouldn't be a problem. A minute later, coming off the banking, it did become a problem. Out of nowhere he drove into a bank of fog so dense he couldn't see the track in front of him. His eyes desperately scanned the road. He continued for a second then, realising he wasn't getting out of it any time soon, he panicked and slammed on the brakes. He tried one more lap before a nervous John Wyer, hearing the screech of tyres and seeing the fog, called him in. Embarrassingly, the attempt was over. Later, while checking over the car, the mechanics made a stomach-churning discovery. Because of the bumpy track a crossmember at the front of the car had fractured nearly the whole way through. "In another half hour or so it would have broken altogether and the suspension would have collapsed," Macklin recalled. It had been a lucky fog after all. Looking at his wounded DB2, Macklin breathed a long, deep sigh of relief.

Continued on page 81

Mia Macklin's wedding, Surrey, England, May 1940. Dressed in his pristine naval uniform, Lance and his sister, Mia Macklin, smile for the camera.
(Courtesy Screen Archive South East)

Spa Francorchamps, Belgium, July 1949. Charles Lewis sneaks Macklin a beer during a brief, unscheduled, stop. He later finished fifth. "What's it worth not to send a copy to Astons?" photographer Louis Klemantaski later asked.
(Courtesy The Klemantaski Collection)

Christopher Columbus 500 Years Grand Prix, Genoa, Italy, May 1951. Macklin battles his way to third place in the HWM. (Courtesy Revs Institute)

Le Mans 24 Hours, France, June 1951. Macklin's third place finish, alongside co-driver Eric Thompson, proved to be a highlight of his career. (Courtesy Motorsport Images)

Tourist Trophy, Dundrod, Northern Ireland, August 1951. Though the new Aston Martin DB3 debuted with high expectations it ultimately proved to be a disappointment. Macklin's first race with the car, here at Dundrod, ended in retirement. (Courtesy Motorsport Images)

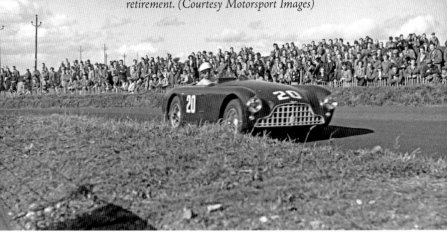

Gran Premio de Modena, Italy, September 1951. An elated – and dirty! – Macklin grins at the camera after finishing in third place, while second-placed José Froilán González chats to someone in the middle of the frame. The race was won by Alberto Ascari. (Courtesy Revs Institute)

Daily Express International Trophy, Silverstone, England, May 1952. The chequered flag waves as Macklin crosses the line to take the victory. (Courtesy Motorsport Images)

Daily Express International Trophy, Silverstone, England, May 1952. Surrounded by reporters, Macklin savours the win. It was one of his proudest moments. (Courtesy Motorsport Images)

A brochure from the 1952 Daily Express International Trophy.
(Courtesy BRDC Archive/SHL)

Daily Express International Trophy, Silverstone, England, May 1953. Macklin checks the HWM's engine during a break in proceedings. John Heath and Duncan Hamilton, in helmet facing the camera, are at left. (Courtesy The GPL Collection)

Belgian Grand Prix, Spa Francorchamps, Belgium, June 1952. The HWMs were up against some stiff competition at this year's Belgian Grand Prix. Macklin eventually finished four laps down in 11th place. (Courtesy Motorsport Images)

Le Mans 24 Hours, France, June 1953. The unusual-looking Bristol 450 was quick but, at least initially, dangerously unreliable. Much to the company's dismay, Macklin liked to call it 'the pregnant grasshopper.' (Courtesy Revs Institute)

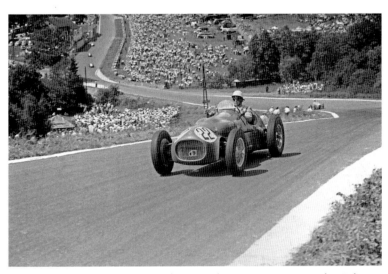

Belgian Grand Prix, Spa Francorchamps, Belgium, June 1953. Another Belgian Grand Prix, another tough race for HWM. Here, Macklin heads around Eau Rouge before his eventual lap 19 retirement. (Courtesy Motorsport Images)

British Grand Prix, Silverstone, England, July 1953. At Silverstone the HWMs proved to be both outclassed and unreliable, with none of the team's four entries making it to the finish. Here, Macklin leads José Froilán González before retiring with clutch problems. (Courtesy Motorsport Images)

Crystal Palace Trophy, London, England, July 1953. Crystal Palace proved to be a happy hunting ground for Macklin, finishing in a strong fourth place this time around. (Courtesy The Klemantaski Collection)

His HWM and Aston Martin obligations all tied up, it was nearly time for Macklin to return to his customary life of leisure. He was about to head back to France when a conversation with Moss changed his mind. A few weeks earlier, and before his stunning Dundrod drive, Moss had followed Macklin's suggestion and gone to speak with John Wyer about the possibility of driving for Aston in 1951. After wishing him well, Macklin pointed him in the direction of Wyer's office and waited for him to come out. When he did, half an hour later, his face was flushed red.

"Did you sign up," Macklin asked, enthusiastically.

"No," Moss said, quickly. Macklin looked at him, confused.

"Mean bloody lot, that," Moss continued, indignant. "They hardly offered me anything except ... they offered me fifty quid a year."

"Well, that's what they pay me."

Moss gave Macklin a withering look.

"Well," he said slowly, "you must be bloody stupid."

Now, a few weeks later, the two laughed. Still, Moss said, wouldn't it be fun if we could take one of the Astons for a spin? Having a think, he asked Macklin if he'd like to have a go at an endurance rally that was coming up in a few weeks. Macklin, always up for a challenge, agreed.

Moss was referring to the MCC *Daily Express* 1000-Mile Rally, a one-off event that spanned several days and wound through the back roads of Britain. Generously, Aston agreed to lend them a DB2 that the factory had tinkered around with and made suitable for rallying conditions. Everything was in order. On November 8, Macklin, Moss and the hotted-up DB2 turned up at the start point at Plymouth, looking well and truly out of place in a mass of tweed-suited gentlemen driving MGs and Fords. Their first control point was around 200 miles away in the seaside town of Eastbourne, and any doubt about what they were involved in was removed when they discovered they'd been given around seven hours to get there. Ignoring instructions to take it easy they promptly tore off, leaving everyone in their wake. Enjoying the freedom of speed-unrestricted public roads, they turned up at Eastbourne four hours early.

Not knowing what to do they drove slowly along the seafront, casting their eyes over the town's long pier and across its tatty arcade stores and tea rooms. After a while they noticed a sign saying "Tea Dance." They looked at each other and, without a word, pulled in across from it. Wandering inside they found themselves in the middle of a hive of activity. While a live band played swing jazz the floor was packed with dancers, including, to the drivers' delight, lots of pretty young women. Sauntering over, the two worked their charm and were soon in deep conversation with a couple of chatty locals. Everyone was getting along swimmingly when they collectively had an idea.

"So, what are you doing?" one of the women asked.

"We're on a rally," Macklin replied.

"What's that? Sounds interesting."

Moss chipped in. "We drive around the countryside from one place to another. It's great fun."

The quartet looked at each other.

"Why don't you come with us?" Macklin asked, enthusiastically. Moss nodded.

The women giggled. "Oh yes," one said. "It sounds lovely."

The drivers were thrilled. Leaving the dance the quartet excitedly rushed over to the DB2, but, straight away, the women's enthusiasm started to wane. The rally gear, the numbers and the realisation that this was a proper racing car made them nervous. Reluctantly they jumped in and travelled down as far as race control, but once they arrived they quickly hauled themselves out of the car. Hurriedly excusing themselves, the women ran off and never returned. Macklin and Moss were crestfallen.

Still, the rally continued. They arrived at the next town five hours early, whereupon they decided to play it safe and booked a hotel room and went to sleep. Hours later they rose, showered and headed off up north towards Wales. Moss slept as Macklin drove down narrow Welsh country roads in the dark, the steady rain making conditions tricky, especially without a navigator to guide the way. At one point Macklin mistook a curve for a straight and, realising his error at the last moment, took to a farm gateway as an escape road. Luckily the gate was open, but the DB2 still ended up in a farmyard surrounded by a lot of noisy upset animals. Moss woke with a start. Not understanding how he had suddenly become surrounded by farm animals, he brusquely asked Macklin what was going on. "Are we wrong, then?" Macklin blurted out. "You're supposed to be navigating." Moss was unimpressed. "There is no doubt that sometimes Stirling Moss' language can be downright bad," Macklin recounted.

After another long stop, the two continued north to Scotland. They were making cracking time when, hurtling over a blind brow, they abruptly found themselves at the end of a long queue of cars stretching into the distance. By now it was snowing, and it turned out that many of the cars were having trouble getting over a steep mountain pass. They were taking it in turns to push each other over, and the resulting delay stretched for miles. Impatient as ever, Moss and Macklin were having none of it. The location wasn't much for passing: a steep bank on the left opposite a steep drop down into a valley on the right. There was, however, a narrow grass verge before the drop, just big enough for a car to fit through. Moss, who was behind the wheel, eyed the verge. "Let's see if we can pass them on the outside," he said. Macklin agreed, and soon the two were tearing up the road past the ragged line of parked cars. Despite the snow and the dangerous drop they went for broke, the other drivers turning and shaking their fists, shouting and honking their car horns as the Aston went skidding past them, splattering their cars with mud. "It was, after all, supposed to be a rally," Macklin said, indignantly, "with people overcoming conditions, not being mastered by them." The others clearly didn't see it the same way.

The last event was a series of manoeuvrability tests. Moss and Macklin came prepared. Before the rally they'd laid out a replica of the tests they knew they'd face – slaloms, reversing into marked out spaces and so forth – and taken turns practising outside Aston Martin's headquarters. Arriving at Torquay for the end of the rally, a coin toss resulted in Moss taking on the testing responsibilities. Afterwards they thought they'd done fantastically and headed to the rally clerk to check the results, sure they'd scored a fabulous and crushing victory. They were to be disappointed. Muttering something about putting a wheel wrong during the manoeuvrability tests, the clerk informed them they'd come seventeenth. They were furious. "We had been fiddled out of a win," Macklin said. "We believed they didn't want it won by Stirling Moss and Lance Macklin in a works Aston Martin. They wanted this first postwar rally won by Mr Everyman in a Ford Zephyr or something like that, which is, I believe, what happened." The two drove home, grumbling to each other the whole way.

– – – – –

1950 had been an astonishing year. In sports, as in life, one small, seemingly inconsequential act can often have far-reaching repercussions. So it proved for Macklin. If Dudley Folland hadn't been prevented by his family from taking part in Le Mans that year, Macklin might never have teamed up with Abecassis, never caught his eye, never sat in a competitive racing car's seat. He knew he'd been fortunate. He'd met the world's best drivers as well as, importantly for him, some of Europe's prettiest women, and was now living his dream as a full-time racing driver. However, he'd also received a first-hand taste of the dangers that were out there, waiting for racing drivers during this most dangerous period of motorsport. In idle moments images occasionally flashed through his mind: seeing Moss on his side, not moving, under the hot Italian sun. Feeling the exhausts of the cars flashing past his stricken HWM when he skidded, helplessly, down the middle of the track at Bari. Looking at the cracked crossmember of his Aston Martin and wondering what might have happened if it had let go while turning a corner at 160mph.

He didn't dwell on them, of course, because, like all the others, he couldn't afford to. Nevertheless, and for more reasons than one, he entered the end-of-year break knowing that he was a lucky, lucky man.

www.veloce.co.uk / www.velocebooks.com
All current books • New book news • Special offers • Gift vouchers

Chapter 9

Dashing round the continent; a podium at Le Mans

On March 10, 1951, Macklin found himself chatting with Moss and the larger-than-life Duncan Hamilton on a cold morning at Goodwood. Having enjoyed a typically lazy off-season the drivers had gathered to check out what Heath, Francis and the rest of the HWM team had been busy with. After an inauspicious beginning the previous day, when the brand new HWM, to everyone's dismay, had refused to start, it was now going like the clappers. Moss and Macklin were delighted as they watched Abecassis tear around the track with a wide grin on his face.

The good mood didn't last. Ignoring the light drizzle that had started to fall, Abecassis began to lap faster and faster when he suddenly lost control. The car spun off the track and into a badly maintained barrier that was missing its bottom half, causing the out-of-control HWM to slide underneath. The top of the barrier hit Abecassis, breaking his collarbone and knocking him out. His injuries were nasty enough but he could count himself lucky: a few more inches would have seen him decapitated. Francis and a marshal jumped a barrier and rushed towards him, fearing the worst when they saw a thin trickle of blood streaming from his ears and nose. "I honestly thought it was the last I should ever see of George Abecassis," Francis recalled. It wasn't, but it did put him out of action for months. For Macklin, who had watched events unfold in horror, it was yet another sobering reminder of the risks he was facing on the track.

Macklin's plan for the year gradually began to fall into place. There weren't to be as many drives for Aston Martin, he'd only take part in the most important ones, while his main focus lay with HWM and its continuing mad dash across the continent. This year HWM started off at the Goodwood meeting on March 26, giving Macklin ample opportunity to catch up with his English family, as well as spend riotous evenings at the Steering Wheel Club with Moss in tow. His first race of the season was for the Lavant Cup, which Moss won. Macklin, unhappy with his car, ended up back in fourth. There was another race later that day, Moss coming in fifth and Macklin seventh. The season under way, HWM then got the road-show rolling and took a trip across the channel to take part in the Grand Prix de Marseilles on April 8. There, Moss took third behind the ever-present Maurice Trintignant and Luigi Villoresi, while Macklin, still unhappy with the car, and probably lacking concentration because of it, was sixth.

Knowing they were back in Macklin's adopted neighbourhood, the HWM team left him to sort out accommodation near the team's next race at San Remo. Heading off ahead of everyone else he drove to Roquebrune and settled down at his mother's villa, then booked the rest of the team into the gorgeous Hotel Les Diodato that stood just down the road. Arriving after a hard couple of weeks everyone was delighted, instantly falling in love with the ancient hotel's charm and its accommodating owners. Chatting to his mother while waiting for the team to show up, Macklin had also learned that Leslie's chauffeur, a middle aged Italian called Richard Milani, had secretly dreamed of becoming a motor racing mechanic. Luckily for Milani, it turned out his timing couldn't have been better. Francis was in desperate need of a mechanic and, much as he loved his current crop, didn't really want to deal with yet another enthusiastic amateur. Milani and Francis met and instantly clicked, despite not speaking each other's language, and, by the time the team rolled out, Leslie was in need of a new chauffeur.

The team spent a week living Macklin's lifestyle, lazing on the beach, taking in the sunshine, going for dips in the Mediterranean and eating long, lazy meals at fine restaurants. To the hard-working mechanics, all of them working-class men from grimy parts of England (save Francis, of course), it was eye-opening. In a comfort-starved postwar world, Macklin's existence was like something out of a story book.

Reluctantly, they had to move on. For April 22's San Remo race they were joined by Louis Chiron, the great prewar Bugatti driver. Although he wasn't far off his 52nd birthday, Chiron still possessed an almost boundless enthusiasm for getting behind the wheel of racing cars, which he flamboyantly manhandled around circuits like a madman. The old fox was still a crowd pleaser. Chiron occupying the third seat came as a badge of pride to the team, showing that they now commanded considerable respect despite the haphazard, shoestring nature of the operation. Chiron's race didn't go as everyone hoped, though, his enthusiasm getting the better of him and leading to him breaking a driveshaft. Moss ended up fifth and Macklin seventh. Moss was absent for the next race, a non-championship outing at Bordeaux, although he didn't miss much. Macklin's car, which had been continually misbehaving since the first race of the season, gave out on him and he had to endure a long walk back to the pits. Chiron, meanwhile, ended up sixth.

The team immediately packed up and headed back to England for the prestigious BRDC International Trophy race on May 5 where, to everyone's disappointment, things went from bad to worse. First, Francis was involved in a collision in the transporter on the way over. Then, according to Francis, John Heath steadfastly refused to listen to his mechanics' advice and insisted on fiddling with the cars' carburettors, setting them up so badly that the team's chances of doing well in the race were ruined. In the event it was only Moss who suffered, coming a dismal fourteenth in the rain-affected six-lap main event. The other two HWMs of Macklin and Abecassis sat lonely and broken in the paddock with a torn-apart gearbox and blown engine respectively. Macklin's year, despite the early enthusiasm, was going nowhere fast.

Picking themselves up off the ground, everyone took a deep intake of breath and headed back to Italy. First up was Monza on May 13, where Moss lifted everyone's mood with an unexpectedly stunning drive into third place, slipstreaming Villoresi's Ferrari for over a hundred miles in one of the two heats. Macklin, though, lingered miserably near the bottom of the field. Mystified as to why he was so much slower, and guessing it was probably the carburettor, Francis, ever dedicated, took the one from Macklin's car and worked on it in his hotel room until he fell asleep. He woke up with a cleaner staring at him. "Do the English always sleep with bits and pieces from their racing cars?" she asked, once she'd eventually stopped giggling.

Macklin's frustration with the team was increasing. Still, he managed to remain fairly laid back while the chaos unfolded around him, enjoying the travelling and the driving itself even if his car was constantly misbehaving. He was hoping the next race, a winding trip through the beautiful, seaside streets of Genoa on May 20, would bring him more luck.

There's a photo of Macklin driving the HWM through Genoa, watched intently by thousands of locals packed tightly together. Looking at the picture today, what stands out most of all is the startling lack of barriers or safety crew. If something went wrong, an axle seizing, say, or even a little over-exuberance from the driver, the results could have been disastrous. At the time, of course, it's unlikely that anyone in the crowd was thinking that, although some onlookers might have been just a little concerned had they known that the driver heading past them could barely see a thing. Despite nearly missing the start – the HWM team had lazily ambled up to the grid just in time for the scheduled 2pm start on the assumption that Italians always ran late, only to discover that this time everyone was bang on time – by the end of the first lap Moss and Macklin were running first and second and streaking away from the Ferraris of Villoresi and Ascari. However, all was not well in Macklin's cockpit. Something had got in his eye, and soon he could barely see. He was still comfortably in second place but, after a few blurry laps, he steered the HWM into the pits. As Macklin pulled up, a confused Alf Francis sprinted over to the car. "I can't see a damned thing," Macklin shouted as he switched off the car's motor. Francis was aghast. "Keep going as fast as you can and try to finish," the mechanic shouted back, pushing the HWM back out onto the pit road. It fired up and off Macklin went, unhappily, back into action.

Second place had gone, but so quick was the car that he comfortably eased into third and stayed there. Moss' luck eventually ran out and he broke down while in the lead, while Abecassis, back in action after his nasty pre-season crash, had car trouble but still ended up fifth. Despite his eyesight, which barely improved throughout the race, Macklin clung on and ended up third as the chequered flag fell. He was delighted. Although he knew it was a race he would have won if he hadn't come in he didn't complain, happily taking his long-overdue trip to the podium and grateful that the car had finally behaved itself. After a hard few months, the champagne tasted extra sweet.

A week later – the travelling never ending – they were back at Aix-les-Baines. While Moss came second in a dinged-up car it was back to business as usual for Macklin, retiring with a seized gearbox. Luckily for him, it at least didn't send him spinning down the middle of the road this time. After their mixed results the team split, Moss and his car heading across the border for the Grand Prix of Rome while Macklin and the rest stayed in France for the Circuit des Remparts race in the tiny town of Angoulême. It was another quirky little European event that ran through the town's bumpy streets, with the race pits lying opposite the town's cathedral. People packed the footpaths, watching the drivers as they headed flat-out through the narrow streets just inches away from them.

Again, the fiery Louis Chiron was called up to partner Macklin, and most of the drama centred around him. He refused to take to the track until he was paid more starting money, then, when he did, he set blindly quick laps, only to hurt his cause by ill-advisedly tinkering with his engine before the race and then getting in a comical argument with Francis about it on the grid. He crashed, then furiously powered back to finish sixth. It was typically Gallic performance. Macklin, in contrast, quietly and successfully went about his business, winning the first heat and coming second to Rudi Fischer in the main event. Still, despite his strong performance there were signs his already-lacking work ethic may have been dwindling even further. Although he drove well he still hadn't been quite as fast as the ageing Chiron (between incidents, that is) and after the race Francis was sure that had Moss turned up, he would have won. Maybe it was time for a bit of a break.

Lance soon got just what he needed. Following Angoulême he had a weekend off, enjoying a spell of 12 glorious, driving-free days until his next race at Le Mans. As usual he spent the time at his mother's villa in Roquebrune, reverting to his playboy lifestyle while the pressure was off and doing his best to block out the knowledge that his next race was a big one. The crowds at Le Mans had been tremendous the previous two years, and were certain to be bigger this time around. On the track, several drivers already had lucky escapes. The average race speed was beginning to creep up. He thought about the drivers who were going to be there – Moss, Fangio, Gonzáles and nearly everyone else who mattered – and he shuddered slightly. These thoughts, plus the tragic memory of ill-fated team-mate Maréchal, came to him in fleeting moments during his sun-drenched holiday in the south of France. He shut them out.

– – – – –

Macklin turned up at Le Mans refreshed, happily catching up with John Wyer and the rest of the Aston Martin team, none of whom he'd seen since their disastrous speed record attempt at the end of the previous year. George Abecassis, who he'd grown close to over the course of the past year, was there too, although the two were split apart despite going so strongly the year before. Abecassis was instead paired with Bryan Shawe-Taylor, an able, if not outstanding, Irish driver. For his part, and to his considerable dismay, Macklin was to be paired with enthusiastic amateur and full-time insurance salesman, Eric Thompson. Macklin was never one to be sour and the two got along, having met previously at the ill-fated 24-hour record attempt, although he still had deep doubts about Thompson's driving ability. "He was really very reluctant," Thompson recalled later. "He'd been racing in Formula Two in HWMs, had done well at Le Mans the year before, and he was a very experienced and very good driver. He resented the fact that I, as an amateur, had been partnered with him."

In reality, Thompson was more than capable. He had entered a DB2 at Le Mans the previous year and, while he hadn't lasted long – only eight laps, in fact – he'd shown enough promise for John Wyer to figure he could get the job done just fine a second time around.

The ability of his co-driver wasn't Macklin's only worry. Aston Martin had been working on developing a successor to the DB2 throughout the year, but, while everyone waited patiently, the new DB3 was taking a painfully long time to appear. Though the team was hoping to have it ready by the time Le Mans rolled around they didn't quite manage it, instead reconfiguring and updating a couple of the old DB2s. These were given to Abecassis and Shawe-Taylor and the third Aston Martin team entry of Reg Parnell and David Hampshire. Macklin and Thompson were going to have to make do, John Wyer curtly informed them, with the very same car Macklin had driven the year before. Macklin's mood, so fully rejuvenated after his French sojourn, was again beginning to turn black.

He needn't have worried. When the race got under way on the afternoon of June 23, 1951, Macklin was pleasantly surprised to find Thompson to be "very fast and very consistent," as he put it himself. The two drove a relatively uneventful but fast race, the supposedly old and heavy DB2 easily outpacing its more modern counterparts. As dawn broke on Sunday morning they had shot up into a handy third place and there they stayed, crossing the line third overall and first in their group. Not only was it both drivers' highest Le Mans finish but it was also the best Aston Martin result at the track since the war. The team were overjoyed and headed to Le Mans proper to party long into the night, Macklin revelling in the atmosphere. His return to sports cars had proven to be a complete success.

Still, there was something unsettling in the air, a feeling of darkness around the edges after the end of that year's race. Tragedy had struck again. Within half an hour of the race getting under way, young French driver Jean Larivière had taken his Ferrari around the sharp Tertre Rouge corner far too quickly. He ploughed straight over the top of an apparently inadequate protective banking, before plunging into a garden below. He was killed instantly. As author Christopher Hilton noted: if the drivers hadn't been entirely aware the circuit could be a killer, they certainly were now.

– – – – –

After his brief sports car sojourn it was time to get back to the never-ending HWM circus. By this point it was very much an all or nothing situation: the HWMs, for the most part, were either finishing well or not finishing at all. The first race back was certainly of the latter kind, an ill-advised trip to AVUS in West Germany on June 1 succeeding in only blowing up the engines of both HWMs. Macklin skipped the next race, an absurd affair in Rouen, where the French officials did all they could to gift the win to a local, then rejoined the team for a dull outing at Mettet in Belgium, where none of the cars ran particularly well. The most noteworthy aspect of all this, for Macklin at least, was a strikingly beautiful French girl he had tailing him around the paddock at the Belgian race. By now well and truly used to the pretty women trailing after his driver, even Alf Francis was impressed. "She was not like some of the empty-headed nuisances who straggle from circuit to circuit, knowing nothing and caring less," he said with approval, although he did have to lie to her when asked why Moss seemed to be the faster of the two. "John Heath," he said, looking around to make sure his boss wasn't around, "always gives Moss the best car." He didn't mention anything about a lack of concentration.

Next up was the non-championship Grand Prix on July 22 at the Dutch Zandvoort track, a race that turned out to be more of the same. Before the cars even took to the grid Francis and Heath became involved in an almighty row about sparkplugs, something that Heath, strangely, held very firm views on despite always turning out to be wrong. In the race itself Macklin broke down (although he was still classified sixth at the finish) while Moss overcame teething problems to end up third. Afterwards, on August 5, came Albi in France where, again, most of the action happened off the track. After another terrifying drive over foggy, slippery mountain passes in Switzerland, the mechanics turned up at the French track to find Macklin nowhere in sight. Concern grew as the hours ticked by, Duncan Hamilton giving Macklin's car a few laps instead. Finally, one of the mechanics spotted a bedraggled, hunched figure wandering slowly over to the HWM pits. It was Macklin. It turned out he'd suffered two flat tyres on his way over and had to walk for miles on the side of the road to make it to the race. Despite looking like a tramp, and with heavily blistered feet to boot, he still hopped in the car in time for qualifying. The next day he showed impressive resilience and drove a solid race to finish seventh.

After a hard season the HWMs were by now on their last legs. At Erlen in Switzerland on August 12, Moss, for the umpteenth time, broke down while in the lead. Macklin trundled home fifth.

Breaking with HWM briefly, he then embarked on a quick trip across the channel to once again drive for Aston Martin in the Tourist Trophy at Dundrod. Here, on September 15, he finally got to test the new Aston Martin DB3 on the track, although it repaid his excitement by breaking down and sending him out of the race. Disappointed, he flew back to the continent with the end finally in sight. He had one more race to get through before he could finally relax. It had been a gruelling season.

The grand finale was the Modena Grand Prix on September 23. Straight away, as soon as the first practice session came to a close, it was clear that something unusual was happening. Maybe he wanted to end the season on the high, maybe he simply liked the track, but for whatever reason Macklin posted the third quickest time and was a whole second quicker than Moss. The same thing happened in qualifying the next day. It was as if Macklin, revelling in being back on the continent, had suddenly found a second wind. Though he had never been slow, exactly, he had clearly stepped up a gear and was now driving extraordinarily well. In the race proper he quickly shot up into second place, harassing Ascari's Ferrari and dicing for the lead, his HWM sliding around, passing and re-passing in front of the startled locals. The tired and underpowered HWM really had no business mixing it with the powerful factory Ferraris, but that day Macklin was driving out of his skin. Ascari eventually got away, and Froilán González, who spent an awful lot of time desperately trying to get by, did too. Still, Macklin crossed the line with a weary smile in third place. Alf Francis said it was the best he'd ever seen him drive, one of the few times he truly and clearly showed what he was capable of. "I am sure that if Macklin had really tried hard in those days he could have equalled Moss on almost any circuit," he said, years later. "The difference was very little." After the race Macklin sat next to Gonzales, his face black from dust and oil, his overalls grimy and smeared with dirt, wearing a giant, ear-to-ear grin. It was the perfect end to his hardest working season.

That evening, after spending a few hours hanging about and chatting with the local drivers after the race, Macklin tidied himself up and headed to a fancy restaurant in downtown Modena to meet the rest of the HWM team. Everyone was in good form, overjoyed to be having a long, luxurious and leisurely meal instead of their usual mad scramble for sustenance on the road. After dinner and a couple of drinks, everyone watched intently as Heath stood up and announced his plans for the next year. As Francis later recalled, they were in for a shock: Heath proudly told the assembled group that he was planning to build an entirely new car for the following year. He wanted better road holding, he told the puzzled team. Prompted by Francis, Moss and Macklin chimed in to say the basics of the car were fine and all they needed was a bit more grunt. "If we could find another 20 brake horse power we might be a match for the Ferraris," Macklin told Heath. The boss, though, was unswayed. It was at this moment, in the afterglow of one of its finest performances, that HWM's fortunes took a dive from which it would never fully recover. "We were at the crossroads and John Heath took the wrong turning," Francis wrote, sadly. "We could have been the Prancing Horse of Britain." While Moss would, of course, go onto greater things, Heath's decision also left a question mark that still lingers over Macklin. What could he have achieved if he'd been behind the wheel of a powerful, giant-killing Grand Prix car? It's one of British motorsport's great 'what-ifs.'

After Heath's announcement a fed-up Alf Francis quit HWM. Moss, in search of something quicker and more reliable, also left, although he would continue to occasionally fill in when he had the chance. The team was now without its best mechanic and its best driver, and although it still had plenty of able backup it would never be entirely the same again. For his part, Macklin took it all in stride. It had been an up and down year. At Modena and Le Mans he'd tasted success and showed what he was capable of, but he'd also experienced frustration at the HWM's lack of speed, its mechanical gremlins, and its unreliability. On the plus side he'd avoided any serious crashes and, as usual, had ended up having plenty of adventures off the track. It hadn't been perfect, but he'd take it.

Chapter 10

Victory at Silverstone

1952 rolled around, and with the new year came an assortment of new drivers. The most prominent of these was a slight, shy teenager who turned out to be staggeringly quick behind the wheel. Peter Collins, who later developed into one of the great postwar British drivers, had been snapped up by HWM during the off-season after an eye-catching series of results in his little 500cc Cooper. Collins and Macklin clicked immediately. "Peter Collins was a splendid racing driver," Macklin recalled later. "He was also a very nice, easy-going, light-hearted, amusing person." They bonded while at HWM and Aston Martin, the two troublemakers getting into all sorts of mischief and quickly becoming solid friends.

It was strange not having Alf Francis, the stern taskmaster, watching over them as they took to the Pau circuit on April 14 for the first Formula Two race of the year. Though Macklin started near the front of the grid – and was even reportedly promised a bottle of wine if he kept Villoresi and Ascari behind him for the first lap – it turned out to be a forgettable start to the season as he wound up seventh and last, while Collins retired in his very first race. The next round, two weeks later at Marseilles, wasn't any better as both HWMs retired. For all their speed issues, the 1951 cars had at least been semi-reliable. John Heath's decision (which had already caused Francis and Moss to abandon ship) to go for broke and build a whole new car was beginning to look more and more ill-advised. Originally determined to improve the HWM's road holding, Heath found that the new cars could barely keep themselves on the road at all.

After the two disastrous French races it was time to head back to England and the *Daily Express* BRDC Trophy event at Silverstone on May 10. Team morale was low. Nobody was expecting much in the face of a very strong contingent of British drivers, among which was a young, dashing and self-confident Mike Hawthorn. Just 23 years old, blindingly quick and thoroughly, unmistakably British, he'd caught the public's eye the previous year and was already being marked down as a star of the future. Events would soon prove this to be correct.

Undeterred by the miserable weather, a record crowd of 125,000 turned up on race day, jamming the roads for miles around. It was proof that postwar racing in Britain, while it had got off to a slow start, was now becoming well and truly entrenched. At the track Macklin looked around, hardly believing his eyes. The atmosphere was electric.

For Macklin, as was the case for many of the drivers, this was to be a double event. Although the main trophy race, where he'd be driving his HWM, was later, his first job was to drive an Aston Martin in the 17-lap production sports car event. Early signs had been encouraging as he lapped the slippery Silverstone circuit quicker than his team-mates, but things quickly went wrong in the race itself. Sprinting across the track for the customary Le Mans-style start, he leapt into the Aston and pushed the start button. Nothing happened. Cursing as the rest of the field sped off around him he sat alone, frantically trying to get the stubborn car to start. Eventually it roared into life, although by now he was over half a minute behind everyone else. Setting off with his foot to the floor, he tore through the field and eventually wound up a very commendable fourth, not far behind Moss and his two Aston Martin team-mates, Parnell and Abecassis.

Tossing his frustration aside, it was time to hop back into the HWM. Perhaps annoyed at his earlier mishap he was now setting very solid lap times indeed, and when the first heat rolled around he found himself lining-up fourth, with Collins up ahead in second. While Collins was passed by Jean Behra's quick little Gordini at the start, the two HWMs spent the rest of the race dicing among themselves, Collins eventually retaking third and leaving Macklin where he'd begun in fourth. Hawthorn, meanwhile, had streaked away in his Cooper-Bristol for the win. The second heat was relatively straightforward, Frenchman Robert Manzon winning commandingly in his Gordini. Everything was set for the final, all signs pointing to an epic duel for the win between Hawthorn, the golden haired Englishman, and the chirpy Frenchman Manzon. Facing a classic French versus English battle in the home of British motorsport, the patriotic crowd was thrilled.

Things didn't turn out quite as anyone expected. After exchanging sharp glances at the front of the grid, Manzon and Hawthorn led the field around the first corner as thousands of screaming fans watched on. However, their battle – which Hawthorn looked to have under control as he rapidly tore off into the lead – didn't last for long. After just a lap Manzon began to limp around, the Frenchman having damaged his transmission at the start in a display of over-exuberance. This left Hawthorn clear out in front, while, further back in the crowded pack, Macklin slowly began to move up. Things were going smoothly for Hawthorn when, changing down gears, the gearlever came clean off in his hand. Left with a one-inch stub with which to change gears, he tried his best to keep his ailing car on the track but had to admit defeat, pulling the Cooper into the pits a few laps later.

Still going strong and his car for once holding together, Macklin sensed an opportunity. He pulled ahead of team-mate Tony Rolt and set off towards the lead, hurtling the HWM through corners, his exhaust blaring as he sawed furiously at the wheel. Coming round one corner, he glanced over to see Behra forlornly sitting on the side of the track in his broken Gordini. He was now in the lead.

The next few laps passed like a hazy dream. Blurry snapshots of the crowd on their feet, British flags fluttering, his pit crew waving their fists and urging him on, broken cars littering the circuit. Rolt lay far behind him, and in front was nothing but clear track. He knew, for the first time, he was about to win something big. Crossing the line as the chequered flag fluttered, he immediately slumped back in his seat and waved at the delirious crowd. He'd done it.

As he pulled into the pits a lap later the HWM was quickly swamped with friends, his crew, cameramen and photographers. John Heath broke through the mass to give him a pat on the back while Macklin pulled down his goggles, grinned wildly and eased himself up to perch above his HWM's seat. Gratefully accepting a beer, he drank it slowly as he carried out a series of interviews, said hello to other drivers, shared a laugh with Abecassis and Heath, and tried his best to gather himself in the middle of the chaos. "I'd make a thousand trips to pull this off," he later said with a wide grin as he accepted the huge, gleaming silver trophy. Years later it was the 1952 BRDC trophy that took pride of place on the trophy shelf in his Wimbledon home, gleaming in the sunlight and polished every week by his young daughter. Looking at it he would think back to that overcast afternoon in May 1952 when, for one fleeting moment, everything went right.

Chapter 11

No fun at HWM

After heading back to London and celebrating his victory at a jam-packed Steering Wheel Club, Macklin woke up the next morning with a lingering sense of satisfaction and a throbbing hangover. Having spent a relaxing few days in London, he headed back to Europe, clear-headed and full of confidence. Getting back to business, his next race was the Swiss Grand Prix in Bern on May 18, not far from his old prewar stomping grounds. Despite all his good memories, he came crashing back to reality as a strong HWM team of Moss, Collins, Macklin and Abecassis suffered a series of mishaps, forcing Macklin and Moss to pull out after 24 laps. Disappointed, he then travelled with the team to France for the Paris Grand Prix a week later. Here his fortunes rose again, driving a shared car with Collins to a fine fourth place.

The following weekend, on June 2, he was back in Monaco, and once again behind the wheel of an Aston Martin. 1952 thus far hadn't been a good year for the team, with the DB3 – which Macklin had partially helped develop – turning out to be sluggish and poor-handling. Still, things were looking up at Monaco as a new, bigger engine helped Macklin set times that weren't too far behind the leading Ferraris. John Wyer and David Brown were pleased, although their smiles soon faded as, under clear, perfectly blue skies and the blazing Mediterranean sunshine, the team disintegrated. In the race each Aston ran hot and broke down: Macklin's three-quarters of the way through, Collins just before the finish, and Reg Parnell at the halfway point. Parnell's exit was particularly spectacular. Throwing a rod, his Aston then skidded on its own oil and ploughed into a barrier down at the famous Ste Dévote corner, quickly followed by four other cars. Ahead of Parnell at the time, Macklin came around the next lap and just managed to swerve to the inside and avoid the treacherous oil slick and the now-huge pileup. Out of the corner of his eye he caught a glimpse of Stirling Moss leaping out of his stricken Jaguar C-Type and up into the stands, fleeing the carnage behind him.

Six days later, on June 8, Macklin again found himself back in an HWM at Aix-Les-Baines. In contrast to the year before, he had a trouble-free run to the finish and – aided somewhat by a slew of retirements – a well-deserved second place. Though he didn't know it yet, Aix-Les-Baines was to be the last time he would achieve any success behind the wheel of an HWM for the rest of the year.

– – – – –

With little time to relax, Macklin and Collins jumped in a car and rushed down to Le Mans. They were to share one of the troublesome Aston Martin DB3s. Upon arriving at the track they discovered the team had yet another problem: the rear brakes of all the Astons overheating so much that the oil in the rear axle was, as Macklin put it, "practically turning to water." Sighing, with the realisation they didn't really have any time to do much about it, the two drivers agreed to drive without brakes as much as possible. It was all they could do. Coming up to the start, they knew they were in for a long and anxious 24 hours.

To their delight, the Aston, despite its problems, actually went pretty well. To most observers things were going smoothly as the two endured a seemingly trouble-free race, easing their way up to third place even with their dodgy brakes. Inside the cockpit, though, was a different story. Just before heading into action for an early stint, Macklin was told that the sister car of Parnell and Thompson had fallen prey to a dreaded back axle failure. The two were unhurt, but their demise conjured images and questions in Macklin's mind. Every time he headed down the flat-out Mulsanne straight, the car getting buffeted as it reached 140 miles an hour, he looked at the none-too-reassuring dirt barriers and wondered: what if it locked up now? He tried not to dwell on it but, when he got out of the car hours later he slumped down in a seat, drenched in sweat and very much relieved. He'd made it.

The same, unfortunately, couldn't be said for the car. Not long after Macklin handed over to Collins the dreaded rear axle began making worrying noises. Collins tried to continue but the problem began to grow worse and, thinking back to its sister car, he knew continuing wasn't worth it. Though they were lying third and had less than two hours to go, it was time to call it quits. Disappointed at having fallen so agonisingly close, the two nevertheless cracked open beers when they met back at the pits and began to party.

As Macklin and Collins began to settle back into their seats, something truly spectacular was unfolding out on the track. Macklin had known Pierre Levegh – really Pierre Bouillin – from his years on the Formula Two circuit. Levegh, in his little Talbot, had been a constant presence, and was clearly ambitious and driven. A look at Formula Two records from the early 1950s shows him turning up week in, week out, without the benefit of a full team to back him up. Even though he was usually about, something always seemed to set him apart from those around him. He was a driver who seemed to linger in the corner, in the shadows. Unlike so many of the others he didn't go out partying after races, didn't spend hours chasing women, didn't socialise. Approaching 50, and with a distinct middle-aged paunch, he was a different generation from the 20- and 30-somethings he was racing against. He turned up to race, and while everyone knew who he was, very few knew him personally. He didn't try to fit in.

What the others didn't fully realise was just how brightly his passion for the track burned. It had begun on a sunny afternoon in 1931 when he watched the mighty prewar drivers in their monstrous cars battle it out around Le Mans. Glued to the track, he couldn't look away. It ignited something inside him, unleashed a determination that accompanied him for the rest of his life. He wanted to win Le Mans and he would do anything it took.

In 1951 he'd come fourth, directly behind Macklin and Thompson, but also, importantly, two places behind another Talbot. As Christopher Hilton pointed out later, regardless of what Levegh said to anyone at the time, the success of the other Talbot was crucial. He knew it meant he could do better. He could, if he really tried, actually win.

His obsession kicked into top gear. For the next year he insisted on preparing his own Talbot, going as far as buying one and doing the job himself when the factory refused to help him. Now, coming into the morning of June 15, 1952, he was doing something nobody had ever done before. He'd decided that if he was going to win he'd do it by himself, and now, after 20 hours of driving, he was behind the wheel, tired, delirious, but hanging on. He was an entire two laps ahead of the chasing Mercedes. The crowd, who had turned up in their thousands, were on their feet willing him on, shouting and furiously waving French flags. His wife and pit crew were aghast, holding their breath and desperately hoping disaster wouldn't strike. They'd been trying to get him to leave the car when he stopped in for fuel stops, but their efforts hadn't worked, Levegh refusing to budge as his hands gripped the Talbot's steering wheel, his eyes hollow. He barely recognised his friends. The dim knowledge that his dream was right in front of him for the taking was the only thing pulling him on.

Macklin, like everyone else that day, stood transfixed as Levegh hurtled round for lap after impossible lap. Then, just 70 minutes from the finish, it all came to a sudden, dramatic end as the Talbot pulled over to the side of the track. Some speculated he was the victim of a mechanical problem that would have happened regardless of who was driving, but it's more likely that the exhausted Levegh made a mistake while changing down gears, missing one and blowing the engine. He was out. The crowd went silent, their nationalistic fervour quickly abating as the two Mercedes came through with the race effectively sewn up. Levegh slowly dragged himself out of his car and, to an almost deafening silence, unsteadily wandered back to his pit. He spoke briefly with the race warden, then, exhausted, fell into a deep sleep. Watching the drama unfold from the Mercedes pit was the tall, rotund Mercedes team manager Alfred Neubauer. "I must get this man," he said to himself as Levegh stumbled back to his team. It was to be a fateful decision.

It wasn't the only fateful decision to occur that weekend. That year's Le Mans turned out to be the last time Macklin would ever drive for Aston Martin. For some time he'd been growing frustrated with the team's financial arrangements, the £50 retainer and sharing of prize money growing less and less enticing the more successful and experienced he became. Throughout his tenure there'd also been a question about who was the team leader, for, while Reg Parnell was ostensibly in charge, everyone knew Macklin was the team's quickest driver. The two had occasionally butted heads, and Macklin, knowing he was faster, felt he should not only be recognised as the team leader but should also be paid what he was worth. "I left for reasons that were purely financial," he later said. "Astons were very mean with their drivers in those days." This stinginess had already cost Aston Stirling Moss, and now, a couple of years later, it was going to cost it Lance Macklin as well. Yet, while Aston Martin later brought Moss back for a vastly inflated sum, Macklin never returned. Only four years into his career and at the height of his powers, he couldn't have foreseen that he'd never drive for a front-line team again. "Looking back," he told Chris Nixon years later, "leaving Astons was probably the worst mistake of my life."

– – – – –

A week later he was back in the cockpit at the Belgian Grand Prix, where the HWMs were soundly blown into the reeds by their Formula One opposition. On June 29 he was at Reims where his HWM broke down, followed by the French Grand Prix on July 6. There he at least managed to overcome problems and finish, although he wound up ninth and a massive seven laps down on Ascari's winning Ferrari. Aside from the the car's unreliability he just wasn't able to get to grips with his HWM, his early-season success quickly fading into a distant memory. His car's engine blew up at the Sables d'Ollone track a week later, while the British Grand Prix on July 19 was little better. Effectively qualifying last, an almost-unimaginable 18 seconds off pole sitter Giuseppe Farina, his eventual climb to fifteenth was only due to others retiring.

His miserable season continued. At Saint-Gaudens on August 10 his HWM again blew up, while at the Dutch Grand Prix a week later he finished eighth, a full lap behind team-mate Duncan Hamilton. Next was La Baule on August 24 where he out-qualified both Collins and local HWM driver Yves Giraud-Cabantous by an impressively large margin, although his engine again blew and sent him out of the race after 36 laps. Next up was the Italian Grand Prix on September 7 where neither Macklin nor Collins – who had been having a slightly more successful year – qualified. To his relief the end was in sight, with a trip to Modena for the September 14th Modena Grand Prix bringing his last competitive outing of the year. At the same track where he'd driven one of his finest races just a year earlier, his year ended on an appropriately drab note as he limped out on the 41st lap with a broken transmission. That evening he thought back a year earlier to the dinner the HWM team shared at the fancy Italian restaurant. He thought of Francis and Moss, of the team laughing and clinking bottles in celebration, of Heath then lowering the mood with his speech full of misguided enthusiasm. It all felt so long ago.

– – – – –

There's a fair chance that Macklin didn't help his cause as the 1952 season descended into the mire. "If his car blew up in practice and couldn't start he wouldn't be disappointed, he'd just say 'oh well, I'll go into town and find myself a bird,'" George Abecassis later remarked. "Sometimes, when he raced for HWM it was a nightmare to get him to come to practice at all. If there was some blonde he was after he just wouldn't turn up." In a season where the car was woefully out of sorts and lacking the precious input of a mechanic like Alf Francis, he'd been more concerned with chasing women than fixing carburettors. Still, at least that had gone well for him. He'd had a great time adventuring on the continent with Collins in tow and, on the whole, he seemed happy enough. Having a laissez-faire attitude occasionally came in handy, especially when good results were few and far between.

At the end of the season he took a short trip back to Britain, where he immediately began frequenting his home away from home at the Steering Wheel Club. Wandering into the club one afternoon, the bartender called him over. "Someone's been looking for you," he said as he handed Macklin a note. It was from a stranger asking him to call what looked to be a number in Bristol, England. Macklin was intrigued. Later on in the week he called the number and, to his surprise, was put straight through to a senior member of the Bristol Aircraft Company. Best known for making a variety of medium and light bombers during the Second World War, Bristol had turned to building cars after the war wound up and, apparently, was now looking to branch out into motor racing. Someone at the company had heard about Macklin cutting ties with Aston Martin, the voice on the other end of the line said, and they would love to have him as their lead driver the next year. The pay would be £1000 plus starting money. Macklin was sold, and, before hanging up, he arranged to meet the team in Bristol a few weeks later for a trial run. He was going to be both well-paid and an undisputed lead driver at last. Things are looking up, he thought, happily.

While Macklin had increasingly struggled as 1952 wore on, battling his failing, underpowered HWM, Mike Hawthorn's star had soared. Competing in the little Cooper Bristol run by his father, he'd displayed a startling amount of speed and supreme self-confidence. It wasn't hard to imagine that if he'd been born a decade earlier he would have been a Spitfire pilot. He had dashing good looks, a wide smile and an arresting mix of charm and arrogance. In a postwar Britain searching for heroes, he was well on his way to becoming one.

Macklin had, of course, already run into Hawthorn, both at the BRDC Trophy race at Silverstone and on the many Formula Two events they had both attended on the continent. The two immediately became good friends. They shared a love of women and, increasingly, booze, often heading out in search of both and usually succeeding. Yet there was something about Hawthorn that belied his friendliness and his charm. Macklin noticed something darker, a mean streak that would occasionally surface when the two were out and about together. "As a person Mike was rather a peculiar fellow," Macklin said. "He could be charming. He could be unpleasant. He could be very hard in many ways."

Nonetheless, the two quickly became firm friends. Hawthorn's scintillating pace throughout 1952 had marked him out as a prospect for the future, and while teams clamoured for him, it was Ferrari who got in first. Fiercely nationalistic, Hawthorn would have preferred to sit behind the wheel of a British car, but there weren't really any competitive options around at the time. BRM, launched with a wave of publicity as the saviour of postwar British racing, had so far turned out to be a hopeless embarrassment, while HWM was far from competitive. Hawthorn would have seen the HWMs struggling around Europe, their two very fine drivers constantly endeavouring to make an impression, and thought 'no thanks.' Ferrari it was.

Meanwhile, Macklin had decided to remain with HWM, despite the team's miserable end to the season. It was clear it was missing the input of an experienced designer or a talented engineer like Alf Francis. Although HWM had never had the quickest cars around, one thing the team could count on during the first few seasons was relatively solid reliability. Now, that was gone, too. Everyone was hoping for a better year in 1953, but, little did they know, things would continue to go from bad to worse ...

Chapter 12

Never, ever interested

The 1953 season got off to a late start. Macklin had kept himself busy over the prolonged off-season by taking frequent trips to the Bristol Aircraft Company's massive Brabazon runway just outside Bristol city. His early delight had been cooled somewhat when he discovered what he was dealing with: the profoundly odd Bristol 450. "I thought (the Bristol) was going to be a very small, very streamlined little 2-litre car," he recalled. "Instead, it turned out to be a large – certainly much too big for a 2-litre car – saloon with two fins on the back. A peculiar thing." Not sure what to make of it, Macklin quickly began calling it, to the company's dismay, The Pregnant Grasshopper. 'Goggle-eyed,' and ever-so-slightly out of proportion, it certainly didn't look encouraging.

The 450 was based on the ERA G-type, an ill-fated Formula Two car that Stirling Moss had driven, with little success, the previous year. Now it was up to Macklin to try and turn it, in its new sports car incarnation, into a race-winner. He'd get up early and head to the factory where he'd take the ungainly beast on long, fast runs down the company's seemingly-endless four mile runway. Unlike most test sessions on racing circuits he didn't have to worry about losing the car under cornering and slamming into barriers, thereby setting the programme back weeks at a time. Surrounded by nothing but tarmac he had all the room he needed to get to grips with his new ride. Despite hours of testing, though, things hadn't been going particularly well. Though he'd told the press that the car could be "driven without hands," he was less complimentary in private. "I got some idea of the handling," he said later. "It was most peculiar, and I didn't like it." He was beginning to get signs that his dream £1000 drive might not be turning out exactly as he'd hoped.

– – – – –

It took until May to finally get back on the track. Setting the tone for what was to follow, his first race of the year, at Bordeaux on May 3, ended in retirement after 80 laps. Five days later he revisited Silverstone for the BRDC Trophy, the scene of his great triumph the year before, but this time he lasted only eight laps before the HWM again gave out. Hawthorn, driving the wheels off his Ferrari, took a popular victory ahead of Roy Salvadori and Tony Rolt. Macklin could only watch from the sidelines. At the Ulster Trophy at Dundrod on May 16, Hawthorn again swept to victory, furthering his claim as Britain's hottest new driving talent as his season went from strength to strength. Macklin and Collins failed to even qualify.

Then came a blip of good fortune during the ten-lap Coronation Trophy at Crystal Palace on May 25. Soaking up the hot weather and enjoying the enthusiastic English crowd, Macklin and his HWM put up their best performance in ages. Lining-up fourth on the grid behind Moss, Macklin aced the start and slotted into a third place that he wouldn't relinquish. For the final, Macklin started in an unexpectedly high second place on the grid. Sitting in his car, he could look directly down the track with his view to the end of the straight completely unobscured. It was a rare moment.

As he waited for the flag to fall he looked around at the crowd, listening as the cars around him revved their engines in a throaty, rising and falling roar. When the flag waved he found himself immediately swamped by the pack around him, quickly slipping back from second and ending up way down in the pack. Determined not to let his good showing go to waste he bit his lip and threw the HWM around as hard and fast as he could, cutting and slicing his way back up through the field. The HWM ended up crossing the line only 0.6 seconds behind Peter Whitehead's third-placed Cooper-Alta. Although agonisingly close to a podium for the first time in months, he wasn't overly heartbroken. What really mattered was that he'd been competitive, dicing with others for the first time in a very long time. That weekend he returned to the Steering Wheel Club happy, even if, as it would turn out, the weekend's success was only temporary.

On May 31, at the forbidding Nürburgring, things swiftly came crashing back to reality as Macklin's run of poor luck resumed. After his car broke down with a magneto problem – not, incidentally, for the first time that year – Collins and stand-in driver Paul Frére aced the circuit and trounced their German rivals, finishing second and third. At the finish Frére was less than two seconds behind the winner, Emmanuel de Graffenried. Suddenly, and for whatever reason, the HWMs were showing that they actually did have some pace. Unfortunately, they often couldn't stay on the track long enough to make it count.

Next up was the Dutch Grand Prix on June 7, which was dominated from start to finish by Macklin's old friend and rival Ascari. The HWMs were no match for the rest of the field, and, after qualifying well down the order – Macklin 15, Collins 16 – they endured a miserable race. Macklin's luck again failed him, ending up the first car out of the race after just seven laps with a broken throttle, while Collins limped home second to last. Moss, driving a Connaught, was last, showing that it wasn't only the HWM drivers who were having a wretched year.

In mid-June Le Mans again rolled around. Macklin's frequent trips to the Brabazon runway at Bristol had yielded relatively encouraging results as the Bristol 450, at first completely unmanageable, now seemed to be running fairly well. Yet he still wasn't completely happy with it. As he lined up for the traditional Le Mans running start on the sunny afternoon of June 13, he looked across at his boggle-eyed car with a sense of trepidation.

On the crack of the starter's gun, he joined the drivers in the mad dash across the pit straight for their cars. Hopping into the Bristol's cramped cockpit, he immediately knew something wasn't right. As he joined the mad gaggle of cars jostling for position into the first corner he couldn't help noticing the pungent smell of petrol quickly filling the car. His stomach began to churn. That day Macklin wore nothing but a short-sleeved shirt, a flimsy crash helmet, a pair of trousers and his usual boxing boots. These were the days before safety equipment, and he knew, like all other racing drivers of the era, that if a fire broke out he would be in deep trouble.

As he drove around the strong smell refused to go away, as did terrifying visions of his car engulfed in crackling, whirling flames. After several unnerving hours he pulled into the pits and handed over to co-driver Graham Whitehead, reeking of petrol. "I ... (drove) the first three hours," he later said, "and I wasn't very happy for a moment of them." Relieved to be done, for the moment at least, he wandered over to chat with the Bristol mechanics and try and figure out where the alarming smell of petrol was coming from. After a few minutes of chatting he suddenly realised that Whitehead hadn't come past the pits. The clock kept ticking as Macklin, thinking of the petrol and the visions he'd had of his Bristol coming to a fiery end, became more and more nervous. A few minutes later news about the car filtered back to the pits. Coming off the flat-out Mulsanne straight, Whitehead had been midway through the flowing Esses corner on his very first lap when the car suddenly burst into flames. The back wheels locked, Whitehead was thrown into a spin at 120 miles an hour, and the car hurtled backwards into a wall. Luckily, Whitehead was thrown clear as the flaming race car spiralled away from him, the lack of safety features ironically saving him from a massive impact and a fiery fate. He was uninjured, though shaken. Macklin was shaken, too, knowing full well that he'd been just one lap away from the fireball that he'd been so nervous about. It had been a near thing.

As it turned out, Macklin and Whitehead were lucky in more ways than one. Ninety minutes later the other Bristol, driven by the unfortunate Tommy Wisdom, was coming down the Mulsanne straight at full tilt when it, too, abruptly burst into flames. This time the driver wasn't thrown out. Desperately trying to keep himself calm as flames enveloped the cockpit and ate through his flimsy cotton clothes, Wisdom steered the car to the side of the track before leaping out. The car continued on down the road, a flaming ball of fire lighting up the night sky as its driver writhed in agony on the side of the track. Wisdom spent months in hospital, his face black and blue and his body racked with burns. "He looked as though he had gone ten rounds with Joe Louis," Macklin, who visited him in hospital, said. They later found out that the problem lay with the crankshafts breaking, sending oil from the sump dripping onto the hot exhausts. The whole episode was a nightmare, a terrifying reminder of what could so easily go wrong.

That year's Le Mans ended with Duncan Hamilton and Tony Rolt taking a famous victory in their Jaguar C-Type after – according to Hamilton, at least – having stayed up all night drinking before the race. Behind them was Moss and Peter Walker, also in a C-Type, ahead of the American duo of Phil Walters and John Fitch in their Cunningham. Another C-Type, that of Peter Whitehead and Ian Stewart, was third. Levegh was there, although the rules had been changed after his heroics the year before, and he hadn't been allowed to attempt the whole thing himself. He finished eighth. Hawthorn was there, too, making his debut alongside Giuseppe Farina in the beautiful Ferrari 340MM. Although

Hawthorn's Ferrari didn't last long, with its brakes failing after all of 12 laps, he still gathered himself sufficiently to partake in the riotous victory celebrations after the race, along with Macklin, Hamilton and the rest of the tight-knit British contingent. There were no early risers the next morning.

June 21 saw the HWM team trek to Spa for a fruitless outing at the Belgian Grand Prix, where Macklin's off-the-pace HWM broke down after 19 laps. Next, a short couple of weeks later, the drivers were all back together again at Reims for a double-header. The Reims 12-hour sports car race was to kick-off on the night of July 4, followed the next day by the French Grand Prix at the very same track. It was a packed schedule that led to some very tired drivers, although most of the leading Grand Prix stars elected to sit out in the sports car race and, sensibly enough, get some sleep for the main event. Macklin was one of the hardy bunch who signed up for both, driving the Bristol in the sports car event and the HWM in the Grand Prix. The two Bristol drivers were still nervous following the team's catastrophic outing at Le Mans, although they'd since spent time up at Bristol and had received assurances that the problem had been taken care of. They could only hope this was true.

On the afternoon of the fourth it was Whitehead who apprehensively took the first stint in the Bristol. With a big weekend ahead Macklin was back at his hotel squeezing in a couple of hours' sleep, having left instructions with the team to call him if anything went wrong. After a couple of hours the phone rang. Groggy, Macklin rolled over in his bed and gingerly picked it up. It was Whitehead. "Don't bother, Lance," he said, sighing. "It's out." Macklin hung up. Though he later claimed he went straight back to sleep and woke up refreshed for the next day's race, the real story is quite different. Whether he couldn't sleep or simply didn't feel like it, at some point he wandered downstairs and ended up in the hotel bar. There he ran into his friend Mike Hawthorn, who had skipped the sports car race but was gearing himself up for the next day's Grand Prix by sinking a few pints. After a few more drinks the two decided to go out and, hours later, were spotted drunkenly stumbling back to the hotel along the banks of the town's canals. Their progress decidedly haphazard, Macklin lost his balance and tumbled into the canal. On getting fished out – presumably by onlookers, since Hawthorn wouldn't have been much help by this stage – he turned up to the hotel sopping wet.

While Macklin was out getting plastered with Hawthorn, the other

Bristol was actually going rather well, enduring a trouble-free run to fifth place overall and first in class. Its progress, though, wasn't enough to convince Macklin to stick around. Still unhappy with the car's handling, and plagued by memories of his near-escape in the Le Mans darkness, he had decided to never race a Bristol again. He did have one final fling with the team a few months later at the high-speed Montlhéry circuit, heading out with Jack Fairman and breaking a stack of two-litre class records. The two covered 200 miles at 125.87mph, 500 kilometres (310.7 miles) at 116.10mph, 500 miles at 112.25mph and 1000km (621.3 miles) at 115.49mph. They also averaged 116.42mph over three hours and 115.43mph over five hours. When they were done, Macklin jumped back in the car and took the thrilled mechanics out on high speed runs around the track, showing them what it like inside the wind-buffeted Bristol. Though it was an impressive outing, he never sat inside a Bristol again.

His entire racing career with the outfit spanned a lot of testing but only a paltry three hours' racing, all of which came at Le Mans. "I decided it wasn't quite the car for me," he said later. "I felt that my reputation was becoming involved and I couldn't see any great future in it." In retrospect, it's hard to understand why he decided to call it quits. Aside from the disastrous initial outing at Le Mans the Bristols actually did very well, easing to fifth at Reims and then crushing class records at Montlhéry. Perhaps his initial impressions proved too much to overcome. Either way, it turned out to be another unfortunate career move. The next time the cars raced, at Le Mans the following year, they dominated their class by finishing first, second and third in class, ending up seventh, eighth and ninth overall. Macklin could only watch on, once again cursing his poor judgement.

– – – – –

The French Grand Prix at Reims proved to be an all-time classic. It was the day Mike Hawthorn truly established himself as one of the world's fastest drivers by duelling with the great Juan Manuel Fangio – then widely recognised as the world's greatest driver – for lap after lap on the long, fast Reims track. Despite Hawthorn's crippling hangover, he drove at a level he never quite reached again. The two went toe-to-toe like a couple of furious boxers, swapping the lead at nearly every corner, their wheels straying onto the grass and sending up clouds of dust as they wrestled with the steering wheels, their brows sweating in the summer heat. They were determined to do anything to win the duel, the likes of which had never been seen in

Grand Prix racing before. On the very last corner Hawthorn threw his
Ferrari into the lead and stayed there, winning by no more than a second.
Froilán González, also, like Fangio, driving a Maserati, was only half a
second back in third, with Hawthorn's team-mate Ascari in fourth. Macklin
got to see Hawthorn and Fangio streaking by at close quarters, although
not quite in the way he would have wanted. After being lapped by the two,
his HWM's clutch gave out and, again, he retired.

Macklin's eventful weekend didn't stop there. Hanging about at the
hotel after the race, he looked up to see a beaming Hawthorn wander over
to his table. Hawthorn sat down. "What are you doing tonight?" he asked.
Having earlier been busy with his racing schedule Macklin, for once,
didn't have any plans. "Well, I've got a date with a little girl who is very
attractive," Hawthorn said, happily. "But her parents will only allow her
out if her sister comes too. The sister is rather nice." He paused. "Perhaps
you would like to come along and make up the four?" Macklin was never
going to say no, and a few hours later he found himself in the passenger
seat of Hawthorn's Ferrari, with two excited French ladies in the back.
The quartet steered clear of Reims itself, knowing they'd be instantly
swamped as soon as they were recognised, and instead drove fifteen miles
out into the countryside for dinner at a small town restaurant. After
dinner they headed back to the hotel at Rheims where Hawthorn, with
a sly grin, went upstairs with the elder Frenchwoman while Macklin and
the woman's sister went to his room to kill time. Demonstrating that for
all his womanising he did have a strong moral streak, Macklin guessed his
date's age was around 17 and decided against trying to seduce her. They
whiled away the hours by talking, the two getting on well while, upstairs,
Hawthorn was occupied in an entirely different way. After a few hours
Hawthorn and his date came back down the stairs, the four piling back
in the Ferrari and driving back to the ladies' place to drop them off. That
done, the two drivers headed back to the hotel for the final time and both
fell into a long, deep sleep.

That night proved to have long-standing repercussions. A few months
later Macklin was at the Paris Motor Show, suited up and hanging-out
with members of that year's British contingent, when he felt a tap on his
shoulder. Turning around, he immediately recognised Hawthorn's French
date, with an apologetic half-smile on her face.

"Can I have a talk with you?" she asked. "I have something serious to
tell you about."

Macklin was surprised. "My god!" he exclaimed. "Yes."

The two moved over to a quiet corner, away from the hubbub of the crowd. "The problem is this," she said in a hushed tone. "I'm pregnant and Mike Hawthorn is the father. I don't really mind about it, but my family know and I've been thrown out by my father."

Macklin breathed deeply.

"The only thing I want is for Mike to recognise the child. It's only a formality, I'm not asking Mike for anything at all. But I wonder, as you are a friend of his, if you could see him and tell him the position and ask if he would recognise the child?"

She paused. From his years of living in France, Macklin knew why she was so insistent. In French society at the time a child would be branded illegitimate if its father refused to recognise it as his own, attaching to it a stigma that would endure for the entirety of the poor child's upbringing. Macklin looked at the girl, noticing for the first time just how young she really was, and immediately felt sorry for her. Of course, he told her. I'll call him as soon as I get a chance. "Thank you," the girl said, giving him a quick hug before scurrying off.

A few days later Macklin called Hawthorn. "Frankly, you know, I think you ought to do it," Macklin said. "It doesn't mean very much to you and the girl is being very reasonable about it. She's not asking you for any money." Hawthorn was having none of it. "Oh no, bugger that," he replied. "I don't want anything to do with it. It's her own fault if she became pregnant, she should have been more careful." Macklin was appalled. Chasing women was, of course, a standard part of the life of racing drivers in the 1950s, forming a sort of holy trinity of racing driver behaviour along with driving fast cars and drinking each other under the table. It was the very laddish behaviour of testosterone-fuelled 20-somethings, making for exciting tales around tables and in biographies. Yet for all the macho talk of "chasing birds" it was easy to forget that their targets were real women with real lives, leading existences of far more substance than simply being bait for sexually voracious racing drivers. There's no doubt everyone involved knew the game, but, as happened in Hawthorn's case, things could and occasionally did go wrong. It's hard to imagine Macklin, faced with a similar situation, doing anything but accepting full responsibility. Hawthorn wasn't quite so accommodating. A year later the young woman got at least some revenge, pushing a pram with her young child – who, by many accounts, was a dead-ringer for Hawthorn – up and down in front of the hotel where Hawthorn was staying. It became a source of deserved embarrassment for the now not-so-smug Englishman.

– – – – –

After all the drama of Reims it was time for Macklin to get back to business. On July 11 he was back at Crystal Palace in London, a track he seemed to have taken quite a liking to, and whose short races helped negate the HWM's terrible unreliability. He drove a solid race to slot in fourth. On July 18 he was back at Silverstone for the British Grand Prix where, to nobody's surprise, the HWM was given a sound thrashing before sparing further blushes and breaking down. Years later, several young boys, including future Formula One World Champion Jackie Stewart, recalled timidly wandering up to him in the pits in search of an autograph, nervous about meeting one of their dashing racing heroes. They needn't have worried. All recalled a dapper Macklin happily bending down and signing their notepads, even sticking around for a quick chat while his mechanics tried calling him away. Meeting your heroes, the boys happily learned, does occasionally live up to expectations.

On July 26 Macklin was back across the channel in beautiful Aix-les-Baines with Collins and local driver Yves Giraud-Cabantous. In a relatively small field he did well, out-racing his team-mates to fourth in the first heat and third in the second, ending up third overall. Stepping onto the podium, even for a relatively inconsequential race, was a pleasant surprise. Things were back to normal at Sables d'Olonne on July 9 when his HWM broke down, followed by the same result on August 23 at the Swiss Grand Prix. A week later, at Cadours, he came fourth in his heat behind team-mate Giraud-Cabantous and the Gordinis of Trintignant and Behra, before dropping out of the main event. The last race of the year, the final World Championship Grand Prix at Monza on September 13, ended in appropriate fashion when Macklin became the first retirement after just 27 laps. Hopping out of the car, he wandered away down the track as his stricken, forlorn HWM sat, as it had so many times over the past two seasons, with steam billowing out from under its bonnet. Despite crashing out of the race on the last lap Ascari still took that year's driver's championship. Hawthorn, after an impressive season, finished fourth. Macklin, needless to say, finished nowhere.

– – – – –

1952 and 1953 turned out to be transformative years in Macklin's racing career, albeit not in a way he would have liked. He went into 1952 coming off an impressive couple of seasons with HWM and Aston Martin, and with a growing reputation as a serious force to be reckoned with. George Abecassis later recalled that during this period, many in the Italian grand prix community thought he had more potential than even Stirling Moss. Nearly two years later, things were very different. It's doubtful he had become any slower as a driver – he could still prove to be blindingly quick on occasion – but having a slow and unreliable car had sapped his momentum. He'd also made terrible career decisions, none more so than when he chose to leave Aston Martin. In two years he'd gone from a serious contender to having little chance of a top-line drive. His career would never recover.

It would be hard to say he was overly fussed by it all. He was still doing what he loved, after all, and also enjoying his extra-curricular activities and partying with his new friends Hawthorn and Collins. Though he obviously wanted to do well on the track, and certainly knew he was capable of it, his focus was never entirely on racing. He had all the talent of those around him – "certainly as good as Collins and almost as good as Hawthorn," according to Moss – but little of the drive. He would frequently cause Abecassis, a constant presence over those years, to scratch his head. "He had this tremendous athletic flair and he could have been a very great driver without any question at all," Abecassis once said. "He had a quite astonishing sense of balance, and I don't believe there's any game he couldn't have played really well, but the extraordinary thing was that he was never, ever interested."

Chapter 13

Adventures with Austin Healey

At the start of 1954 Macklin no longer had a sports car drive, and his options were alarmingly few. Ferrari and Maserati were never really in the equation, and the top two British teams, Aston Martin and Jaguar, were out as well. He knew he was still on people's radar, with *Motor Sport* magazine's Bill Boddy rating him one of the top 25 Grand Prix drivers in the world, albeit in the lowest of three categories alongside Collins, Parnell, Prince Bira, Behra, Maglioli, de Graffenried and Roy Salvadori. Still, he glumly realised that public recognition didn't automatically entitle him to a drive. One afternoon he was pondering the problem over beers at the Steering Wheel Cub when he had a thought. What about Donald?

Macklin had known Donald Healey since he was a toddler. Healey had been a great friend of Noel's, for whom he drove Invictas, and had been a frequent visitor at Fairmile. Healey was very much of the old school: a tough yet kind Cornishman with a strong work ethic and an inventive mind. He was a terrific driver, too. The stories he told hearkened back to the early, adventurous days of motor racing: ploughing an Invicta through massive snowdrifts in Norway and Sweden; getting covered in mud on the long, torrid Monte Carlo rally; going flat-out, foot to the floor, around Brooklands. He was someone who would appear, clad in overalls and goggles, on sepia-tinged photographs from motoring's golden days. He was a man who got things done.

After the war Healey had turned to building his own cars. Like most things he'd turned his hand to they'd proved successful, both in production and on the race track. Healey's early postwar cars had turned out to be especially popular in the United States and, after a chance meeting on-board the Queen Elizabeth in the middle of the Atlantic, he ended up entering into a partnership with Nash Cars that proved exceptionally fruitful. Together they made the Nash Healey, which sold well – in the United States, that is, since it was export-only – and competed with distinction on the track. In 1950 a Nash Healey driven by Duncan Hamilton and Tony Rolt finished fourth at Le Mans, just in front of Macklin and Abecassis' Aston Martin, while the following year the same combination came in sixth. Healey's little sports cars didn't have the grunt of the big players, and were never able to mix it with the Jaguars, Ferraris and Mercedes for the overall win, but at the same time they were never really designed to. They were simply tidy little sports cars that Healey brought to the track for, more or less, publicity. Healey actually drove the first competition Nash Healey in the fearsome 1950 Mille Miglia, after which he enlisted drivers and kept the racing programme going. By 1954 the team had competed all over the world, and was gearing up for a busy programme with its latest model, the beautiful Austin Healey 100. Macklin, searching around for a drive and running out of ideas, figured he'd give his old family friend a call.

The chat obviously went well; a few months later, in early 1954, Macklin found himself leaning over a rail on the Queen Elizabeth, looking out over the vast mid-Atlantic with a cocktail in his hand. He was accompanying Austin Healey team manager Mort Goodall and an Austin Healey 100 to New York City, in his new role as an Austin Healey works driver, having called Donald Healey and discovered the team did need a driver after all. Macklin was back in business. The trip to New York proved to be pleasantly lazy, although both Macklin and Goodall knew they were in for a bit of a haul once they arrived. After docking in New York the two planned to hop in the Austin Healey and drive it all the way down to Sebring in Florida for the annual 12-hour sports car race on March 7, a drive of 20 hours or so. Still, they weren't too fussed, figuring that if they really put their foot down they could shave a few hours off the time. It was a racing car, after all.

Sebring was Macklin's first race of the year, and his first opportunity to see what the Austin Healey was really made of. The large field was heavily stacked with local drivers, although, as a round of the World Sports Car Championship, a fair few internationals – including Moss, Collins and Fangio – were going to be there. He looked forward to the parties that would inevitably happen once he arrived in Florida. He was a long way from home, and knew he would appear even more exotic than usual, at least so far as the locals were concerned. It was going to be a lot of fun.

The ship arrived in the middle of the night. After unloading and filling out the requisite paperwork, Goodall and Macklin hopped into the little Healey, which had been fitted out with a small windscreen and a flimsy hood to offer some semblance of protection, and blared off into the looming dawn. They took it fairly easily, not doing over 3000 revs for the first 1000 miles to protect the brand new engine – Macklin did later comment about how ridiculous driving a brand new racing car 20 hours to an event was, although nobody considered it at the time – and quickly settled into a steady 70mph groove. As they drove down the New Jersey Turnpike dawn broke, filling the sky with a golden crimson glow and illuminating the little Healey, which was the only car for miles around. To the two Englishmen, being on a six-lane superhighway was an event unto itself, let alone having it all to themselves. They looked around in wonder, basking in the early morning air.

After a while another car distantly appeared in their mirrors. Gradually it gained on them until, after a few minutes, they looked over and realised it was right beside them. A siren cut through the cold early morning air. It was a "great, tall ... Neanderthal cop," as Macklin later recalled, and he didn't look happy. The two pulled over to the side of the road and turned off the Healey, sitting uneasily as the hulking police officer strode towards it. Since the Healey was English the steering wheel, of course, was on the other side of the car. Not realising this, the officer mistakenly headed over to speak with Goodall on the passenger's side.

"I'm going to book you for speeding," he said, in a curt New Jersey accent. "You were doing 70."

"Really?" Goodall replied.

"Yeah. Gimme your licence."

Goodall handed his licence through the window. The cop looked at it with a furrowed brow.

"Where you from?"

"England."

"Well, this is going to cost you fifty bucks."

"I don't see that it's got anything to do with me."

The officer raised his eyebrow. "Whaddaya mean it ain't nuthin' to do with you?"

"Well," Goodall said, repressing a giggle, "I'm just sitting here."

Growing confused, the officer peered into the Healey and across at Macklin, who was sitting on the other side of the car behind the steering wheel. With a grunt he brusquely handed back Goodall's licence then stormed over to the other side of the car. The two Englishmen shared a quick smile, although their grins quickly disappeared when the increasingly frustrated officer reached into his belt and pulled out a revolver. He pointed it directly at Macklin's head. "Step outside," he said. Macklin hesitated. "Christ Lance," Goodall told him. "You'd better step out. He's not joking." Nervously, Macklin eased himself out and headed over to the police car, where he sat as the officer sternly called up headquarters to check out their details. After a few anxious minutes they were back on the road, shaken up and $50 poorer.

The next day they passed through the South, the air thick and humid, the roads lined with tall Georgia pines and an occasional run-down shack. After the previous day's adventure with the New Jersey police they decided to take it easy and follow the road rules, even if they found the 45mph speed limits difficult to stick to. At one point, deep in rural Georgia, they drove over a rise to see the road stretching off into the distance and out of sight. There was nobody else around. Macklin leaned over to Goodall. "I think we can safely wind it up a bit here, don't you?" he asked. Goodall agreed, and off the two went, barrelling down the road at a more comfortable 100mph. After a while they noticed a town in the distance and carefully slowed right down, travelling through its narrow streets at a sedate 30mph before winding it back up again as they entered the open road. Soon, though, Macklin glanced in his mirrors and became alarmed. There, far behind them in the distance, was a pair of flashing lights. The two Englishmen nervously pretended to ignore them, hoping desperately they were aimed at someone else, and continued on their way.

Of course, the lights weren't for anybody else. After a while a police car pulled alongside them with its sirens blazing and, in a repeat of the day before, forced them to pull over. This time the officer – who turned out to be a sheriff – had a huge ten gallon hat, a deep southern accent and didn't pull any guns, but Macklin and Goodall still had to turn around and follow him back to the small town they'd come through half an hour earlier. When they pulled up at the town's courthouse, Goodall leaned over. "You'd better go in, Lance" he said, earnestly. "I'll stay here." Macklin flashed him a look and hopped out.

The main part of the courthouse was a long, large hall, with a couple of small windows and bare wooden beams. It was hot. The echo from Macklin's shoes ricocheted off the bare walls as he wandered to the far end of the hall in the direction of a small, cluttered desk. Behind the desk, leaning back in a leather chair and resting his shoes on top of it, was a man whose face lay buried behind a comic book. "Judge," the sheriff called over. The judge lowered the comic book.

"Yeah?" the judge asked, annoyed.

"Judge, I was doing a hundred miles an hour for twenty five miles and I had a tough time trying to catch him."

The judge's jaw dropped. "A hundred miles an hour?" he thundered. He turned to Macklin, who was standing uncomfortably beside the sheriff.

"What do you say to that?"

"I don't think I was doing a hundred miles an hour," Macklin said, hesitantly, before figuring he should probably concede something. "We've only just arrived from Europe and frankly, you know, there's no speed limit outside the towns in Europe."

The judge raised an eyebrow. "Didn't you see the signs saying 55?"

"I thought they were for trucks. In Europe we have speed limits for trucks, not cars."

The judge didn't buy it. After a back and forth he imposed a hundred dollar fine, adding a parting shot as Macklin was about to head back outside. "If you hadn't been British and just arrived in this country I'd have put you in jail as well," he said menacingly, before putting his feet back up and returning to his comic. Hopping in the car, Macklin sighed. "I should have just put my foot down," he told Goodall as he swung the Healey, very slowly, back onto the road.

– – – – –

They were caught speeding one more time before finally arriving, hours late and over $200 down, in Sebring. Donald Healey, who had sensibly flown on ahead, was horrified, although the other members of the British contingent thought it was hilarious.

Like many of the British postwar tracks, Sebring was held on a former army air base, and with its rough surface and bare minimum of safety provisions it had already developed a reputation as a car breaker. The field was large, hitting 63 even despite a large number of no-shows, and it soon became clear that the mighty Ferrari and Lancia teams would be the ones to beat. Macklin was teamed with a local driver, a genial, thoroughly competent amateur called George Huntoon. Huntoon had actually raced at Le Mans in 1951, as well as a host of other high-level stateside events, and he turned out to be a more than able partner.

Rain pelted the track overnight but eased off as race day came round, leaving the air cold and windy and the track wet. The first lap was chaotic, with over 60 cars crowded together and jostling for position. The Lancias quickly cut through the field and shot off into a race of their own at the front, with Moss' wonderfully curvy Osca holding down fourth and Huntoon touring solidly around in the middle of the pack. As night fell the retirements came in waves. The entire Aston Martin team was out early, quickly followed by various locals, the Ferraris, and then, most importantly, the Lancias. Soon the only Lancia remaining was that of Piero Taruffi and Robert Manzon, and bad luck soon befell them, too. Forced to come in to fix a broken headlight, they headed out again only to break down. In an impressive display of determination Taruffi pushed his car a mile and a half to the finish line, but it was all in vain as he ended up disqualified. Moss, not believing his luck, suddenly found himself in the lead. He stayed there, taking the chequered flag after 12 hectic and exhausting hours. When the winners took to the podium Moss and co-driver Bill Lloyd shared the top step, followed by the sole remaining Lancia of Porfirio Rubirosa and Gino Valenzano. In third place, having worked their way up and, most importantly, stayed on the track, was the little Healey of Huntoon and Macklin. It was a wonderful debut. The Healey, a middle-class, everyday sports car, had outlasted its hugely expensive upmarket rivals. Seeing the win as marketing gold, Donald Healey quickly capitalised on the team's success by producing the 100S – S for Sebring – a fast, powerful Austin Healey that has gone down as one of the company's greatest cars. It boosted Stateside sales of the Healey and gave the marque its most famous win. Despite the drama getting there, it had turned out to be well worth it. The team left Sebring tired, hungover, and happy.

A month later Macklin came crashing back to earth, failing to qualify the Healey against strong opposition in the British Empire Trophy at Silverstone on April 10. On April 19 Macklin rejoined HWM, which had spent the off-season developing a car for the new Formula One rules, in the seven-lap, non-championship Lavant Cup race at Goodwood. It was an encouraging start to the year, Macklin finishing fourth behind Reg Parnell, Roy Salvadori and Ken McAlpine. Still, the result would prove to be a bit of a red herring. Though no-one knew it at the time, Macklin's fourth place would prove to be the highlight of HWM's short, final Formula Two season.

Next up on the horizon lay something completely, utterly different. Stretching for a thousand miles through the Italian countryside, the infamous Mille Miglia was one of the longest, fastest and most dangerous road races in the world. Running over hilltops and down valleys, winding through small villages and big cities, it was unquestionably one of the greats in an era of epic races. It involved around twelve hours of flat-out driving, and was kind to local drivers who had driven the course's hundreds of corners before. For this reason the field was always stacked with Italian drivers, although it tended to attract top international talent, too, especially after joining the World Sports Car Championship in 1953. In 1954 it was running a round-trip route between Brescia, where it started and finished, and Rome. A staggering 483 cars were entered in the event, ranging from the powerful Lancias that had set the pace at Sebring to diminutive Fiat 500s. It was eclectic, dangerous and completely wild. Macklin couldn't wait.

Unlike most of the non-Italian entries, Macklin elected to forgo a co-driver and tackle the race himself. He set off from Brescia at 5:50 in the morning on May 2, 1954, just 12 minutes ahead of pre-race favourite Ascari, roaring off into a drizzly, foggy Italian morning. He hurled the Healey through the twisty Italian roads, going as hard as he could but also constantly checking his mirrors and trying to stay out of the way as the much faster, full-blooded sports cars that frequently came flying past. Among them was Ascari's Lancia. Perhaps, just for a second, Macklin thought back to their surreal duel at the Targa Florio a few years earlier. This time the circumstances couldn't have been much more different.

He battled on through the fickle weather and through the crowded, dangerous roads to cross the line thirteen hours and thirty eight minutes after he'd started. Exhausted, his face covered in grime, he gently eased out of the car to learn that he'd finished 23rd overall and fifth in class. The result wasn't as saleable as Sebring's third place but, put in perspective, was more impressive. Driving the entire, treacherous event himself, he'd managed to beat nearly 160 others despite not even having a top-flight car under him. It was one of his finest drives.

1954 was turning out to be much less busy than the previous few years. No longer was he tied up every weekend with HWM, jumping from circuit to circuit in a fog of travelling, womanising and partying. Now, for the first time in nearly six years, he had a bit of time to relax. True to form he spent it either at home in France, partying at French racing driver's club the Action Automobile, or at its English equivalent, the Steering Wheel Club. He was no workaholic. His womanising had already become legend in the Donald Healey racing outfit, and so had his lack of interest in doing any driving he didn't particularly feel like. "Lance would drive Donald (Healey) mad," Shelagh Montague Browne, who, in 1954, was beginning to re-emerge onto the motor racing scene, recalled. "It was this very lackadaisical attitude of his. Manufacturers wanted their cars raced and wanted their cars to win. Normally you'd turn up for practice and start trying and beat the other guy, but Lance wasn't at all fussed by that. He could take it or leave it." Having a laid-back schedule certainly did Macklin's work ethic no favours. Free time, and the partying that ensued, proved to be a dangerous combination.

– – – – –

Le Mans almost didn't happen for Macklin in 1954. After the year's early success, Donald Healey had been preparing his cars for the race when he had a sudden change of heart. Watching from the sidelines, he'd grown increasingly frustrated by what he perceived to be the race organisers' lax entry regulations. Sports car racing in general had begun to turn into a two-tiered system, pure-bred, exceptionally fast sports cars on one level, and much slower, production-derived cars on the other. It had created a situation that was quickly becoming dangerous, with impossibly fast sports cars and slightly modified road cars sharing the same track. No serious crashes had happened yet, but Healey didn't like the way things were headed. When it came to Le Mans, the most popular of all sports car races, he withdrew his cars in protest.

Macklin, however, was undeterred. After a bit of scrambling he managed to secure himself a last minute seat in an Osca – the same quick little car Moss had driven to victory at Sebring a few months earlier – alongside regulars Pierre Leygonie and James Simpson. After getting off to a solid start on the afternoon of June 12, the Osca was circulating rather uneventfully when, 257 laps in, it slid off the road in the middle of a rainstorm. What exactly happened next is unclear, but it's likely a helpful yet misdirected marshal gave the stricken car a push back onto the track. The Osca made it back to the pits, but when officials found out the car had been given a helping hand it was disqualified. The team's race was over.

Donald Healey's withdrawal from Le Mans had extended into a general withdrawal from the World Sports Car Championship. His team's absence was due to last until the forbidding Carrera Panamericana in

November, meaning that Macklin had to scrounge around if he wanted to pick up a drive. Additionally, his single-seat career with HWM was over. After a couple of minor non-championship races the team had come to realise how completely out of its depth it had become, Heath's gamble on updating the engine to fit the new Formula One regulations having failed. HWM's final race, with Macklin as the sole entry, was at the French Grand Prix on July 4 at Reims. It was a miserable weekend. The HWM was a staggering 30 seconds a lap slower than pole sitter Fangio in his new, all-powerful Mercedes W196. In the race the team's blushes were spared as the engine, as it had been doing so often over the past two years, blew after ten laps. Under resourced, the team had tried valiantly to keep up but it just hadn't been enough. HWM's days as a competitive racing outfit wasn't yet over – by this stage it'd at least set up a successful sports car outfit – but as a Formula Two concern it was done. So, too, was Macklin's time as a works Grand Prix driver.

The year continued to drag on slowly as his next three races, for three different teams, all ended in retirement. Beginning on July 4 with another double-header at the Reims 12-hour for HWM, he moved on to Dundrod's Tourist Trophy in an Osca on September 11, and, when November finally rolled around, the Carrera Panamericana for Donald Healey. In an era of dangerous long-distance races, the Mexican Carrera Panamericana was widely recognised as the most dangerous of the bunch. Racing through deserts and up through windy, isolated hill country roads, it started south in Tuxtla Gutiérrez, Chiapas, and ended nearly 2000 miles away in Ciudad Juárez, Chihuahua. Every year there were deaths. In 1953 there had been nine, mostly comprising of spectators mowed down by an out-of-control Ford while they stood gawking at another crashed car. It was brutal.

Despite the danger, and a growing chorus of outrage over the event in Mexico, it had been designated as the final round of the World Sports car Championship in 1953. In 1954 Donald Healey, feeling adventurous, planned to join Macklin as his co-driver in the event. Unfortunately, the team's championship comeback came to nought as Macklin and Healey's car suffered from ignition problems and didn't even make it to the end of the first stage. A glimpse of what might have been came from the other Healey entry driven by the hard-charging American Carroll Shelby and his co-driver Roy Jackson-Moore. Behind the wheel of a Healey that had just been upgraded to 100S specifications, the two tore up the competition and were a startling fourth place at the end of the first stage. Unfortunately, though, it wasn't to last. The next day Shelby was charging hard when he lost control and crashed heavily, allegedly after becoming fixated on an attractive woman in the crowd. Macklin would have understood. The race was eventually won by Umberto Maglioli in his Ferrari 375 after 17 hours and 40 minutes of driving, where he averaged an incredible 107.9mph (173.7kmh). Seven people – four competitors, two spectators and one team member – were killed. Though not everyone yet recognised the risks posed by the sport's great increases in speed, the local authorities did. 1954 was the last year the great race took place.

With the Carrera Panamericana done and dusted, the Sports car Championship was over for the year. Ferrari had taken the championship victory from the fast yet fragile Lancias, while Austin Healey, despite skipping most of the year, had finished in an impressive tie for seventh alongside Cunningham and Aston Martin. For the tired drivers and their battered cars there was the option of one last stop on the tour before their year was finally over, and it was one that few turned down. The drivers hopped on planes and headed east, to sun drenched beaches, lazy hotel pools and plentiful margaritas: the Nassau Cup in the Bahamas beckoned.

Macklin signed up immediately, for not only was Nassau his kind of scene but he was due to meet a special friend there. Hanging about after the Sebring race earlier in the year, his eyes had fixed themselves, as they tended to do, on a beautiful young woman at a party. She turned out to be a native of Waco, Texas called Linda Kay, and the two hit it off immediately. Kay was a world traveller, devout Francophile and, to top it all off, a fanatical skier. Macklin was immediately infatuated, and the feeling was mutual. A few months earlier, Kay had driven 200-odd miles just to have dinner with Macklin while he had briefly stopped over in Houston. During the visit he had told her to meet him in Nassau and, although she'd been nervous about her parents vetoing the idea, come November she found herself on a flight to the Bahamas. While she was on her way there Macklin hurriedly set about rearranging the Healey team's sleeping arrangements in preparation for her arrival. Donald Healey had generously booked rooms in the grand-sounding British Colonial Hotel overlooking the Nassau seafront, although to Macklin's dismay he had put a Healey mechanic next to his driver's room. Soon the mechanic had been banished to the sixth floor, while his now unoccupied room was all ready for Kay's arrival.

Driving to Nassau's small airport to greet Kay, Macklin became intrigued by the large amount of traffic clogging the island's small roads. His curiosity rose further when he wandered inside the main terminal and straight into a chaotic hubbub of calypso bands, brass bands, restless crowds and, vainly attempting to look orderly, dignified looking men in suits and top hats. "What's going on?" Macklin asked someone in the crowd. It turned out to a reception for the 100,000th visitor for the year, although nobody was entirely sure who the lucky ticket holder was just yet. "Whoever it is will be taken out and given a great time," the man told him. Macklin shuffled alongside and, along with the rest of the crowd, waited.

Half an hour later the bands piped up as a Pan Am jet from Houston touched down on the runway. After a few minutes its door opened and, to Macklin's complete surprise, out stepped a beaming Linda Kay. By a stroke of luck she had bought the lucky 100,000th ticket. Macklin could only wave as she was ushered into the mayor's Rolls-Royce and driven to a luxurious suite at the best hotel in town, where she spent hours being treated to the finest hospitality that Nassau had to offer. What are the chances, Macklin wondered, scratching his head as he drove back alone to the team's hotel.

The races, held on November 11 and 12, took place on a disused airfield that hadn't been touched since the end of the Second World War. As such its surface was rough, with weeds poking out from cracks in the concrete and surrounding the circuit, giving the track itself a forlorn air of abandonment. Still, in light of the meeting's festive atmosphere nobody was really complaining. Donald Healey, clad in shorts and a plaid shirt, watched on as Macklin mixed it fiercely with the international contingent. He finished an encouraging sixth in the first heat before crashing out, in dangerous fashion, with a broken front stub axle in the second. "I was lucky," he told the *Nassau Tribune*. "I could have been killed by something like that." After the race the drivers trooped back to the British Colonial Hotel for a suit and tie ball, the revelry lasting long into the next morning. It was a celebratory end to a long, dangerous season.

Chapter 14

Tragedy

Despite some impressive drives the previous year, by the start of 1955 Macklin's career was on the wane. Though his driving talent hadn't vanished by any means, as startling drives at the previous year's Sebring and the Mille Miglia races had demonstrated, his opportunities had dried up. He'd been surpassed in the public consciousness by a new breed of young British racing heroes spearheaded by Hawthorn and Moss, a group that was soon to include his friend Peter Collins. The days where he spent every weekend behind the wheel were long over. It was almost as if he had crossed an invisible line and become a high-level gentleman racer – albeit an exceptionally talented one – instead of a seriously committed racing driver. He was no longer aiming for the heights of Formula One, instead happy enough to do his best in the small Austin Healey. He still had all the talent to be driving competitively at the front of the field, but not the ambition ... or the judgement ... or, especially, the luck.

Macklin's first race of the year came with a return to the Sebring 12 Hours on March 13, 1955. After the previous year's success, Donald Healey was hoping his drivers would do well, and so they did. With the old firm of Moss and Macklin teaming up behind the wheel, the little Healey powered to sixth place, beaten by only the winning Jaguar D-Type of Hawthorn and Phil Walters, and a selection of pure-bred Ferraris and Maseratis. Three weeks later, on April 2, came the British Empire Trophy at Oulton Park where Macklin finished 14th, before heading back across to Italy for the Mille Miglia on May 1.

While Macklin battled valiantly in the Healey, the 1955 Mille Miglia became famous for what was perhaps Stirling Moss' greatest drive. Rocketing off from Brescia with co-driver Denis Jenkinson in the brand new Mercedes 300SLR – a fearsome, streamlined silver bullet that was a slightly modified version of the W196 Formula One car – they proceeded to completely demolish the opposition, winning by over half an hour from Fangio's (admittedly sick) 300SLR, and breaking nearly every race record. One of the cars they passed on the way was Macklin's Healey. Looking in his mirrors and seeing the distinctive Mercedes quickly pulling up, Macklin pulled over and waved to his old friend as the Mercedes flew by.

Macklin eventually finished 36th, which, considering the problems he faced, was a startling result. Not only did he again drive the race by himself, but he also had to deal with a broken throttle cable, forcing him to turn off the ignition whenever he came up to corners or had to slow down. It was as impressive as anything else he'd done behind the wheel but, buried in the pack as he was, it went almost entirely unnoticed.

Next came the Silverstone International on May 7. While Macklin finished a respectable 17th, it was his old Aston Martin team that stole the show. Though it had had a relatively miserable 1954, Aston Martin spent the off-season developing the promising new DB3S, and, at Silverstone, it reaped the benefits. Trouncing even the mighty Jaguar team, Reg Parnell and Roy Salvadori powered their way to a 1-2 finish. Macklin looked on at what might have been.

On May 22 he headed to Monaco for the grand prix, where he failed to qualify by the barest of margins, despite driving a car with some serious power in the form of Stirling Moss' Maserati 250F. A week later he took a trip to Albi, the track he'd raced on so many times before, one last time. Yet again, though, his chance to make the most of having a powerful car didn't last long. Qualifying a solid fifth, he was out after 36 laps, the victim of a broken water hose. As he hopped out and wandered away from his broken car, little did he know that it would turn out to be the penultimate time he'd ever race a Grand Prix car. In exactly two weeks his life, and motorsport all over the world, was going to change forever.

– – – – –

Donald Healey's unease about the safety of sports car racing, which had manifested itself most obviously at Le Mans a year earlier, had only grown stronger since. By mid-1955 he'd become concerned not only with the dangers posed by faster and slower cars, but the types of drivers who were entering as well. Because of their relative affordability, his Austin Healeys had become popular among amateur drivers, some of which, Healey noted in dismay, didn't particularly seem to know what they were doing. Again, like the year before, there was to be no official works Austin Healey team at Le Mans in 1955.

In hindsight it's tempting to wonder what might have happened if Macklin had accepted that he didn't have a drive and relaxed, maybe heading to his mother's villa at Roquebrune, maybe even watching the race from the confines of a friendly team's pit. He didn't. Something about Le Mans pulled him in, drew him towards it even when he had to go out of his way – something he wasn't keen on doing, especially at this stage of his career – to find a way to get there. Maybe it was a desire to get another taste of his great success in 1951. Maybe it was to atone for his nearly-moment with Peter Collins in 1952, where he came so close to setting foot on the podium one more time. Maybe, like so many other drivers, he'd fallen for the oldest and greatest sports car race of them all. Whatever the reason, he didn't call it quits when Donald Healey gave him the news about the team pulling out in early 1955. Instead, with Healey's reluctant blessing, he worked in conjunction with French Austin importer AFIVA to enter a Healey – the 100S he'd driven in the Carrera Panamericana – under his own name. After a bit of dithering the organisers accepted the entry, to the delight of Macklin and his jack-of-all-trades co-driver Les Leston. While he knew he couldn't realistically challenge for the overall lead with the Mercedes, Jaguar, Ferrari and Aston Martin teams out in force, he figured he had a pretty good shot at taking his category. Anyway, strange things had happened at Le Mans before. He went in with his hopes up.

Alfred Neubauer had received his wish. He'd signed up an astonished Pierre Levegh, giving him the equipment to finally mount a serious challenge for a Le Mans win at the age of 49. It was a drastic step up for the Frenchman, going from his comfortable little Talbot to the single fastest sports car on the planet. For him it was a dream come true, although he was soon to find that his dream would have unexpected, and unwelcome, downsides. The Mercedes, with its staggering pace, frightened him. He was an amateur driver handling a high-tech machine built for professionals, and he struggled to cope. Eyebrows had been raised when he'd been announced in the third Mercedes car for Le Mans – Karl Kling and André Simon took another, while a super team of Moss and Fangio took the lead drive – and they stayed up when testing began. Visibly nervous, Levegh's times had proved to be not only far slower than the other drivers but also wildly erratic.

To his credit, though, Levegh had been quicker than his team-mate, the widely respected American driver John Fitch, and had begun to settle down by the time Le Mans came around. Much was later written about whether he deserved to be there at all, whether he was too old, too nervous and too slow. Yet while there's no doubt he wasn't in the class of the regular Mercedes drivers, few were. Levegh was no mug. He'd spent years battling on the Formula Two circuit, and had driven well at Le Mans in the past. Though he'd overdone it when he tried to run the race all by himself that obviously wasn't going to happen again. Besides, he'd shown he could drive quickly and maintain concentration for far longer than he'd normally need to, which was exactly what Neubauer wanted. Above all, would someone as astute as Neubauer really have let a driver behind the wheel of his most precious car if he thought they weren't up to it?

– – – – –

It's important to remember that the race was taking place only ten years after the end of the Second World War. Many of the drivers competing had taken part in the war itself, and the ones who hadn't had still grown up in a postwar world replete with its after-effects. It was part of the reason safety was so lax. Consider Macklin: for all the terrifying incidents he'd had throughout his racing career – the spins, the heavy crashes, the time at Le Mans where he'd driven through the darkness surrounded by the smell of petrol – nothing could ever compare to the terrifying nights he spent on his MTB in the darkness of the English Channel. In racing, death could come to you if you weren't careful, but in war it could come even if you were. Compared to what had happened in the not-too-distant past, the hazards that came with motor racing were nothing too special to worry about.

Nationalism also came into play. The prospect of three Mercedes' dominating the French home of motorsport was something that made the German team nervous, fearing it would dredge up unwelcome memories from the decade before. Indeed, the main reason Levegh was even in the team was as a tonic for the French fans in the crowd. Neubauer, canny as ever, could see the obvious PR benefits of having a Frenchman drive one of his cars at France's most famous race, even if the driver himself wasn't the quickest in the field. For his part, the devoutly nationalistic Mike Hawthorn fiercely disliked the German team. The man who looked and acted like a Spitfire pilot was never going to take kindly to being beaten by, in his view, the old foe. "Damn it," he said, after becoming momentarily overawed by the Mercedes team. "Why should a German car beat a British car?" At the helm of his giant-killing Jaguar D-Type, he was determined to stop the German juggernaut. He was going in to bat for England.

The speeds at Le Mans had been rising drastically since the war. 1954 had seen a lap record of 117mph, compared with 1949's 96.5mph, and everyone knew Mercedes would blow even that out of the water when it took to the track in 1955. Macklin, along with the many production-car drivers in the race, realised he was going to have his work cut out not just racing other cars but checking his mirrors and staying out of the way. He was going to have to be especially careful along the dangerously narrow pit area coming onto the main straight, a part of the track that created a bottleneck, and that other drivers had singled out as being particularly hazardous. Photographs from the time show cars flying down the straight at huge speeds, just feet away from relaxed-looking team members ambling around cars parked outside their pits. It's a state of affairs that appears almost inconceivably dangerous now, and was beginning to cause concern even at the time. Not enough concern, however, for race organisers to do anything about it.

– – – – –

On the afternoon of June 11, 1955, Le Mans was bathed in heat and surrounded by a festive air. The pits were crowded, mechanics rushing about the cars and making last-minute adjustments as the drivers chatted away among themselves, some relaxed, some with their stomachs churning. The grandstands were packed. Behind them lay hundreds of stalls in a hodge-podge of sound and colour, the smell of French festival food wafting through the air and mixing with the sound of guitars, mandolins and the excited chatter of thousands of racing fans. There were stalls selling food, some playing host to snake charmers, others for bearded ladies, and some for plain-old ordinary souvenirs. Sometimes, people later said, it was easy to forget there was a motor race going on at all.

Gradually everyone wandered over to the stands to catch the start. At 3:50 the drivers headed over too, standing, as they did every year, across the road from their cars on the main straight in the shadow of the mighty stands. Macklin looked over at his Healey and waited. Further up the road Hawthorn kicked his heels, while Levegh nervously stared at the Mercedes. They were nearly ready to go.

At 4pm the crowd erupted as the starter gun cracked and the drivers sprinted to their cars. Macklin reached the Healey quickly, jumped in and was off, as was Hawthorn, Levegh and everybody else except for Fangio. Attempting to emulate the ever-athletic Moss he had flamboyantly leaped into his car only to feel the Mercedes' gearlever go straight up one of his trouser legs and become stuck. By the time he disentangled himself he was dead last. Furious, he roared off in hot pursuit.

At the front, Eugenio Castellotti, a tall, dark and handsome Italian driver, quickly took the lead in his Ferrari 121LM, followed by a hard-charging Hawthorn. Very quickly the two began to pull away and started trading blows, passing and re-passing each other while setting increasingly faster lap times. Fangio was quickly working his way up through the field, frightening other drivers out of the way as his massive Mercedes loomed up in their mirrors. Macklin settled into a comfortable groove about midway through the field, dicing with some of the smaller cars but mostly trying to keep his nose clean while running as quickly as he could, while Levegh lay somewhere between Macklin and Hawthorn. He was going nowhere near as quickly as his team-mates but he was never really meant to. He had been sent out to play the long game. In the early years of Le Mans there was always the danger that those who decided to go too hard at the start risked blowing up their cars before the race had even reached halfway. Sometimes teams would even play tactics, deliberately getting their drivers to lure competitors into fast-paced battles hoping to blow their engines and send them out of the race. Levegh, who didn't have the raw pace to get drawn into such battles anyway, had been told to play the long game and focus on keeping the car on the road. It was a 24-hour race, after all. If his Mercedes was still going in the latter stages of the race, he would almost certainly be in with a shot at the win.

Fangio, on the other hand, was going for it. He tore around the field and was quickly back up with the leaders, then in front of them. Castellotti couldn't keep up and dropped back. Soon it was just Hawthorn and Fangio, battling in a way that the Le Mans crowd had never seen. 300,000 people watched, transfixed, as the two great drivers threw caution to the wind and took each other on, driving as hard as they could. This was no longer a 24-hour race. This was a Grand Prix. They swapped places, broke the lap record time and again, streaking through as a flash of silver and green mixed together as one. Everyone was awestruck.

They went at it for nearly two and a half relentless hours, neither giving an inch. According to Jaguar driver Norman Dewis it was all part of Jaguar's cunning plan. Hawthorn had been sent to lure the Mercedes into a race in order to blow it up, taking Fangio and Moss out and opening up the strong possibility of a Jaguar win. It was certainly plausible. However, there was also the chance that Fangio was simply driving his natural race and that Hawthorn was desperately trying to take it to him. Either way, what's certain is that Hawthorn was burning with a single-minded determination. He was driving like he rarely had before.

After two and a half breathless hours it was time for the first round of driver changes. Moss and Ivor Bueb, Hawthorn's team-mate, wandered down and waited in the pits for their team-mates to pull in. Bueb, though a good driver, was nowhere near the calibre of Moss. With the cars neck and neck Mercedes already had a decisive advantage. Jaguar flashed Hawthorn a sign. He knew he had just three more laps.

At 6:26pm Macklin, glancing in his mirrors, saw the combined green and silver flash coming steadily towards him. Having been lapped by them three times already, he immediately knew who the drivers were. As they came closer he pulled his Austin Healey over to the right, well off the racing line, to give them room to pass. He cracked a smile as he realised his friend Hawthorn was in the lead. "Fabulous," he thought to himself. "Mike's doing a great job." The Healey drifted into the right-hand Dunlop curve at top speed, around 135mph, while Fangio and Hawthorn closed up at an even quicker 150mph. Looking once more in his mirrors, Macklin realised there was another car between the two. It turned out to be Levegh, who had just been lapped by Hawthorn but was just in front of Fangio. He, too, was going flat-out at 150mph.

As they came to the pits, the four by now in tight formation, Macklin looked over and saw Hawthorn pull alongside him. He watched out of the corner of his eye as the green Jaguar, glinting in the sun, dragged the Healey off and shot past. Later, Macklin remembered it felt like the Jaguar took forever to pass, even though it was only really a few seconds. In his mind, everything had already slowed right down. It was 6:27pm.

Then it happened. Without warning Hawthorn cut right in front of Macklin, heading, as he'd known for three laps he was going to, into the pits. His narrow red brake-lights flicked on just 25 yards in front of the Healey. Macklin immediately slammed on his car's brakes, desperately hoping Hawthorn would look in his mirrors and see the Healey looming behind him. He didn't. Macklin now knew he wouldn't be able to stop in time without ploughing into the back of the Jaguar at near-full speed, so he did the only thing he could and tugged the wheel to the left. Everything was happening in slow motion. The Healey slid left, missing Hawthorn's Jaguar by inches but now almost out of control. Fangio, who had sensed the danger and backed off slightly, watched in horror as the Healey drifted towards a hard-charging Levegh. Levegh had no time to do anything but quickly throw his arm in the air, saving, Fangio said later, the Argentinian's life by alerting him to the nightmare that was quickly unfolding.

The Healey slid directly in front of the Mercedes and instantly became a mobile ramp as the front wheel of Levegh's car travelled up its curved rear, sending the Mercedes flying into the air. Macklin felt the impact, followed a split second later by the Mercedes' hot exhaust sailing by just inches from his cheek. The Healey was sent spinning backwards down the track while Fangio ducked inside it, away from the danger to his left and so close to Hawthorn's car that green streaks were found on the Mercedes after the race. Time stood still as Macklin looked up to see Levegh hunched over the wheel, 15 or so feet above him, his Mercedes hanging suspended in mid-air.

Then it all happened fast. The Mercedes came down and hit an earthen bank that acted as a second ramp, sending it flying towards the completely defenceless crowd. It reared up in mid-air, standing nearly vertically, before landing among the fans with a sickening thud. 14 people were killed instantly. Propelled forward, the car then exploded as it hit the concrete entrance of a tunnel running under the track, turning it into a giant grenade. Broken, jagged pieces scythed through the crowd, brutally chopping down anyone standing in the way. People were bowled over by the wheels, decapitated by its spinning bonnet. They were mown down in groups. It lasted only seconds, but to those there it felt like an eternity, and when it was over the ground was littered with the mutilated bodies of the dead and dying. It was unlike anything anyone had ever seen at a race track. It was like the war all over again.

Back on the track Macklin held on as the Healey skidded out of control down the main straight. In a blur he saw the chaos around him as he wrestled with the car's steering wheel, finally pulling it in a straight line, albeit backwards. He heard the giant explosion as Levegh's car hit the concrete entrance. Clinging on to the wheel with his foot pinning the brake pedal to the floor, he braced for the impact that he knew was coming, and, when he hit the concrete barrier seconds later, he was still going at least 60mph. His head felt like it was being torn from his shoulders. One of the Healey's wheels was ripped off as the car was sent spinning back onto the track where, eventually, it came to rest in front of the main grandstand and opposite the Mercedes pit.

Knowing the stricken Healey was completely exposed, Macklin jumped out and launched himself onto the nearest barrier. He looked around, trying to gather himself. About 150 yards away he saw the grandstands aflame and, glancing further up, a driver's body lying prone on the track. In his confusion he wasn't sure who it was, although he suspected it was either Fangio or his dear friend Moss. Whoever it may have been, he sprinted past it as he made his way back across the track to the pits and to safety.

A pall of smoke billowed across the track as what was left of the Mercedes burned itself into the ground. Medics rushed among the carnage in the grandstands. Hawthorn had seen everything and, fixated, had overshot his pit before jumping out of the car. As there was no reversing allowed the reluctant driver was forced, through some strong words from Jaguar team manager Lofty England, to get back in and bring it around again, a lap that proved to be one of the most surreal of his life as his mind swam with what he'd just seen. Adding to the chaos, an MG driven by Dick Jacobs had overturned on the other end of the pit straight in a completely unrelated accident, sending yet another pillar of smoke up into the air. Everything had been turned upside down. Confusion reigned.

Accounts from the immediate aftermath vary, which is understandable given the shock everyone was in. According to Porsche driver Jaroslav Juhan, Macklin fell inconsolably into the arms of Porsche's press chief before being helped into the pits and out of sight. Norman Dewis, a staunch Hawthorn defender, recalled Macklin running down the pit shouting "It's all Hawthorn's fault" at everyone around him, a scenario that seems, to put it mildly, extremely unlikely. It's interesting to note that even at this early stage people were attempting to apportion blame.

Shaken and trying to come to terms with what had just happened, Macklin eventually staggered over to the Healey pit. There he was met by Donald and his son Geoff Healey, who were relieved to see their friend in one piece. According to Christopher Hilton, Donald Healey was the first to reach him, his normally smiling face now completely serious.

"Christ almighty, Lance," he said as the smoke continued to billow across the track. "What happened?"

"That bloody idiot Mike Hawthorn ..." Macklin trailed off for a second, struggling to find his words. "I don't know what the hell he was up to, but he just suddenly pulled straight across in front of me and clapped his brakes on."

"Well, are you all right?"

"I'm bloody lucky to be all right, but I am."

He paused for a second.

"I'm afraid the car's rather badly damaged," he added as an afterthought.

Healey dismissed him. "Oh, I shouldn't worry about the car," he said. "Let's go and have a drink."

The two headed slowly around to a marquee at the back of the pits where Macklin's girlfriend at the time, a young Californian woman named Rosa Koth, was nervously waiting. Macklin slumped wearily into a seat as Healey searched around for a bottle of champagne and cracked it open. Soon, Geoff Healey and Macklin's brother-in-law, the Duc de Caraman, arrived. The party sat around sipping on their drinks, silently, until the canvas door burst open. It was a wide-eyed Les Leston.

"Oh my god, you've never seen anything like it," he said, breathlessly. Everyone stared at him. "It's like a bloody butcher's shop out there. There are bodies everywhere, bits and pieces. It's a terrible sight."

Macklin was furious. "Les, for Christ's sake," he shouted. "It's people like you who give motor racing a bad name. You exaggerate so much."

Leston stared at Macklin. "I'm not joking," he said, slowly. "There must be a hundred people killed."

"For God's sake, Les, don't be ridiculous. The car didn't even go into the crowd."

But it had, of course, and Macklin's initial disbelief soon wore off as he spoke to Leston and came across a steady stream of friends who had seen the accident happen at close quarters. One had been leaving the bathroom when he was abruptly confronted by people carrying shattered arms, legs and torsos. The more he spoke to his friends, the more horrified he became. After a while a former HWM mechanic, who was now working at Jaguar, came into the marquee searching for his old friend. Apparently, over at Jaguar, Hawthorn, who had by now handed his undamaged car over to Bueb, was having a breakdown. The Jaguar crew didn't particularly know what to do and figured that maybe some kind words from Macklin – who was, after all, a close friend – might calm him down. Macklin was in no mood to cheer up Hawthorn. "I don't honestly think I could do any good if I did come and talk to Mike Hawthorn, because he bloody nearly killed me too, and I'm not feeling all that happy towards him," he told the mechanic who, disappointed, shuffled off back towards the Jaguar team's caravan.

A few minutes later the Jaguar caravan door swung open. This time it was Mike Hawthorn himself. He looked pale, his normally confident aura having completely deserted him. He staggered over to the marquee and slumped down in a seat behind Macklin, placing his hand on the latter's shoulder.

"Oh my god, Lance," he said in a shaky voice. "I'm terribly sorry. I bloody nearly killed you and I killed all those people. I'm really sorry. I'm certainly never going to race again."

Donald Healey stepped over. "Mike, for Christ's sake, pull yourself together," he shouted.

Looking at Hawthorn, seeing him completely shaken up and almost in tears, Macklin's anger dissipated. "In a racing car travelling at 150mph anything can happen," he said. The two then talked among themselves, Hawthorn gradually settling down. When a Jaguar member came to grab him a while later he went off feeling much better. Despite what he'd said earlier about quitting racing, two hours later he found himself back behind the wheel of the D-Type and in the race.

Once he'd gathered himself Macklin hopped in a car with Donald Healey, the Duc de Caraman and Rosa Koth and headed away from the track and back to the town of Le Mans itself. They drove quickly, accompanied by the frequent rise and fall of ambulance sirens, with Macklin slumped back in the rear seat. His brother-in-law had told him that he'd been reported killed on one of the early, jumbled news reports, so the first thing he did when he reached town was head for a phone. Despite the lines quickly becoming overloaded he managed to reach his mother and assure her he was okay. She had heard the reports of his death and was shocked – and then relieved – to hear his voice.

After finally getting through to her Macklin jumped in the car and reluctantly drove back to the circuit. There he bumped into Earl Howe, president of the BRDC and one of the grand old men of British motorsport, who pulled him aside and mentioned that it would be a good idea to make a statement to the organisers, the Automobile Club de l'Ouest, while he was still there and the events were fresh in his mind. He did, having a quick talk with the police while at the club's offices. After finishing up he was wandering back to the Healey pits when he ran into

Fangio. The two chatted briefly, going through the events and agreeing not to blame anyone in particular. "Let's face it," Fangio said. "If motor racing is going to go on, we must be careful not to make anybody responsible for the thing. It's much better to play it down and say you can't tell who is to blame for an accident that happens in motor racing. Things go much too fast." Macklin agreed.

Finally, exhausted and still in a daze, he left the circuit for the day. He headed back to the town again, this time to relax in a local restaurant for dinner. That night Macklin slept badly, tossing and turning, his mind filled with images from the day: the Jaguar's brake-light suddenly glowing bright red, Levegh's exhaust flashing past his face, Hawthorn, pale, sweating, inconsolable, the ambulances rushing past him on their way to the hospital. It was a nightmare from which he couldn't escape.

– – – – –

The next day he woke with the news that Mercedes had pulled out and Hawthorn, now apparently fully recovered, was in the lead. It wasn't until he flicked over the morning papers over breakfast that he truly realised the full extent of just how terrible the accident had been. He'd known it was bad, of course, but he hadn't seen the carnage itself, and nobody at the circuit knew entirely how many people had been killed until many hours after it had happened, by which time he'd left. Communications at the track had been plunged into chaos, to the point where the outside world had a much better idea of what was going on than people actually at the scene. Reading the headlines and seeing the statistics, Macklin was temporarily overcome by shock. He began to realise just how lucky he was to have escaped.

After breakfast he once again reluctantly returned to the track where he immediately saw something that repulsed him. People stood crowded on the spot where Levegh's Mercedes had exploded the day before. The ground people stood on was still damp with blood. "There was this awful smell of death you get in the air when there had been a lot of blood around," he recalled years later. It was a smell he knew well from his wartime experiences, and one that he'd hoped he would never have to come across again. And yet here he was at a race track, less than a day after a horrible accident, and people were happily standing around in it, basking in being so close to the action. It was a sight he never forgot.

His sense of fury and disgust never dimmed. "I suppose they thought it must be a good place to be," he told Mark Kahn 20 years later. "To me,

Continued on page 145

12 Hours of Sebring, Florida, USA, March 1954. The Healey gets a pre-race inspection. (Courtesy FlaGator Collection)

12 Hours of Sebring, Florida, USA, March 1954. Macklin hurls the Healey around Sebring on his way to a fine third place. (Courtesy FlaGator Collection)

Mille Miglia, Italy, May 1954. Macklin powers his Healey through the Italian countryside on the way to a remarkable 23rd place. Unlike the vast majority of that year's competitors, he drove the nearly 14-hour event without a co-driver.
(Courtesy The Klemantaski Collection)

French Grand Prix, Reims, France, July 1954. HWM's last race turned out to be a bust, with Macklin lapping 30 seconds a lap slower than polesitter Juan Manuel Fangio before his engine blew. At least the countryside was pretty.
(Courtesy Motorsport Images)

Opposite: RAC Tourist Trophy, Dundrod, Northern Ireland, September 1954. Macklin relaxes in the paddock. (Courtesy The GPL Collection)

Le Mans 24 Hours, France, June 1955. Macklin's Healey heads past the Dunlop
Bridge during the opening stages of the ill-fated race.
(Courtesy The Klemantaski Collection)

Le Mans 24 Hours, France, June 1955. Seconds after the collision, Macklin spins
out of control as Pierre Levegh's airborne Mercedes scythes through the crowd.
(Courtesy The Klemantaski Collection)

Le Mans 24 Hours, France, June 1955. The heavily damaged Healey lies on the side of the track following the horrific lap 35 crash. (Courtesy The Klemantaski Collection)

British Grand Prix, Aintree, England, July 1955. Macklin looks out at the crowd during the pre-race drivers' parade. (Courtesy The GPL Collection)

British Grand Prix, Aintree, England, July 1955. Macklin tears around the Aintree circuit in a Maserati 250F. He eventually finished in eighth place. (Courtesy Motorsport Images)

Paris Motor Show, France, October 1956. Macklin chats to a colleague while manning the Facel Vega stand. (Courtesy Revs Institute)

motor racing was a sport. I was doing it because I enjoyed it. When there was an accident and somebody got killed or put themselves in hospital, I was genuinely upset. I thought what a tragedy (it is) that such a great sport has to be spoiled by somebody being killed or maimed. But I always got the impression, especially in Latin countries ... that most of the crowd went there as they went to a bullfight, hoping to see the matador gored to death. They went to motor racing hoping to see someone killed, or at any rate have a bad crash. The car catches fire or goes end over end and the driver is burned alive – that makes their motor racing day ... looking at astonishment at the crowds packed in where so many had died a few hours before, I couldn't feel sorry. They had come to see me die, or my friends die, and instead eighty of them had been killed. I knew it was terrible and my mind was horrified. But," he stressed the next part, "I couldn't feel sorry." Looking over the crowd standing on the blood-soaked bank, his faith in people was horribly shaken.

— — — — —

Hawthorn won the race. Photographs of him sitting in the cockpit of the Jaguar happily holding an open bottle of champagne with alcohol dripping down his chin were treated with scorn by the French press, which uniformly felt his behaviour was utterly inappropriate in light of what he'd earlier been involved in. The next day he saw his face on the front of several newspapers underneath vicious headlines. The French, at least, had already decided who was responsible.

The crash made headlines all over the world. Motor racing was immediately banned in Switzerland and throughout France, the Carrera Panamericana was cancelled, and the future of the current Formula One season was suddenly looking very shaky. So, too, was the future of Mercedes' racing programmes. 84 people had been killed, including Levegh, and 120 injured. The tragedy was an instant shock to the foundations of motor racing, the like of which had never been seen before. An official inquiry was immediately set in motion. In the press Jaguar immediately began its defence of Hawthorn, Lofty England quickly grasping the need to protect his driver's reputation, even if Hawthorn himself apparently couldn't.

Levegh's funeral was in Paris the Thursday after the race. It was a sombre affair. Macklin turned up, as did others from the motor racing community, including Moss, Trintignant, Simon and Fitch. Neubauer was there, too, consoling Levegh's distraught widow. The incident turned out to be the beginning of the end for the Mercedes sports car programme and the mighty

300SLRs. At the end of the truncated year Mercedes would leave the Sports Car Championship, not returning for another three decades.

A few days after the accident, Shelagh Mulligan – by now Shelagh Cooper, having since married motoring writer John Cooper – walked into the Action Automobile in Paris. She had been in the Le Mans press box when the accident had happened, and although she didn't see the crash itself she couldn't avoid the smoke rising over the track. Looking across to the pits, she'd seen Hawthorn stagger over to the Healey pit. At the time she thought it odd but now, of course, she knew exactly what had happened.

As she wandered in she spotted Macklin, sitting alone with a drink. She pulled up a chair.

"Oh, Lance," she said. "That was a terrible accident. I'm so sorry."

Macklin managed a weak smile. "That's okay," he said. "I survived anyway."

They didn't speak much. Fangio, who happened to be in the club that day, wandered over and sat down, proceeding to tell her how he really felt. Though the drivers had agreed not to lay any blame publicly, privately, at least for the two directly on the scene, they blamed Hawthorn. "Hawthorn knew he was coming in that lap," Fangio said, "but he still recklessly pulled in front of Macklin anyway." Macklin nodded, mentioning that there was about to be an inquiry to clear the whole thing up. "I'm going to have to go back to the track," he said, before taking another sip of his drink. It was a track he'd already seen more than enough of.

A few days later he walked around the scene of the accident, pointing out brake marks and tyre tracks, and reliving the experience in detail for the official inquiry. Beside him walked Zadoc-Kahn, the French judge in charge of the inquiry. He was impressed. "I must say that the evidence of the British driver Macklin was very, very good," he later said. "Very clear and given very much as a gentleman." In public Macklin continued to refuse to blame anyone, whatever his private sentiments, instead pointing to the dangerous speed of the cars as the key factor in the disaster. Back in Paris, at the inquiry, he gave a statement similar to the one he'd released to the French police immediately after the accident. He'd been surprised by Hawthorn, moved left when he realised he was about to collide with the back of the Jaguar, then been hit by Levegh, sending his Healey spinning down the track. Afterwards he was seen leaving with Koth, looking as dapper as ever. It would turn out to be a year before the results of the inquiry came to light. Despite everything, life, and motor racing, had to go on. It was soon time for the drivers to return to the track, no matter how reluctantly.

Chapter 15

One last shot

It didn't take long for at least a semblance of normality to resume. Just over a week after Le Mans came the Dutch Grand Prix at Zandvoort on June 19, a race that featured many of the drivers who had been involved in the tragedy. Fangio won, with Moss second, and a struggling Hawthorn seventh. Macklin wasn't there, recuperating at his mother's mansion in Roquebrune and trying to come to terms with what had happened by placing himself far away from the motor racing circuit. For the moment, at least, he needed to be alone.

In early July Macklin travelled back to England for the British Grand Prix. Though he was struggling psychologically, he had decided to power through and continue to drive Moss' Maserati 250F during the main race on July 16. It was clear from the moment he sat in the car, though, that something wasn't quite right. Alf Francis was on hand, having become Moss' personal mechanic, and he could tell that Macklin was off. During first practice he was nearly nine seconds off the lap record and miles off everyone else's pace. "In my opinion (he) had been badly shaken by his shocking experience at Le Mans and was right off form," Francis wrote. The race itself went little better. Having settled into seventh place, he was travelling around far too slowly for the team's liking, and was given a hurry up signal that, in the event, he never saw. Midway through the same lap he hit a patch of oil and slid off the road. As he lost control and skidded towards the crowd, his mind flashed back to a few weeks earlier. For a moment he saw himself again in the Healey, out of control and backwards, the Mercedes flying towards the crowd beside him. This time, though, he felt he was in the Mercedes, the crowd in front of him getting closer and closer, disaster only seconds away. He was brought back to reality with a dull thud. He'd hit some hay bales, not the crowd, and felt himself being gently showered with little pieces of straw. He sat back and slumped in his seat. He was almost laughing out of sheer relief.

Easing himself out of the car he strolled back to the pits, where he met a determined Alf Francis. The Maserati, it turned out, was still perfectly good to go, with a little push, and after a few strong words the two were soon sprinting back towards it. Macklin hopped back in as Francis and another mechanic pushed and, seconds later, he was back in the race. He was now going slightly quicker and finished eighth, which, as Francis later said, was probably where he would have finished anyway had he not been given a hurry up. It was, to say the least, a less than impressive outing. Something had changed. It was the last time he would ever race a Grand Prix car.

The nightmare season continued as the shadow of Le Mans hung darkly over everything. Although by this time the French ban on motorsport had been lifted, the French, German, Spanish and Swiss Grands Prix had still been cancelled, leading to a severely curtailed Formula One season. Regardless of which driver people pinned the accident on – be it Hawthorn, Macklin or Levegh, depending on the individual's point of view and/or loyalties – one thing everyone agreed on was the need to look into the safety of racing circuits. The accident had proved to be a belated wake up call. The idea that driving a racing car was safer than going to war simply didn't cut it anymore. While there were many factors that had led to the accident, everyone knew it wouldn't have happened had the entrance to the pit straight not been so dangerously narrow, and moves were immediately under way to check other circuits for obvious safety issues. It would be many more years before safety in motorsport was finally brought to something approaching an acceptable level, but all things have to start somewhere. No matter how slow or how initially lackadaisical it was, Le Mans 1955 was the beginning of an era of responsibility.

The racing went on. On August 20 Macklin returned to Goodwood for the Nine Hours sports car race, picking up a drive in one of John Heath's new HWM-Jaguar sports cars. Alongside him was an enthusiastic, 21-year-old up and coming Englishman by the name of Bill Smith. The two got along well, Macklin recognizing the enthusiasm of his younger self in his new co-driver. Having someone positive alongside him may have helped, and he seemed to regain a little of his enthusiasm, slotting into a solid fourth place and beating the works Jaguar D-Type of Norman Dewis.

Still, deep inside him a battle was raging between his love of racing cars and the horrors he'd been through back in June. For now he continued, but every race seemed harder and harder. The deaths kept coming. Less than two hours into the race at Goodwood, the talented young British driver Mike Keen had gone into a turn too fast in his Cooper Bristol and lost control. Maybe if there'd been barriers and run-off areas he would have been fine, but, of course, there weren't. His car ran off the track, overturned and caught fire. He didn't burn alive inside the car – every racing driver's worst fear – but he did succumb to his injuries and die in hospital later that day. Another race, another death. It was the same old story. There's no doubt that Macklin, his anxieties building, would have noticed. A week later, on August 27, he was back in the Healey for an uneventful outing at Oulton Park where he came in a respectable 12th. It proved to be a brief moment of respite, for, less than a month later, on September 18, 1955, everything was to come to a head.

That weekend the circus was back at Dundrod for the annual Ulster TT. In the wake of Le Mans the organisers had orchestrated several spectator-free zones, particularly in hazardous spots like the high speed, hilly section known as Deer's Leap. Still, they hadn't done anything to sort out the hazards posed by slower cars or drivers, and in practice several drivers were far off the pace and clearly completely out of their league. Dundrod was a narrow, twisting circuit, making the presence of inexperienced amateurs even more hazardous than usual. Going in, Macklin felt nervous.

Race day was warm, if a little overcast, a full capacity crowd coming to watch the resumption of the World Sports Car Championship. It was the first sports car race since Le Mans, and everybody, with the media spotlight now shining brightly on motorsport, was hoping for an incident-free race. They weren't going to get it.

The race started well enough. Mercedes was back in force, and Moss made his customary fast start, streaking into the lead and heading the field around the first corner, with a hard-charging Hawthorn not far behind. Rumour had it that Hawthorn, like Macklin, was psychologically struggling after Le Mans. Appearing in the public spotlight was hard enough, but the pressure of being blamed for a terrible tragedy was colossal. For all his continued gung-ho attitude, Hawthorn was suffering.

The race at the front was fierce, the leading teams mixing it together, while Peter Collins spectacularly dragged himself up the field after a delayed start. Further back, Macklin circulated in the midfield, running a relatively uneventful race in tandem with Ken Wharton's Frazer Nash. They wound their way round the narrow track, surrounded by open fields and high banks, with the burgeoning crowd and dangerously close power lines providing constant reminders that there was little room for mistakes. After a while the two came up behind a silver Mercedes 300 SL. It wasn't one of the huge, powerful cars driven by the works team, but was instead a road-going version entered by a member of the French aristocracy, the Vicomte Henri De Barry. De Barry had already made himself noticed throughout the weekend, but not for the right reasons. Although not completely inexperienced, he'd proved to be terribly slow, lapping his powerful car behind even the small Panhards at the back of the field. After Le Mans many of the leading drivers, especially Moss, had spoken out against inexperienced weekend racers going up against the world's finest in championship races. De Barry was proving to be a prime example.

As Wharton and Macklin's attempts to lap the Mercedes came to nothing, they quickly realised they were dealing with an amateur. De Barry would slow right down going through corners, not entirely sure how to handle them with any sort of speed, then use the massive grunt of his Mercedes engine to power away on the straights, moving slightly to the centre of the track and preventing any sort of pass that the two frustrated drivers behind him would try to conjure up. Half a lap went by, then one, then two. Wharton and Macklin still couldn't find a way past, and De Barry clearly wasn't looking in his mirrors. Macklin was looking in his, though, and after a couple of laps he was alarmed to discover a group of Lotuses and Coopers quickly racing up behind him. Before he knew it they were upon him, one diving past him on the inside and one on the outside, their outside wheels on the grass, throwing up clumps of dirt and stone. Sensing danger he backed off. If they were going to get into trouble, he didn't want any part of it.

He drove on as the group quickly moved past and headed up a corner or two ahead. He wound up the Healey. Coming up to Deer's Leap, the area that had been cleared of spectators, the Healey's engine whined as he hauled along at 140mph with his foot flat to the floor. Driving up and over the rise for the umpteenth time, he felt his car lift under him as it nearly became airborne. When he grounded out on the other side he was greeted by a violent, blinding flash. The road in front of him was a picture of chaos, of spinning cars and flying bodies. Later, what he remembered most of all were the long, high flames streaking 40 feet into the air, covering everything. It was yet another nightmare come true, one he was rapidly heading straight towards.

There was nowhere to escape. Thinking fast, he slammed his foot on the brake and swivelled the car round a full 180 degrees. The Healey went into the inferno backwards at somewhere near 90mph, Macklin doing his best to keep it in a straight line. He ducked down as far as he could inside the cockpit. When the car eventually ground to a halt he poked his head out and found himself completely surrounded by a thick fog of flame and smoke, with three or four battered cars lying next to him. He knew their fuel tanks were at least half full. Quickly scanning around he managed to make out the shape of a grass bank through the haze, and in no time he'd leapt out of the car and sprinted to safety. He ran through the fire, the flames licking at his face and singeing his overalls. He ran past the other cars, past the burning bodies on the road, past the spilled oil flowing across the track and kept going even when he reached the safety of the bank, running away from his fuel-laden car and away, finally, from his racing career.

It turned out that he had been right to keep his distance from the drama around him. When the gaggle of cars had descended on the baulking Mercedes a couple of them, in contrast to Macklin and Wharton's cautiousness, had grown impatient. Young British driver Jim Mayer had been the first to crack, deciding to take his Cooper-Climax part-way onto the grass – as he had done when passing Macklin earlier – and having a go around the outside. This time his luck deserted him. He'd failed to spot a small stone milestone on the side of the road, and, when he pulled out the front of his car collided with the marker and sent him flying into the air. He landed with a thud in the middle of the track, everyone piling into him and creating the massive inferno Macklin was forced to drive into. Mayer was dead and Wharton, who'd also been caught up in the crash, was badly burned. They weren't the only casualties. Bill Smith, the young Englishman Macklin had become so fond of only a month before, was dead, too.

One person who made it through unscathed was the very driver who had caused it all. Henri De Barry merrily continued on his way, completely unaware of the chaos he'd just unleashed. On lap 39, several laps after the accident, he was disqualified for 'poor driving' and forced to come in. Even though he hadn't been paying attention, others clearly had. He furiously set about trying to clear his name, quickly getting signed statements from Hawthorn, Moss, Fangio and Mercedes driver Karl Kling to the effect that they hadn't seen anything wrong with his driving. Everyone knew better, however. In all likelihood the statements were less about defending De Barry's driving skill and more about the drivers maintaining a united front, as they had at Le Mans, and refusing to blame anyone in particular for accidents. De Barry never took part in a serious race again.

Macklin was shattered. It was as if all the nervousness he'd felt after Le Mans, all the fear that came over him every time he sat in a racing car, had been realised in the most horrible way possible. Dundrod was almost worse, in a way, for his psyche than Le Mans was, the pain more immediate, more nightmarish. If Le Mans was a powerful right to the kidneys of his racing career, Dundrod was a left to the jaw. For all intents and purposes, it was over. He just couldn't do it anymore.

– – – – –

In December Macklin was due to race a Healey in the Bahamas, the same place he'd travelled to under such different circumstances a year earlier. Back then he'd led a life of leisure where accidents only happened to other people, but now he was a shaken man, haunted by what he'd seen and been through. Things weren't quite so much fun anymore. Now he could finally understand why his father had been so obstructive all those years ago.

Unsurprisingly he wasn't up to driving at Nassau that year, although his friends still managed to convince him to come along for the ride. He did, enjoying the company and the warm Caribbean sunshine, all of it proving to be an effective antidote to the strain he'd been under for the latter part of the year. He drank copiously. One infamous night he was having dinner at the seaside Pilot House Club with Rosa Koth and a bunch of friends when, after a few drinks had gone down, several of his friends loudly asked why the two didn't get married. Thinking about it, his mind clouded with drink, Macklin couldn't come up with a reason not to. The next day he headed with Koth to the Nassau town hall, fully prepared to get married there and then. To his dismay he found out there was going to be a delay. It had emerged that his bride-to-be was a divorcee, and the Bahaman authorities were obliged to call up her hometown in the United States – La Jolla, California, now a suburb of San Diego – to double check if the divorce had gone through. Koth said it had, so in the meantime they got together with Donald Healey and planned a fabulous wedding party for the next day. Word travelled quickly around the small island and through the racing community. Lance Macklin, the famous ladies' man, was about to get married. Who would have thought?

At 9am the next morning, just two hours before the wedding was due to take place, Macklin was interrupted in his preparations by a phone call. It was the town registrar. Contrary to what Koth had said, her divorce hadn't gone through, since either she or her husband hadn't signed the divorce papers and she was still legally married. The wedding was off. Donald Healey was furious, having already planned the party and invited everyone in the racing community to it. "Well," Macklin said, after having a think. "Why don't we just say we got married? Nobody's going to know whether we did or we didn't." This is exactly what happened. Unlike the marriage itself the party went off without a hitch, the racers drinking and carousing long into the night with no idea that the supposed groom was still a single man. Though Koth and Macklin planned to marry as soon as they returned to the States after Nassau, they never did, splitting shortly afterwards. It was the start of a tragic downward spiral for Koth. She returned to her life in England, where she'd evidently been living with Macklin, this time taking up with *Daily Express* gossip columnist Robert Pilkington. The new relationship, mirroring her return to UK society, didn't work. After a while she returned to America with her son Jed where she vanished into obscurity. Occasionally, vague, unsettling rumours about her would surface. People said that Jed grew up and was killed in a car crash, while Koth, racked with grief, turned slowly into a lonely and broken alcoholic. Her memories, of exotic cars, long nights under starry Caribbean skies, Lance's gentle eyes and charming smile, gradually faded into the past. Sometimes, as she sipped on her whiskey late at night, she wondered whether it had ever happened at all.

– – – – –

One afternoon, Shelagh Cooper's phone rang. It was Stirling Moss.

"Did you hear?" he said, almost breathlessly, "Lance Macklin has got married?"

Cooper was surprised. She knew about Macklin's womanising reputation as well as anybody. "Good heavens," she exclaimed. "Who to?"

"To some American girl. But he's back in this country without her, it doesn't seem to have lasted very long."

After the two chatted Cooper hung up, intrigued. She'd enjoyed a solid friendship with Macklin since becoming reintroduced by Shelagh's husband, John Cooper, at the sophisticated jazz club at 100 Oxford Street in London one evening. She had seen him at the Action Automobile just after Le Mans, of course, and had kept in touch periodically since then. Like Macklin, her personal life had been through ups and downs. In late 1954, tragedy struck when John Cooper was killed in a car accident, leaving his wife widowed at the young age of 23. As soon as he found out Macklin called to offer his condolences, furthering the growing friendship between the two. As soon as he returned to England, and shortly after Moss had rung, Macklin gave Cooper a call to let her know about his escapades in the Caribbean.

"Did you hear that I've got married?" he said.

"Why, yes, congratulations!"

"Well, I don't know about that." Macklin, Cooper thought, didn't sound particularly enthusiastic. "It doesn't seem to be going very well."

"I'm sorry about that."

Macklin explained that the relationship had fallen through; after a bit of chatting he also mentioned to Cooper that he'd once again agreed to drive at Sebring for Donald Healey, although he wasn't taken by the thought of it. "It's a ridiculous way to make a living," he said, sadly. Nonetheless, feeling like it was expected of him, he was reluctantly going through with it. "Would you like to come?" he asked Cooper, hoping to at least have a few friends alongside him for moral support. She agreed, and a month later she found herself on a plane to Florida alongside her friends Bernard and Joan Cahier and Louise King (who was soon to become Mrs Peter Collins). Macklin and Cooper's friendship was growing.

The party turned up in Florida with the rest of the racing crowd on March 22, 1956. Though nearly everyone was re-energised after the long, unsteady trudge that the 1955 season had turned into, Macklin was an exception. Sebring was certainly beautiful, with clear blue skies and a scattering of palm trees, but he just didn't want to be there.

Teamed up with the remarkable but ultimately ill-fated Archie Scott Brown, he reluctantly hopped back into the Healey. The race, on March 24, didn't go too badly, with the two circulating around mid-pack before retiring after 110 laps. Yet when he hopped out of the stricken Healey he took one final, long look around him. His racing career, he knew, was over.

Chapter 16

Life after racing

With his driving career done and dusted, Macklin was at a loss about what to do. The one thing he'd been fixated on since boyhood – driving fast cars – was out of the equation, and he suddenly found himself aimless and with an awful lot of time on his hands. Fortunately, he had someone to help. In late 1955 and early 1956 his relationship with Shelagh Cooper had blossomed, the two spending more and more time together in England, continental Europe, and, of course, the US. They were quickly and unavoidably falling in love. One day in early 1956 Cooper was staying with Bernard and Joan Cahier at their villa in Évian-les-Bains when the phone rang. It was Macklin. "I'm going to be passing through Geneva to see my mother in the south of France, I might just swing by Évian," he told her, matter-of-factly. She was delighted to see him, unaware there was an ulterior motive to his visit. When he turned up he revealed his plan. "Why don't we get married?" he asked, brazenly. Cooper was initially taken aback, but after a bit of thought, she warmed to the idea. Why not indeed? The Cahiers were delighted. Bernard suggested a wedding across the border in Switzerland for practical reasons, although – he looked across at Macklin, wearing a grin – being Swiss every paper would need to be exactly in order. Everyone laughed. Of course, nobody had forgotten Nassau's disorganised wedding-that-wasn't. The date was set for August 1956.

A few months after the meeting in Évian, Shelagh Cooper was sitting in the Steering Wheel Club, having a late afternoon drink, when racing driver and RAC member Hamish Orr-Ewing wandered in. An old friend of Cooper's, he immediately strolled over and sat down next to her.

"So," he said after a while, "do you have any plans on the horizon?"

"I'm going over to Europe to marry Lance Macklin," she replied, excitedly.

There was a pause. "Oh, no," Orr-Ewing said, becoming agitated. "You mustn't do that."

Cooper looked at him, furiously. She wasn't one to appreciate having anyone question her judgement so boldly, at least not without explanation.

"And why on earth not?"

Orr-Ewing looked down and muttered darkly. "They're a bad lot, those Macklins," he said.

After a bit of apologising Orr-Ewing explained himself. It turned out that his mother was Esme Stewart, Noel Macklin's first wife. Noel, Stewart told her son, had been a less-than-faithful partner. Evidently she had remained in love with him even after the divorce, but the hurt Noel's womanising caused remained long after they broke up. Like everyone else, Orr-Ewing knew Lance had a similar reputation, and he didn't find the stories of his womanising amusing in the least. Cooper was no fool, though. Saying goodbye, she walked out forcefully. Lance, she told herself, had met his match.

Though Macklin had already made up his mind, Cooper made it extra clear that she didn't want him racing again, even threatening to call off the wedding if he harboured thoughts of getting back behind the wheel. She didn't want to deal with the premature death of a loved one again. It was a request he gladly acquiesced to, although he wasn't entirely sure about how to go about it at first. Racing had been his life for years, and his dream for even longer, and after deciding to quit he faced the same problem almost every athlete does when leaving the sport they've devoted themselves to. How, he wondered, would he adjust to life without constant competition? Initially he had no idea. In the meantime he was content to keep attending fancy parties and kicking about with his racing driver friends at exclusive clubs. Though he was no longer racing, and was soon to be married, he wasn't quite ready to give up the playboy lifestyle just yet.

One evening Cooper received an unusual call. It was her friend Jean Daninos, the ever-enthusiastic Frenchman in charge of manufacturing outfit Facel. Daninos was a man of big dreams. Short and stocky but with a powerful inner drive, he'd spent years toiling away at various car companies dreaming of creating his own automobile. He wanted it to be something big and fast, yet also beautiful and luxurious, a car important people would want to be seen in. He already knew what he was going to call it: Facel Vega. After years of frustration, an opportunity to live his dream had finally opened up, and putting a call through to Shelagh Cooper was one of his first moves. He told her that he'd heard she was now Lance Macklin's girlfriend, and he was wondering if she'd be so kind as to put him in touch with Lance's mother, Leslie. Daninos was on the search for engines and wanted to use something American, in the way that Noel Macklin had used American engines in his prewar Railtons, and he figured Leslie might still have some connections that could prove useful. Cooper put him onto Leslie, who, in turn, happily passed him on to a contact at Chrysler. Soon a deal was done, and a happy Daninos, whose project was now under way, asked Cooper if there was anything he could do in return. Her mind wandered over to her aimless husband-to-be.

"Well, Jean," she said. "Have you got any jobs going on this new Facel Vega project of yours?"

He thought for a moment, then told her there would probably be openings on the export front, selling his Facels throughout the continent and as far away as New Zealand and the United States. Macklin had of course been a car salesman before, courtesy of his short-lived, though successful, Chipstead Motors foray, so a few days later Cooper put the idea to him. He'd still get to be involved with cars, she told him, and it would give him a solid job to go to. Plus, the Facels that had already made public appearances were looking very good indeed. He demurred, but his girlfriend wasn't having it. "Lance," she told him, sternly. "You know full well I'm not going to marry a racing driver. You've got to get a job. You're bilingual, very charming and very personable. You could get any job. We're going to Paris." He did as he was told. The duo swiftly headed to France to meet Daninos where, after a few days of not-particularly-intense deliberation, Macklin signed up. He was now Facel Vega's official export manager, which suited him perfectly. He would live in France, which he always preferred over England, and spent most of his time driving the fabulously exotic and quick Facels and charming prospective clients over long, lazy European lunches. Really, he couldn't have asked for much better.

Their timing worked out well. Around the time Macklin landed his job at Facel, a rustic French cottage that sat on the Duc de Caraman's estate came up for sale. "When we first went in it was like going into something out of *Great Expectations*," Cooper recalled years later. "There were mice, spiders … everything that could live in there lived in there. It was extraordinary." The cottage had been at the centre of a family feud, and had sat, untouched, since the previous owner had died well before the Second World War. His mark was still on the place – his clothes were in the cupboards, the beds were made, his coffee still in the coffee machine. "Ah, c'est rien," the French builder tasked with tidying the place up said when he arrived. "I see this all the time." He got to work, and within days the place was looking thoroughly rejuvenated. It was beautiful, with brick walls and wooden floors surrounded all around by the flowing French countryside. Only 30 minutes from Paris, it was the perfect place to kick-start the couple's life together. Maybe, Macklin thought to himself, life after racing wasn't going to be quite so hard to take after all.

In August 1956 the two were married. This time there wasn't to be any drunken after-party, no crowds of rowdy well-wishers. It was simply a small, intimate gathering in Geneva with a few close friends. Lance Macklin, finally, was off the market.

His new job proved to be ideal. While he'd never had a particularly strong work ethic – something that was to prove problematic in the coming years – the Facel job was different. It was multi-layered and tailored to his skills, utilising him as part salesman, part engineer. The Facel itself was a truly extraordinary car. It was fast, good looking and luxurious, and exactly what Daninos wanted. In France at the time there wasn't anything like it, and Facels turned heads wherever they went. The Macklins drove them everywhere. Often Shelagh would take orders and drive Facels to their new owners, sometimes delivering them to wealthy people in the French countryside, sometimes going for longer trips through the Alps and further afield.

When selling, Lance was particularly talented at using the Facel's allure to his advantage. He'd drive up the Champs-Élysées, park up by, say, the George V, and wait until intrigued passers-by stopped and wandered over to take a look. When he wanted to – which, during the early years of his time at Facel, was often – he could be a terrific salesman. He was never brusque or pushy. Instead he used his considerable powers of charm to do the trick. "Jean always said Lance could sell ice cream to an Eskimo or coals to Newcastle," his wife later said. "Often he didn't bother, of course. But when he did he was very good indeed." He had the benefit of his racing connections, too, helping him sign up George Abecassis and HWM as the official UK Facel Vega distributors.

He wasn't just a salesman, of course. Not only did he have a terrific technical mind due to his years of driving cars and sailing boats, but he also had a wonderfully inventive one, too. It was something he inherited from his father, and it came in handy when working for a small, relatively hands-on car company. He helped design the Facel Vega's tubular-framed chassis, and was often the first to suggest and try out new modifications. Sometimes testing would take both Macklins far afield, through the French countryside, through far-off towns and cities, in torrential rain and beating sun. Working for Facel Vega was often an adventure.

One day, Daninos called Lance into his office. He wanted to try new tyres on the Facel, he told his employee, Dunlops instead of the usual Michelins. If they worked he'd place an order, so take the car as far as you need to figure out if they work. "Just drive and drive," he said, "until you wear them out." Forget about the expense account. Lance and Shelagh happily jumped in the car, drove out of Paris and kept going. They headed south to Biarritz, across the ragged Pyrenees, along the sparkling Mediterranean coastline, through beautiful Burgundy. They were gone for weeks, travelling through hot sun and violent thunderstorms alike. They stayed in fine châteaus. It was travel in the utmost style, complete 1950s European glamour, and it was all for work. "When we got back I said 'god (Daninos) is going to be furious when he sees this expense account,'" Shelagh later said. "But he didn't bat an eyelid, because he had the report. It was exactly what he wanted."

– – – – –

In November 1956 the long-awaited result of the Le Mans inquiry finally came out. To many people's dismay the report didn't say much, finding all parties free of blame. It said the organisers had set up the race according to the regulations then in force, Hawthorn's move hadn't been unduly troublesome, Macklin's swerve couldn't be counted as bad driving, and the unfortunate Levegh was simply in the wrong place at the wrong time. A lot was made of the inquiry investigating a mysterious driver "X" for culpability, most people assuming – probably correctly – they were referring to Hawthorn. However, he was completely cleared. Macklin wasn't impressed. After initial enthusiasm he'd gone on to describe the inquiry as a "farce," feeling there had been a lack of willingness to get to the truth of the matter and a greater desire to clear everyone and make the whole thing go away. The final report was brief. For all the widespread comment about inexperienced drivers, slower cars and a complete lack of safety features on and off the track, the worst crash in motor racing history was labelled a racing incident (though the circuit's design did come in for some criticism). There would have been more than a few pairs of wide eyes the morning the report came out, Macklin's among them.

Macklin and Hawthorn's friendship never recovered. "My father was a very honourable man," Macklin's daughter, Miranda Kelly, would later say. "He felt Hawthorn had behaved in a very ungentlemanly way. To him, you didn't do that, you didn't behave like that. You put your hand up and said 'I boobed'. But on the contrary Hawthorn didn't say that, he was kind of passing the buck."

Other authors have done forensic analyses on the Le Mans crash, going over the events second by second, trying their best to work out who was where, who did what, writing up speeds, angles and everything else in precise scientific detail. Even now there are still elements of debate. Was Macklin looking in his mirrors when he should have been watching Hawthorn in front of him? Did Levegh really raise his hand in warning to Fangio as he saw his fate rapidly approaching? Crucially, did Hawthorn leave enough room when he chopped in front of Macklin on his way to the pits?

It's hard to look back and pin the blame for the accident on Macklin. Yet, by the same token, it also wasn't Hawthorn's fault there was a tragedy. That was a much wider issue encompassing lacklustre safety standards, poor driver quality and high car speed disparities. Even though the report shied away from placing blame, people in high places knew better, and changes began taking place with immediate effect. It was the beginning, however slow at first, of a new era of responsibility.

Macklin sued Hawthorn a couple of years later when Hawthorn's book, *Challenge Me the Race*, appeared to absolve himself of all blame. Since Levegh was dead Macklin assumed Hawthorn was pointing the finger at himself and began proceedings to, as he saw it, clear his name. Everything ended abruptly with Hawthorn's tragic early death in January 1959, when his Jaguar lost control on a public road and hit a tree. Even if the lawsuit had gone through the full process it's unlikely Macklin would have won, given Hawthorn failed to point the finger at anyone in particular. Instead, the lawsuit can be seen more as a public demonstration of Macklin's indignation and hurt. He became famous in a way he'd never been before, and in a way that he never wanted to be. What happened at Le Mans followed him around for the rest of his life. Some of his children's first memories were of their father standing up and walking away from people asking what that day was like, trying to get him to talk about a moment he never, ever wanted to revisit.

Chapter 17

The (wayward) family man

The first few years of Lance's time at Facel were mostly idyllic for the married couple. On September 18, 1957, their first child, a boy they named Patrick, was born. He would turn out to be like his father in many ways: occasionally wayward, yet athletic, smart and an extraordinary sailor. The aftermath of Shelagh's labour was made easier by a friendly Facel customer from Burgundy, who sent a special delivery of expensive wine – 12 bottles of red, 12 of white – directly to her hospital bedside. Facel customers were rarely short of money.

When Patrick, or Paddy, as the family quickly began calling him, was young, Lance would jiggle his son on his knee, telling him adventure stories and sending him gently to sleep. It was a much more hands-on parenting style than he'd ever received from his own mother and father. Thinking back to his own frosty childhood, he decided early that his own children weren't going to be brought up in an emotionally vacant Victorian atmosphere. Still, he wasn't fully prepared to sit back and play the role of the dutiful, responsible father. He never fully integrated into family life to the extent that his wife would have liked – the idea of working 9-5 and acting like a typical '50s nuclear parent was one he could never stomach – and, with a few concessions, he retained the debonair playboy lifestyle he'd had since the end of the war.

He was also, to his wife's distress, still a ladies' man. Discussing his life in France with Mark Kahn years later, he was unflinchingly honest about his indiscretions. "For a man living that sort of life in Paris the temptations, the sexual temptations, are very great," he said. "Paris is very well organised from a man's point of view." He longingly admired the French way of dealing with marriage, which was that both husband and wife would take on an extra lover at some point in their relationship. "It was very different, being stuck to the same person month in, month out," he said. "Very constricting. And my wife, Sheila (sic), was not a French girl, and when she sometimes caught me out it created problems." In one celebrated incident he went to a beach-side party with two pretty young women, discovering upon arrival that they were attending what was supposed to be a fancy dress party. Realising they'd come unprepared, all three stripped off, covered themselves in axle grease and rolled around in beach-side sand, re-entering the party as croquette de pomme de terres. Hours later, around three in the morning, Shelagh was woken by a knock on the door. Opening it, she was startled to find the trio, who had drunkenly ambled back to the family home, stumbling around stark naked. She slammed the door in their faces. It just went to show: if the constraints of married life didn't suit Lance, he simply ignored them.

The years rolled lazily along. On April 27, 1959, the couple welcomed their second child into the world, a girl they named Rita Miranda. This time they weren't together for the birth. The moment Miranda was born Lance was in London, sitting in a television studio and waiting for his turn in the spotlight. He was there to celebrate a special evening for his old friend Stirling Moss, who was about to be the subject of popular British TV show *This is Your Life*. The show's format was always the same, with a well-known guest watching on as significant figures from their past were dragged out to chat about the subject's life. Sitting backstage, Lance watched as Moss awkwardly made his way through the first couple of guests, his primary school headmistress and parents, Alfred and Aileen Moss, before it was his turn to stroll through the thick red curtain and onto the stage. When Moss heard the voice of his old friend over the studio's speakers his face broke into a wide smile. The curtains opened and out strode Lance in a perfectly fitted suit, his curly hair neatly trimmed and with a huge grin spread across his face.

The two, with presenter Eamonn Andrews, talked racing. "I remember the first time I tried to follow Stirling round in about the same car," Macklin, whose debonair charm was tempered by a slight nervousness, recalled. "I followed him in practice and I thought to myself 'this fellow certainly doesn't hang about.'" Moss jumped in. "That's how I felt about Lance and his girlfriends, I might say," he said with a laugh. The two shared a knowing look. "We know something about that, too, so I wouldn't say too much about Lance if I were you," Andrews added scratching his head, with a smattering of laughter from the audience. If the world didn't know about Lance Macklin as a ladies' man, it certainly did now. That evening, Moss and Macklin hit the town with some old friends, partying the night away at the

Steering Wheel Club and revelling in the carefree, boozy atmosphere. The family responsibilities could wait.

Macklin returned home to France a few days later, overjoyed to meet his new little girl. Still, the extra responsibilities of a growing family did nothing to change his lackadaisical attitude towards home life. "He was certainly not a good husband," Shelagh recalled years later. "He wasn't at all averse to me going out to work. He did as little as he could. He would get up late in the morning and have a nice late-morning drink, then would head down to the Action Automobile at lunchtime and have a long, lengthy lunch." Daninos wasn't particularly impressed with his salesman's work ethic either. If Macklin was interested in who he was dealing with he could be superb – he once sold a Facel Vega to Ringo Starr, for instance – but often the clients were neither famous nor interesting. "Often they were just boring little provincial manufacturers of ball bearings who wanted a Facel to show off," Shelagh said. "He wasn't interested in that one bit. But if it was a glamorous film star …"

Sometimes Daninos would send Shelagh, who was also juggling parenting duties and a day job as a model, on trips to speak with potential clients instead of her absent husband. For some things, though, Lance was irreplaceable. He would take the press on road tests, visit factories to try to sort out problems with different parts of the car, and speak in technical terms to the firm's engineers. Much as his laziness and fondness of the good life drove everyone around him mad, nobody doubted that he was an integral part of the Facel operation.

Sales of the Facel, outstanding as the car itself was, were middling. The company didn't have much of an advertising programme, instead, relying on word of mouth and hoping its cars were bought and seen by the 'right sort' of people. They certainly were. The list of people who bought Facels reads as a who's-who of late '50s/early '60s style and sophistication. There was Starr, of course, as well as Ava Gardner and her husband, Frank Sinatra, plus Sinatra's partner in crime Dean Martin. Royalty, including the Shah of Persia and King Hassan of Morocco, loved them, as did Pablo Picasso. It was the sort of exclusive company the Macklins liked to keep. At one point Lance even convinced his old friend Stirling Moss to buy one, a sale that pleased Jean Daninos no end. Why, the company figured, did it need advertising executives when it had clients like these?

However, Facel was never entirely accepted by the French themselves. There were several reasons for the rejection, most prominent among them being Facel's use of American Chrysler engines as opposed to French-sourced ones. In the eyes of many fiercely-nationalistic Frenchmen, the car was a bastard child. Sales, never exceptionally high to begin with, began to dip. Already struggling, the company then suffered a blow on the evening of January 4, 1960, from which it would never recover. That night a Facel Vega driven by publisher Michel Gallimard made its way down a dark, tree-lined highway just outside the small French town of Villeblevin, with Nobel Prize-winning author Albert Camus occupying the passenger seat. Camus had accepted his publisher's offer of a ride instead of taking the train as he had planned. It was to prove a fatal mistake. As the Facel drove down the quiet road something abruptly went wrong, sending the car careening off into a tree and tearing it apart. Camus was killed instantly, while Gallimard, fatally injured, later died in hospital. As the world reacted in shock, a horrified Jean Daninos quickly dispatched Macklin to the scene to try and figure out the cause of the accident.

To the company's dismay, the problem lay with a fault in the car's steering. It hinted at an ugly, underlying truth. Facels, for all their power and style, weren't especially safe cars to drive around in. Camus' death tore Daninos apart. "I just can't sleep at night thinking about it," he told Shelagh. "It upset him more than I could ever explain," she said. The crash led to bad publicity for the brand, disastrous for a company that didn't advertise and relied on its reputation to sell cars. Stocks sank further.

Desperate to shore up his rapidly disintegrating company, Daninos came out with something new. In 1961 Facel released the smaller, sprightlier Facelia. Daninos ditched his American connections and instead turned to a French company to build a powerful 1.6-litre engine, finally making an entirely French automobile. Maybe now, Daninos hoped, the French would finally accept his car as one of their own. He was to be disappointed. Getting rid of Chrysler turned out to be a disastrous move as the French powerplant he'd pinned his hopes on proved hopelessly problematic. The Facelia sold fairly well but was beset by problems, while the company lost money on every one it sold. Facel had always operated on fairly thin margins, and the failure of the Facelia nearly sent it under. It was the end for Daninos, who was forced to resign from his beloved company in August 1961. His dream of a French supercar had turned into a nightmare. The company limped along until, at the end of October 1964, it finally shut its factory doors for the last time. "Everyone figured (the Facel Vega/Facelia) would sell itself," Shelagh said, "which it didn't, of course." It was a sad end for a terrific car.

The Macklins weren't there to watch the company fall apart. They could see what was coming and left even before Daninos was given the boot, Lance generously being gifted a Facelia to take with him as a farewell present. Watching as the prospect of unemployment loomed ever-closer, Lance had developed an adventurous post-Facel plan. One day he had fallen under the spell of a mysterious Dutch entrepreneur who claimed to have developed an additive for batteries called Electrolyte, making them last much, much longer than usual. Lance was convinced that the additive, which was more or less a perpetual motion supplement, was going to make millions. His wife wasn't buying it. To her, the shady Dutchman was, as she always called him, "The original conman."

"Look, Shelagh," Lance said as the two talked over the issue one evening. "It's going to be absolutely fantastic. It means the batteries can never wear out."

"He's a conman, Lance. I don't trust him an inch."

"No, no, no. He's a very nice man."

"Most conmen are nice to meet," his wife shot back.

Lance, though, was determined. "What we have to do," he said matter-of-factly, "is sell this house and put all the money into Electrolyte."

"But I don't want to sell the house," Shelagh protested. With all the stress of their young family, plus work and Lance's erratic lifestyle, the beautiful farmhouse was a shining beacon of stability and normality.

Lance was firm. "Well, we're going to have to sell it."

And that was that.

At Paddy's christening Lance had met Tony O'Reilly, a sharp Irish lawyer who was best friends with Shelagh's brother, Andrew Mulligan. The two had stayed in contact, and, when the Electrolyte business burrowed its way into Lance's head, he gave O'Reilly a call. It turned out that his friend was now working closely with the Irish government in trying to get investors to move to Ireland, so he knew how to sort out favourable business conditions and tax breaks. Macklin hadn't particularly thought about Ireland as a place to live before, but O'Reilly was convincing. "There's a factory in good working order," O'Reilly told him. "It's going for a song. It would make a perfect factory for your battery additive." In later years O'Reilly would become fantastically wealthy, accruing and then losing several fortunes through a combination of perseverance and savviness, even becoming Ireland's first billionaire. However, at this early stage he was still evidently finding his feet. Despite the shoddiness of the proposition – there were, apparently, no guarantees – Lance was sold. To his wife's further dismay the Macklins were now headed to Ireland.

Chapter 18

An Irish misadventure

In early 1961, Lance Macklin and his young family packed up and headed to Mitchelstown in County Cork, Ireland, to embark on his new adventure. Dubious about her husband's idea from the beginning, Shelagh knew things weren't going to work the moment they set foot in their new home. "I was absolutely shattered by this idea of coming back over to Britain," she said. "I had visions of Lance not even being able to afford school fees or anything." Driving around downtown Mitchelstown, their future dependent on a shady pseudo-entrepreneur with an unproven, fantastical idea, Shelagh was blunt. "I think we're making a mistake," she said. "No, no, it's not a mistake at all," Lance replied, full of confidence. "We're doing the best thing possible." Shelagh wasn't having it. "No. This is crazy. Absolutely crazy."

Their relationship becoming increasingly fraught, Shelagh headed back to France to work on selling her beloved farmhouse while Lance sailed on to England to take care of business matters. It was left solely to his wife to pack up the house and take its contents, plus a dog, a cat and two small children, across the channel to Ireland via England. By the time she'd taken care of everything and paid French taxes she was nearly broke, arriving in England with just enough money to drive her overcrowded car to her parents' place in Kent. She was exhausted, both emotionally and physically. "This isn't very funny," she thought to herself as she drove through the countryside, listening to her screaming children in the seat behind her and keeping an eye on the fuel gauge in front.

The family gathered in London, where they rented an apartment in the fashionable suburb of Wimbledon while Lance attempted to get his business off the ground in Ireland. While her husband was busy with his money-making scheme, Shelagh, the more practically minded of the two, went to work doing part time secretarial work in the day and cooking at night. For her it was an exhausting life, although her husband never seemed under an excessive amount of strain. They became like ships passing in the night, while the time they actually did spend together was filled with tension. Lance was determined to make his far-flung Electrolyte business work, whereas Shelagh, on the other hand, was just as determined to make him realise it was never going to. Things eventually came to a head one night in the Wimbledon flat during a particularly heated quarrel. Lance, attempting once more to bring his family to Ireland, attempted to put his foot down.

"I'm going to go live in Ireland," he said, firmly.

"Well, I'm not going to go live in Ireland," his exasperated wife shot back.

"And why not?"

"I know it's not going to work, Lance, it's just not going to work." Shelagh, finally, had had enough. "I'm not going to spend any more money getting over there, setting up a house in Ireland, to be left in Ireland doing what? What am I going to do when the factory's gone? This is mad."

Undeterred, Lance muttered that he was going to take the children and head over there regardless.

"All right," Shelagh said, readily. "You take the children and I'll stay here and file for divorce."

It's exactly what happened. In late 1961 Lance Macklin left for Ireland with his children, while Shelagh stayed in England and went straight back to full-time work. They divorced soon after. "He was frustrating," Shelagh said. "He didn't like hard work at all, and wasn't a particularly good husband. But he was always so full of charm. I'm not going to say I didn't have a very good time with him because I did. We had some really wonderful times. But if you wanted someone to bring in the money, to work, he wasn't the right man."

– – – – –

Undeterred, Lance continued on to Ireland. After a bit of searching he found a wonderfully idiosyncratic place to live on the main road between Mitchelstown and Dublin, a crumbling, yet elegant, Georgian-style manor, with a long driveway and surrounded by flowing fields of green. It was a countryside idyll where he could lay down his roots and, he hoped, make his millions. The business was getting off to a slow start with the factory taking a little more time than he would have liked, but the mysterious

Dutchman – whose name time has mercifully forgotten – assured him that everything was coming along smoothly. After all, the man said, these things didn't just happen overnight. Macklin wasn't overly concerned.

Macklin's house was near the small country town of Kilbeheny. The locals hadn't seen anything like him. A good looking, smooth, bilingual ex-racing driver, he appeared wonderfully exotic. Driving his Facelia around the area's rural, often dirt roads, he couldn't help but stand out. "On the corner, around from his house, was a little post office run by two old ladies who used to work the telephone exchange," his cousin-in-law Michael Harrison remembered. "Sometimes you'd ring up and they'd say 'Ooh, we think he's at the vet,' and then they'd ring around to find exactly where he was. 'Ooh, his car's just gone past. He'll be home in two minutes.' It was that sort of thing." Local tongues started wagging, and because of his recent arrival from France he quickly became known around town as The Frenchman. With no mention of Le Mans, his new-found fame didn't bother him at all.

Friends and family would occasionally fly over from England and pay a visit. Among the more regular visitors were Macklin's cousin, Sally Harrison, and her husband. Michael, friends since his childhood. Heading into Kilbeheny and looking as if they were from a different world – which, in a way, they were – the trio would spend hours hanging-out with locals in the small town's few bars, telling stories and sinking pint after pint of Guinness. Macklin's charm was so effective that the locals would waive their antiquated men-only bar policy and allow Sally to enter, making her uniquely privileged among the town's womenfolk. For Macklin and his guests it was a carefree, almost innocent existence.

One time Michael Harrison drove over in his bright red Austin Healey. Macklin, ever-scheming, challenged him to a race. Harrison agreed, and the two were soon flat-out on the main road towards Mitchelstown, kicking up stones as their exotic cars travelled along the loosely-sealed surface. They were neck and neck until coming around the final corner, where Macklin's Facelia pulled ahead slightly, although they were still going full tilt when they flew by a local pub. To Harrison's astonishment, he looked over to see a horde of animated locals sitting outside, cheering while sloshing around glasses of Guinness. Pulling up, he found Macklin waiting with a wide, cheeky grin on his face. It turned out he'd spread a rumour throughout the town that Stirling Moss was coming to visit and there was going to be a race, causing the locals to set up outside and take bets. To them it was a great contest: The Frenchman versus Stirling Moss. This time, of course, The Frenchman had won. Harrison – who looked nothing like Stirling Moss but accepted the plaudits anyway – thought it was hilarious.

While Macklin's life as an exotic country squire was going swimmingly, his business – the reason he was there in the first place, after all – stuttered. After its slow start the Electrolyte scheme collapsed entirely, with the mysterious Dutchman quickly disappearing with all the investment money. It had turned out just like Macklin's wife – and others – had warned him. Yet again, his judgement and business sense had proven to be woefully inadequate. "He was incompetent," Michael Harrison said, bluntly. "I tried to advise him on business matters. I remember going over to Paris with him once and having a business meeting with his brother in law, the Duc de Caraman, and the Duke of Suffolk. Of course, nothing ever came of it." With little to keep him and his young children in Ireland, Macklin packed up his gear, sold the Facelia and headed back to England. His entrepreneurial dream, which had lasted for three fruitless years and came at such a high cost, was over.

Chapter 19

In love

Macklin and the children arrived back in London in 1964. Though he was nearly broke, he had enough left over to move into a nice apartment in Wimbledon, and, after only a few months, he picked up a job at the prestigious Jack Barclay Motors showroom in central London. This time he was purely a salesman, and he spent much of his time wandering around the showroom and charming high-flying potential clients. Having someone like him was gold for the company, since name recognition alone was enough to prompt people to walk through the showroom's doors out of curiosity. Although he'd been out of the cockpit for nearly nine years, his name hadn't been forgotten.

Even though he would spend much of his time doing it over the next 15 years, he never truly enjoyed his career as car salesman. "He should have done very well at Jack Barclays," Michael Harrison said, "but he didn't actually try very hard." For him it was a means to an end, since he would much rather have spent his time back on the continent, driving fast cars and chasing pretty women. He had the talent to be a good salesman but, like at Facel, if he wasn't interested in who he was dealing with then he wouldn't put in much effort.

Occasionally, though, there were days where he wouldn't have to do much at all. One day around 1967 he bumped into Shelagh – the two, at least at this point, remained on good terms – and excitedly told her about a sale he'd just made. Earlier that day a young hippy with flowing long hair and a wildly colourful cape had wandered into the dealership. Unfazed, Macklin wandered over to see what his unusual customer wanted. "My manager says I should have that one over there," the man said, with a disinterested pout, pointing to a top of the range Rolls-Royce at the centre of the showroom. Macklin, who made a commission on everything he sold, was startled. Asking if he wanted anything else, the stranger looked around.

"How about a personal record player," Macklin asked.

"Yeah, sure. What else?"

"How about a Waterford set of crystal decanters?"

"Sure. What else?"

"A handmade, personalised luggage set?"

"Okay. What else?"

The conversation continued in that vein, the customer adding every additional extra Macklin could think of as his commission sky-rocketed. The eventual total came to around £70,000, a colossal sum for the mid-late 1960s. "It's okay," the man said, with disinterest. "My manager says I must spend the money." Finished, he strutted out with a small posse behind him, leaving Macklin dumbfounded. It turned out later that the man was a young Mick Jagger, on a mission to spend as much as possible for tax purposes. It was probably the easiest day of Macklin's career as a salesman.

He had plenty of downtime, much of which he spent in his beloved France or at the ever-popular Steering Wheel Club. The wounds from his failed marriage had mostly healed, with his lifestyle continuing in much the same way. The only real difference was that he now didn't have to deal with a constantly unimpressed wife or hide any women he brought home.

His life as a bachelor came to an end soon after returning to the UK, though, when he fell under the spell of a dazzlingly pretty woman, 23 years his junior. 21-year-old New Zealander Gill McComish had been enjoying the freedom and excitement of her first European trip, seeing the sights and mingling with groups of people who seemed intoxicatingly sophisticated, especially compared to the relatively staid New Zealand of the mid-1960s. During her socialising McComish had been spotted by some of Macklin's friends, seeing in her someone who, they hoped, could settle down the free-wheeling racing driver. They told Macklin about her and quickly organised a meeting, although it unfortunately fell through. Macklin, liking what he'd heard, wasn't to be deterred. "One night I got a phone call," McComish remembered. "The voice said 'You don't know me, but we were going to meet at Pat's party and I would like to take you out for the evening because I'd like to get to know you.' I'd earlier told my flatmates that I'd go along and do all our laundry that night, which is what I told Lance. He said 'Well, where do you go? We can take the laundry and then head back to your flat and go out'. So that's what we did."

The two met in a laundromat, an inauspicious place for a first meeting, but they clicked immediately. Later that evening they went out and McComish fell in love. "I'd been going out a little bit but everybody seemed to have such big egos," she said. "We went out to a pub to have a drink, and this guy came up and started raving on about Lance, telling me what a great guy he was and how he'd done this and that. When he went to the loo Lance said 'that was so embarrassing. Come on, let's find another pub,' and we slipped out. I just thought it was so refreshing to find somebody who didn't have an ego and didn't need to be built up, so immediately I liked him. We had a really nice night and after that we were together every evening."

McComish, it seemed, wasn't another one night stand, and the two began spending an increasing amount of time together. It was a cultural experience for Gill, too. Although Lance's fun-filled, star-studded life was completely normal to him, for Gill it was something out of a storybook. To spend time in Europe with a handsome racing driver, mingling with some of the most sophisticated people on the continent, was mind boggling.

The two spent a lot of time on Macklin's social circuit, meeting up with his old racing colleagues at racing club gatherings in England and on the continent. "It was a lot of fun," she recalled later. "I can remember one day heading south from London in a Ferrari with Lance, along with a Lamborghini and an Aston Martin, and all three were racing along the road south to go and have lunch out in the country. We all went out afterwards and watched Prince Philip play polo. There were a lot of the older racing drivers there, mostly European – Prince Bira was there, Fangio was there one time, Moss too ... we had a lot of adventures."

They also spent a lot of time cruising through the canals that cut across France, whiling away their afternoons on the deck of Macklin's boat as he gently manoeuvred it through the array of locks he'd come to know so well. Selling cars paid the bills, but sailing through France with an abundant supply of wine and a 21-year-old girlfriend was more his style.

He also made time to work on his inventions, usually having a few on the go at any given moment. Around this time he came up with his most famous invention, or at least the one that ended up achieving the most recognition, the Turbo Visor. Apparently conceived while thinking about his MTB/MGB experiences during the war, Macklin designed the Turbo Visor in order to keep perfect, crystal clear vision even in torrential downpours. It did this by fixing a clear, circular rotor to the front of a helmet, which would spin and then throw off any water coming towards it. Ungainly though it was it did actually work, to the extent that it became mildly fashionable in motorcycle racing for a short time. An advertisement for it in *Motorcycle* magazine from April 1965 went as far as having World Champion motorcycle rider Jim Redman promoting it. "100% vision at any speed!" the ad enthusiastically said, underneath a picture of a smiling Redman wearing one. Graham Hill, who had become good friends with Macklin, even raced with one on several occasions. Most notable was his outing at Snetterton in 1964, where the Turbo Visor did nothing to help as he embarrassingly crashed out in the pouring rain.

Macklin's inventions had one overarching similarity. They were all brilliant and had solid technical foundations, but there was often a teething problem that proved insurmountable. So it proved with the Turbo Visor. While it worked perfectly well at lower speeds, making it suitable for go-carts and certain bike races, it had a tendency to pull to one side or the other at high speeds as the wind caught the visor and gave it a tug. Because of this it quickly died off in most serious forms of motorsport, although it did prove so useful in lower-level carting that it's still used frequently today. Despite its continued manufacture, its unlikely Macklin ever made any money out of it. At some point he presumably sold the design, and whatever he would have gained from its continued manufacture – which, given it's still going, might have been a tidy sum – was lost.

After a two-year love affair, Lance Macklin married Gill McComish on April 2, 1965, in an intimate ceremony in London. Earlier in the year she had bowed to family pressure and returned to New Zealand, but had been convinced to come back to London by Lance's marriage proposal. She couldn't say no. The wedding was a relatively small affair, with a few close friends and family, although Lance's old friend John Pertwee livened up proceedings by bounding around with a small hand-held camera taking inopportune photos, flustering guests as well as the elderly registrar. When news of the wedding broke tongues wagged, although the idea of Lance Macklin marrying someone less than half his age wasn't hugely far-fetched, at least not for those who knew of his romantic history. Still, even by his standards the difference was vast – Gill was 22 and Lance was now nearly 45, making her nearer his children's age than his own. People warned Gill about what she was getting into, but she ignored them. Besides, her new husband had already explained the situation to her himself. "I've been a bit of a playboy all my life," he told her. "When I got married I settled down and didn't stray ... but don't expect me just to be faithful to you. If I want to play around I will." He certainly hadn't been faithful to his first wife, and neither was he going to behave himself with his second. Although no doubt disconcerted, his young wife took it with a stiff upper lip. They were in love and her husband's petty affairs, as she referred to them, wouldn't change that.

– – – – –

After they married the newly-wed couple took a skiing trip to Switzerland. Gill had been a talented skier back in New Zealand, and the two had bonded over their mutual love of the sport at their first meeting. They took Paddy and Miranda as well as Gill's mother, who, in all likelihood, paid for the trip, both Gill and Lance being too broke to fund a major outing at that point. There was an embarrassing mix up when Gill's mother was set up in the same hotel room as Lance, the hotel staff figuring she was his wife and Gill one of his daughters. Embarrassed, the incident didn't do anything for Gill's mother's misgivings about having a much older son-in-law, although the married couple saw the funny side and quickly fell about laughing. The rest of the trip went smoothly, Lance using some of the tricks he'd learned from his skiing days to help Gill. "He loved skiing, he loved jumping, he loved doing the Cresta run, loved doing anything that had a bit of excitement," Gill said. "When I skied with him I'd do things and fall over, and he'd growl at me and say 'you didn't even try not to fall over. If you really worked on it you'd find you could really do a lot of things.'" Gruffly spoken though they were, her husband's words helped her find another gear, spurring her on to ever-greater success. After her first time powder skiing she turned around and looked back up the mountain that she'd just come down, staring at her tracks that wound down the slopes and cut through the thick, deep snow. She'd done it at Lance's behest and she was thrilled.

However, for all the trip's successes, the two never skied together again. In England they were simply too broke, while in New Zealand the more hands-on skiing club culture didn't appeal to Lance's somewhat pampered sensibilities. New Zealand skiers were forced to join a skiing club, most of which made members perform small tasks around the clubhouse before letting them hit the slopes. Lance was appalled. He went skiing to have fun, not, as he brusquely told his wife, to work. On clear mornings at the couple's home in Havelock North he would look out the window and see Mount Ruapehu, a popular New Zealand skiing spot, rising in the hazy distance. While Gill occasionally skied it by herself, her husband stubbornly refused to be brought down to what he considered a footman's level.

Shortly after they married Gill moved in to Lance's Wimbledon flat, the two settling down and, for a while at least, leading the life of a happily married couple. Years later Miranda Kelly recalled a happy and relaxed home life, sitting on her father's knee as he jiggled her up and down. There were fun evenings in the Wimbledon flat, Lance cooking spaghetti for the family as he revelled in his fatherly duties. Granted, he wasn't always the most active parent. On his daughter's eighth birthday he told her that since she was now all grown up, her job was to make a breakfast of boiled kippers at the weekend for him and Gill. It was a classic lazy father trick, although she, of course, bought it hook, line and sinker. "My mother always used to say he was very good with children but very bad for them," Miranda said, "which I think was probably quite true." Years later she recalled getting up early on Sunday mornings and heading to her father's trophy cabinet with a jar of silver polish in her hand. There the trophies stood, proudly reminding everyone of his years behind the wheel, the huge *Daily Express* Trophy standing front and centre. Though her father rarely spoke about them, they were his pride and joy. Miranda would polish them weekly for sixpence, slaving over them with a rag and seeing the names of exotic races – places that seemed utterly foreign, mysterious glimpses into the past – glinting in the early morning sun. A couple of years later they were all gone, sold off to pay the bills for a future adventure. Though he never said much about it, selling them broke Lance's heart.

– – – – –

Lance, often with his family in tow, still made frequent trips to the continent. In May 1966 he stayed at his mother's villa in Roquebrune and caught that year's Monaco Grand Prix, which he spent hobnobbing on luxury yachts with the Formula One glamour set. He also found time to catch up with his niece, the young, glamorous Christina de Caraman, who was in town with her larger-than-life husband, Taki Theodoracopulos. Taki – as he's widely known – later recalled that Lance seemed to know everyone who was anyone in the close-knit racing community, even introducing his niece and her husband to both Jim Clark and Jackie

Stewart. "He was very, very reserved," Taki recalled. "He was very much an old-style Etonian. But he was very fun and very nice, and everyone was very fond of him." At one point over the weekend Taki introduced Lance to Giovanni Volpi, an ambitious and wealthy Italian friend who was attempting to form a team to compete in that year's Le Mans. "He had built his own car and he wanted to start a scuderia," Taki said. "I said 'you have to get Lance Macklin. He's been in the game and he was a great friend of Healey's.'" The two met, but even though Lance had told Taki he'd be interested nothing came of it. "Being an Italian, Volpi expected somebody to sell themselves to him," Taki said. "Lance was very bad at selling himself. Vopli told me afterwards that he didn't seem to want it, and I said 'Of course he wants it, but he's not a travelling salesman.'" In the event Volpi's planned team came to nought, but Lance's interest is revealing. Even after the trauma he'd suffered at Le Mans, with all the misery it caused, the magnetic grip of the race still held some sway over him. It's hard to believe, but a racing comeback at nearly 50 was, ever so briefly, a very real possibility.

– – – – –

As glamorous and smooth as married life was, Gill was again beginning to come under pressure from her family to return to New Zealand. When she nervously discussed the matter with her husband she was surprised at his reaction. Despite not having been anywhere near New Zealand before, the idea of heading there immediately excited him. By the mid-1960s New Zealand and Australia had become part of the international racing community, although they had been well and truly off the map during Lance's racing days. Still, he was bound to have heard stories from other drivers who had ventured out there – which, by this stage, was a great deal of the current Formula One crop – and, considering his interest, they must have been good. In 1967 Lance bade farewell to the European motor racing scene one final time, taking an HWM-Jaguar out in a support race before the British Grand Prix (where, true to form, it blew its engine after a single lap), before beginning to pack up his belongings. He had decided to go for it. Lance and Gill were heading to New Zealand.

There was one major problem. The two were determined to bring Paddy and Miranda with them and keep the family unit together, but they knew Shelagh would baulk at even the suggestion of taking her children to the other side of the world. They spent months thinking about what to do, then struck upon a plan. "We thought that once we were away and on the high seas Shelagh wasn't going to be able to do much," Gill recalled. It was outrageous but, they figured, it might just work. They were going to steal the kids!

Of course, they had to keep their plan a complete secret. They were living in small circles, and if anyone found out word was bound to get back to Shelagh who would scupper the whole thing. They sorted all the logistics in secret, then, one day, in early 1968, they decided it was time to go. Lance told his children that the Wimbledon flat was going to be rented out to an American couple – at "vast cost," he told them, meaningfully – and that they needed to pack up for the summer. Everyone quickly got to work, cleaning up the place and packing everything they had into boxes. The operation was under way.

At this time the children had been made wards of court – at Shelagh's behest – meaning they weren't allowed to travel abroad without court permission. They did frequently travel to the continent to see Lance's family in France, however, and Lance figured he could use that as an excuse to sneak the children out of Europe altogether. "We were due to go and stay with my godfather in France," his daughter remembered. "Shelagh was already in France at the time. My father had been quite relaxed about when we were going to go, talking to my mother, so she waited. And the dates he was going to let her know came and went. After a while she made a few phone calls to London asking people if they'd seen Lance, and, of course, nobody had." Shelagh had been tricked. "Lance said, 'Could I have the children's passports?'" Shelagh remembered. "I said, 'No, they're wards of court, you're not allowed to take them out of the country without the court's permission. I have that permission, you haven't, so where are you taking them?' And he said 'Are you trying to stop me from taking them to see their grandmother in the south of France? Oh come on, be reasonable.'" His charm worked. "Like an idiot I said yes, okay. I gave him the passports and I didn't see them again for two years."

By the time Shelagh figured out what was happening they were gone. One morning the family were packed in a car with Michael Harrison and driven down to the docks at Southampton, the kids excitedly expecting a trip to France, their father's stomach churning as he hoped their plan hadn't been rumbled. As they hopped on to the boat, the ill-fated Achille Lauro, Lance gave the kids a map of the world so they could follow their trip. Everything seemed normal as they headed for the south of France, as per usual, but then everything took an unforeseen turn. They quickly headed out of the Mediterranean's familiar waters and travelled south, far away from anywhere they'd been before. Every day the kids would look at the map their father had given them and try and figure out where they were heading. They went further south, passing into the cold southern waters, Paddy and Miranda charting their progress with an ever-increasing sense of fascination. The options for their destination became fewer and fewer the further south they travelled, but it wasn't until they passed Australia that they finally knew where they were going: New Zealand.

Back in England it was beginning to dawn on everyone that Lance and his young wife had carried off a magnificent heist, while, on-board, the kids were having the time of their lives. "It was fucking great," Paddy remembered years later. "Kids like adventures, don't they? What's not to like?" They pulled into Auckland in late 1968, exhilarated. Lance and Gill were relieved. Walking down the gangplank and into the New Zealand customs shed, they shared a smile. They'd made it.

Chapter 20

New Zealand days

Although Auckland was more sophisticated than most of New Zealand back in the late 1960s, it was still a vastly different place from the grand centres of Europe that the family was used to. Nevertheless they slotted in nicely, the kids proving to be adaptable and Lance, naturally enough, happily easing into the laid back Kiwi lifestyle. Their first port of call was Gill's family over on Auckland's North Shore. Although it later became a sprawling, seemingly endless suburbia, the North Shore of the 1960s couldn't have been more different. Though it was gradually beginning to change, the suburbs that would later transform it starting to pop up in scattered clumps, it was still relatively isolated and made up primarily of acres of flat, green farmland. Gill's family lived in Takapuna, a gorgeous beach-side community that later became a hub for wealthy Auckland elite, yet, back in 1968, was a small and profoundly lower middle class suburb. Gill and Lance loved it. Years later the kids recalled walking to school in the morning along Takapuna's long, sandy beach, their toes sinking into the soft sand, and the sea breeze whipping their hair into scraggly messes. It was a world away, both literally and figuratively, from the regimented English boarding schools they were used to. It was completely liberating.

Their father, meanwhile, got to work clipping tomato plants for his brother and sister in law. It was tedious work. Occasionally Paddy would help him out, although, as an introduction into the working world, it wasn't particularly auspicious. "It was the most boring job," he said, bluntly. "I didn't know much about work at the time and little did I know it could be so boring." The two would sit together in the heat of a greenhouse, spending hours clipping away and attempting to keep themselves from going crazy with boredom. Even at the age of 11 Paddy realised his father wasn't particularly fond of manual labour. "I can remember him working, but he wasn't really a great one for labouring, dad," he said. "I suppose you could say he was lazy, although I would say he just didn't do more than he believed was worth doing."

In the evenings, after a long, sweaty day in the greenhouse, Lance would down tools and sit with his brother-in-law Brian on the porch of Brian's Otahuhu home. They'd sit back and drink glass after glass of cheap Villa Maria rosé wine, chatting and lazily watching the afternoon slip away. After a while Lance would bid farewell and hop on his little 50cc Honda bike he'd picked up and somehow find his way back across the harbour bridge to the North Shore, not having to worry too much about the spectre of checkpoints and breath tests. In the Auckland of 1968, nobody was especially bothered by that sort of thing.

After a while Lance began to scout around for a job that was less physically strenuous and more suited to his previous experience. Naturally he looked towards car sales. Local dealerships were delighted to have him, his exotic air proving to be a big hit in isolated New Zealand. After a few months the family left Auckland, heading south for the small town of Havelock North in the sunny Hawke's Bay region of the central North Island. Lance had bagged a job at Barclay Motors (no relation to his previous employer Jack Barclay Motors) and signed on as its chief salesman, primarily selling Fiats. He had a little Fiat 850 himself, and would occasionally take his kids and their friends on rides around the golden Hawke's Bay countryside. "Who wants to go fast?" he'd ask, then, smiling as everyone squealed in delight, would chop down a gear and go soaring off around the area's winding roads. They spent weekends down on the Tukituki River outside Hastings, splashing around in the cool, clear mountain water, feeling like one big, happy family.

After arriving in Havelock North the family quickly made friends with others in the neighbourhood. Neighbour Hugh Barlow, who as a ten-year-old quickly became firm friends with Paddy, remembered seeing Lance working in the backyard of their Tauroa Road home, carrying out some extensive landscaping during a rare spell of prolonged labour. One day Lance came round to the Barlow household to borrow a landscaping rake. Years later, Barlow remembered seeing Lance's Volkswagen Variant station wagon coming up the drive and being disappointed that he hadn't come with Paddy. The Barlow family chatted happily with Lance before he drove home, kindly refusing a cup of tea by saying he didn't want to interrupt anyone's morning more than he already had. A few hours later, in the afternoon, Barlow walked into the family kitchen and saw his mother sitting at the bench, looking dreamily out the window. "You know what?" she said, without turning around. "I imagine Patrick's father cut quite a dash with the ladies in his day". "What does that mean?" her confused son asked. She turned round and smiled. "Oh, nothing," she said.

— — — — —

While at Barclay Motors he reportedly convinced the company to look beyond its normal range of British cars and start selling Toyotas. "People at the time weren't buying Japanese cars," Miranda remembered. "There was still a big hangover from the war, it wasn't that long after it had finished. There were an awful lot of people who had an awful lot of memories, and people didn't want to buy Japanese, but Lance convinced them otherwise." Naturally, he knew a good car when he saw one. "You know, you really ought to import these," he told a sceptical sales team, brought up in the fading myth of British automotive superiority. "They're good cars." Reluctantly they agreed, and were amazed when the little Japanese cars began outselling the more established Austins and Fords they regularly dealt in. Barclays quickly picked up a franchise, in doing so becoming the first Toyota dealership in New Zealand. It wasn't long before others followed, starting a reaction that would eventually see Toyota top the New Zealand sales charts for years to come. "It's a shame he didn't really do that for himself," Miranda later said, ruefully, "because that would have been a really good move." Even on the rare occasions his business sense was on point, it appeared, it did little to benefit him personally.

The family's time in Hawke's Bay was relaxing. A bit too relaxing for Lance, perhaps, as his second wife found him no more willing to work than his first. He didn't put much effort into something unless he felt like it, a laissez-faire attitude that grated on his much more practical New Zealand wife. "He didn't know what hard work was," Gill said. "It wasn't really his fault. The way he'd grown up, Eton and Swiss finishing school ... he'd drop his clothes on the floor and we'd tidy up after him, things like that. He'd never really had to apply himself, and he didn't know how. He tried a couple of times with his inventions, but when the business hadn't worked after a couple of months he'd give up and go back working for someone again." It wasn't just his childhood that had instilled this lack of application. Even during his racing career he had often been taken care of by others on a personal level – living in hotels, his mother's servants looking after him in Roquebrune – and his pure talent had taken care of him in the cockpit. When he left his comfortable existence as a commitment-free, upper-class racing driver, he simply didn't really know how to take care of himself. It drove others mad, although his irrepressible charm and kindly nature tended to keep him out of too much trouble.

When he left the UK he mostly lost touch with much of the racing community. Years later Stirling Moss even refused to believe that his friend had ever visited New Zealand, much less ran off with his young wife and taken his kids. Macklin did, however, get the occasional chance to catch up with some of his racing friends. Around this period Australia and New Zealand had become a regular go-to region for international racing drivers, thanks to the increasingly popular Tasman Series. The New Zealand Grand Prix, a non-championship Formula One event, was part of the series. In 1969 Jochen Rindt, Graham Hill and Piers Courage flew out for the race, and all three made contact with Macklin and came to visit him at Gill's mother's place up in Auckland. The trio sat around the kitchen table with Lance and Gill, staying up long into the night laughing, swapping stories and talking about motor racing. Graham Hill, who'd partied with Lance in London and in Monaco, couldn't understand why he'd swap his glamorous life for a much more sedate existence at the bottom of the world. "Really, Lance," he said over dinner. "I can't understand why you'd want to come out to New Zealand." Lance smiled. "Well, it's all very well for you" he replied. "If you want to go somewhere you just hop in your helicopter or your plane, whereas we were just stuck in London and had to drive a long way to get anywhere. But out here in New Zealand you've got access to so much stuff and, really, it's a very nice life." At one point Miranda wandered into the kitchen to be warmly greeted by the others, who had all met her before. Smiling, Graham Hill signed a photo of him sitting in his Indianapolis-winning Lola for her. Years later she still had it hanging on her wall, a memory of the long ago night when three of the great Formula One drivers sat around a kitchen table laughing and chatting with her father. She didn't see them as great racing drivers. To her, they were simply her father's friends. "It was all we knew, really," she said. All three drivers would die young, two within two years, a sobering reminder of just how lucky her father really was.

– – – – –

"Although the family had become a tight-knit unit, under the surface tension was bubbling. Lance's distinct lack of any sort of work ethic, plus having to look after two young, rambunctious kids, was beginning to slowly take a toll on 24-year-old Gill. As his first wife said, he wasn't a bad parent, just a laissez-faire one. "He was quite good, although he was a little bit unreliable," Gill remembered. "He'd let them get away with murder sometimes. Other times he'd be quite tough, but he was very protective of the kids and really put himself out to try and be a father and provide for them." At one point the couple became involved in a terrific fight and almost split up, although, this time, they ended up reconciling later in the evening. "I was terribly upset about all this," Miranda remembered, "but we had a big discussion and group hug, with Lance saying 'thank goodness there's one sensible member of the family.'" Though things were starting to look just a little shaky, there were still plenty of bright spots, and on January 7, 1970, the couple's only child, Perry, was born.

Unexpectedly for Lance, his worlds were about to briefly collide. Furious about her ex-husband's brazen theft of her children, Shelagh hopped on a plane and flew out to New Zealand to take them back. She stayed in New Zealand for over four months, travelling around the country with her children and attempting to coax them back to England. After a bit of wrangling she went home, but only with the job half-done: Paddy, who had never been entirely comfortable in New Zealand, had gone with her. Miranda, on the other hand, hadn't been so easily swayed, especially after she'd been given her first pony on who to patrol the beautiful New Zealand countryside. The family was now back to four.

An increasingly weary Gill was hoping Perry's birth was going to settle family life. It didn't. What happened next turned out, to Gill's considerable dismay, to be quite the opposite. In an echo of his earlier flight of fancy with the Electrolyte business, Lance came up with an idea that he was sure would solve all their problems. Tired of working for other people, he'd seen a fish and chip/fried chicken shop – The Golden Chicken, a sort of B-grade KFC – advertised for sale down in Otaki, a small coastal town outside Wellington. "I've had enough," he announced to his startled family one afternoon. "I've given them my notice. I'm going to buy a restaurant down in Otaki." Gill was horrified. "It was ridiculous," she said. "He had ideas of it being like it was in England, cooking up nice fish and chips and that sort of thing, but down there everyone wanted everything in a rush. The neighbours, who'd done that sort of thing before, said 'he can't do it, it's hard work and Lance doesn't know what hard work is. It'll be a disaster.'" She tried to be firm. "I don't think we should do it, Lance," she said. "Well, it's too late," he replied. "I've signed up." Appalled at his thoughtlessness she stormed out, threatening to end their relationship on the spot. After a tense few hours she grudgingly reconsidered, and within a few weeks the family had packed up, piled into their Fiat and headed south. On the way to Otaki Gill desperately hoped the move would save their marriage, yet her growing feeling of despair was becoming harder and harder to ignore.

Otaki was beautiful, a small town of quaint buildings, long golden beaches and endless views of the shimmering Tasman Sea. The family moved into a house opposite Otaki College, the local high school, which had a tiny food shop – a tuck shop, in New Zealand parlance – attached to it. Miranda would be put in charge of the shop during lunchtimes and after school. For her, the family's time in Otaki proved to be a busy, pleasant experience, selling ice creams down by the beach, freely riding her pony around the sun-kissed countryside, and babysitting Perry in the evenings. For the adults, though, it was different matter. After a very brief honeymoon period the fish and chip shop experiment quickly went awry. To nobody's surprise Lance proved to be singularly unsuited for the hard work it needed to turn a profit, and quickly lost interest, handing off most of the day-to-day operations to his overworked wife. His appearance in the area created quite a buzz – Lance even made a brief appearance in *The Dominion*, Wellington's biggest newspaper, pictured poised over a deep frying vat with a familiar grin on his face – but not enough to ever make The Golden Chicken profitable. While Gill did most of the work at the shop Lance often spent his afternoons in a local pub down the road, sinking a few pints before coming back to sip on gin and tonics at the shop counter. Motor racing fans would often make appearances, although many were apparently more impressed by Lance's fancy Eton-inflected accent and his family history than anything he'd done behind the wheel.

For him it was fun. During the day he would socialise with the customers, a gin and tonic never far from his hand, before occasionally disappearing off to local fairs to do some small-time commentary over a PA system. His easy manner did make the shop a popular spot for locals, especially ones who had been given a hard time by the highly unpopular

Continued on page 193

Circa 1954. Macklin leans against his Austin Healey while on his way to Sebring.
(Courtesy Gill Macklin)

Circa late-1950s.
Macklin relaxes
poolside with sister
Mia and brother-
in-law Peter Hodge.
(Courtesy Gill
Macklin)

1964. With John Gordon at Cannes. Macklin is steering with the automatic pilot, one of his inventions, in his hands. (Courtesy Gill Macklin)

Opposite, top: 1963. Ready to head off to the Mediterranean. (Courtesy Gill Macklin)

Opposite, bottom: 1964. Second summer in the Mediterranean on John Gordon's boat. (Courtesy Gill Macklin)

February 1965. Lance and Gill, newly married, stand outside Battersea Registry Office. Sally and Michael Harrison attended as witnesses, along with Jon Pertwee. Much to the registrar's consternation, Pertwee also insisted on signing as a witness. (Courtesy Gill Macklin)

Opposite, top: Circa mid-1960s. Crowded conditions as the family stop over in St Tropez. (Courtesy Gill Macklin)

Opposite, bottom: Circa mid-1960s. Lance and Gill looking dashing on a night out visiting friends. (Courtesy Gill Macklin)

Circa late-1960s. Lance and Gill watch the Oxford-Cambridge boat race.
(Courtesy Gill Macklin)

Opposite, top: Circa mid-1960s. Lance,
Paddy and Miranda with Gill's mother,
Joyce, on a Swiss skiing trip. Macklin
was a fine skiier in his youth.
(Courtesy Gill Macklin)

Opposite, bottom: Circa mid-1960s.
Lance and Gill Macklin in their
Wimbledon flat. (Courtesy Gill Macklin)

1967. A rare shot of Lance and Gill on the beach. (Courtesy Gill Macklin)

Circa mid-1970s. Macklin on his boat. "You may have trouble recognizing The Frigate now," he wrote. "During the last few years I have done a lot of work on it, and it is much more comfortable to live on." (Courtesy Gill Macklin)

former owner. "When Lance came the locals thought he was fantastic," Gill recalled. "They thought he was a hero. The guys used to say 'Can we come in and play the jukebox?' but they didn't buy much. So we told them it was all right, but if customers came in and wanted the tables they'd have to leave, which was always fine. The local youths didn't cause us any trouble, whereas they caused [previous owner] Tomlinson plenty of trouble." Though they loved Lance, often unsuccessfully attempting to convince him to ride on the backs of their motor bikes, they didn't spend much money. Neither did many people. The shop quickly became bogged down, its debts growing larger by the day.

Few people in New Zealand recognised the Macklin name, which came as a great relief to Lance, since such recognition usually led to a conversation about Le Mans. There was, however, the odd exception. Alastair Jones, who had recently moved to Otaki as well, was a classic British sports car fan who had developed a love of Noel Macklin's wonderful Invictas. One Friday night he stopped by the Golden Chicken and discovered it had changed owners. Speaking with Lance, he quickly realised he was talking to Noel's son. Lance was taken aback that someone had picked up the family connection, although he was disappointed when he learned Jones hadn't actually known Noel in person. When Jones excitedly asked if he could swing by for a chat in the future, Lance – "with not a lot of enthusiasm," Jones recalled – reluctantly agreed.

For his next visit Jones wisely decided to turn up in his 3-litre Bentley, a car that brought old memories flooding back for Lance. The latter's initial wariness dropped, and soon the two got along well. Jones later surmised, and probably correctly, that Lance's guardedness stemmed from a fear of being asked about Le Mans. Once he realised Jones was curious about his actual racing exploits, he became a lot more forthcoming.

Despite his relaxed approach to life, Jones thought Lance looked worn out. "My first impressions were of a fellow who had fallen on hard times and had the stuffing knocked out of him," he recalled, years later. "Being quite small in stature and wearing small round spectacles created a mental image far removed of what I would have thought he would have presented." Still, he soon realised he was dealing with a polite, friendly man with an endearing charm. As one of the few people at the time who spoke to Lance about his father, he also saw a glimpse of the effect Noel still had on his son. "(He was) quiet and reserved, and one can't help but wonder whether living in the shadow of such a resourceful, clever father didn't have a dampening effect on him," Jones said. It's a valid point, for in later years Lance would occasionally talk about how he felt that he'd failed to live up to his father's expectations. Noel cast a long shadow, one that his son always felt hanging over him.

— — — — —

It's no wonder Lance looked tired, as his hastily envisioned dream was rapidly turned into a nightmare. As the shop became saddled with increasing amounts of debt Lance's alcohol consumption grew as well. Along with having to deal with her now-boozing husband and a failing business Gill also struggled to look after her newborn son, which was proving especially difficult with her husband constantly absent from any sort of parenting duties. She tried to hang on to what remained of their relationship but the stress eventually became insurmountable. One evening, after a typical hard day at work, she lay in bed and a compelling thought crossed her mind. "Wouldn't life be so easy if it was just Perry and me?" she said to herself. "Wouldn't it be nice to be able to come home at night and sit and watch television?" She hadn't had a night off in months. Finally she decided she'd had enough. In mid-1971 she demanded a divorce.

Realising his error Lance begged her to reconsider, but this time his pleas were falling on deaf ears. It was too late. After a brief exchange of words Gill packed up, grabbed Perry and left for Auckland, while Lance stayed behind in Otaki, heartbroken. They sold the fish and chip shop for a hefty loss while Lance half-heartedly tried to keep things going, installing a deep fryer in the tuck shop in order to sell fish and chips. It didn't last long. Even before his interest flagged, as it undoubtedly would have, local health and safety authorities informed him that he hadn't installed his fryer by the book and that he was in breach of all sorts of regulations. He was forced to tear it out. Finally seeing the writing on the wall he quit altogether, selling the house, taking Miranda and heading on a boat back to England. His New Zealand dream was over.

He later blamed the failure of the fish and chip shop on the building's owner – "that unscrupulous Tomlinson," as he angrily wrote to Gill – but he probably knew deep down that it was primarily his fault. "Lance was a damn fool to even entertain the idea in the first place," Gill later said. "A business like that is hard work, it takes a lot of graft to make it successful, and you also have to know what you're doing. We had no idea at all. We certainly did make mistakes." As for his marriage, even after Gill left and the Otaki débâcle came to a close, Lance still figured that if he went back to England and sorted himself out financially he could rekindle their romance. After everything that had happened, though, that was never going to happen. "As a friend and a lover he was great," Gill remembered, "but as a husband and a provider he was a disaster."

Chapter 21

Years of struggle

Macklin had grown to love his time in New Zealand, and his reluctant return to England in mid-1971 plunged him into a deep depression. He was all alone, Miranda having rejoined her mother before being sent back to boarding school. It was an unpleasant reality check. Without a place to live he went back to his old boat, The Frigate Bird, that had remained moored on the river Thames off Twickenham while he was away. Being back on the boat was a tough experience, filled as it was with memories of happier times with Gill. He was still in love with her. "I hoped that once I got back here and with the passing of a month or two, memories would fade and the sadness would go," he wrote to Gill that August. "It doesn't seem to work out quite like that. Time seems to have the effect of diminishing the memories of unpleasant incidents and accentuating the pleasant ones." He was also jobless and broke, and, although he knew he could probably get another car salesman job fairly easily, he wanted to avoid doing so for as long as possible ("Perish the thought!" he said). His prospects, he found, had also been dented by his angry ex-wife. "Shelagh ... is determined to grind me into the ground," he wrote to Gill. Apparently, in his absence, Shelagh had let her vast array of contacts know about his running off with the children, and the shambles that was the fish and chip shop. He had returned with a shadow hanging over him.

He got back in touch with his old friend Donald Healey, who was in the middle of the fiasco that was the Jensen Healey project. Though it seemed as if everything was going wrong with the car at that point, Healey nevertheless mentioned there was the possibility of some development and marketing work going in a few months' time. Macklin, buoyed by the news, even went so far as to meet with some senior Jensen executives, but, possibly due to a gradual breakdown in the relationship between Healey and Jensen, nothing ever eventuated. In the meantime he struggled by with what little money he had, largely spending his days working on an array of inventions and drinking on his boat. He found out that the fish and chip shop débâcle was continuing back in New Zealand, Gill now facing the wrath of creditors after shutting down the shop. He would send money when the Healey venture got off the ground, he told her, but couldn't do anything until then.

In late 1971 he finally became fed up with his relentless poverty and, at the urging of a friend, went to inquire about a possible sales position at London car dealership HR Owen. It turned out it was looking for someone, and so, within days, he found himself back on the sales floor, suited up and ready to go. Using his charm he sold a Rolls-Royce and a Bentley within a week of joining, immediately getting him in everybody's good books and putting him in line for a promotion to branch manager. Yet, although he was financially off the floor, his life was continuing to spiral downwards. He had few friends, he was still broke, and his only real companion was a rat on his boat that, he grudgingly wrote, chewed through most of his food. Everyone, it seemed, was after him for money: people tied up with the Golden Chicken back in New Zealand; his ex-wife (or wives); various family members; an assortment of banks and even creditors still sorting out the long-ago Electrolyte business mess; and on top of everything, his eyesight was beginning to fail. Life, for the moment, was proving to be a struggle.

His work with HR Owen didn't last long, Macklin's initial excitement at having a job gradually overcome by his dislike of the sales business. Around 1974, after a few years of stability, if not financial prosperity, he quit. Deciding to do something completely different, he became involved in a Spanish property business, handling sales of Spanish villas from London. Like all of Macklin's business adventures it didn't last particularly long, this one falling victim to political and economic circumstance, but it did ignite a spark within him. He fell in love with Spain, and, even though he stuck around England for the time being, he kept a constant eye on the country he'd become so enamoured with.

In the meantime, he spruced up The Frigate Bird and added an extra mast to make it look smart, even if it didn't particularly help its sailing properties. He then chartered it out to people over the summer, bringing in a steady income that just about maintained his Spartan lifestyle. The creditors gradually backed off, his income from the car business and occasional grants from his elderly mother helping him ease his way out of the worst of the financial pressures. Still, money continued to be a never-ending problem, and, in late 1976, he was forced to pick up yet another sales job, this time with Fiat in London. Colleagues from the time remembered him as charming and polite, albeit frequently absent from his desk and – true to form – lacking in any real work ethic. "I kind of got the impression that Lance was there on sufferance," his colleague David Fox later said. He *was* there on sufferance, of course, and his obvious lack of enthusiasm made itself clear to all. The firm's Italian managing director was far from impressed, making it obvious that he didn't appreciate having a slacker working under him. "Ah, Macklin," he'd say, rolling his eyes and shrugging his shoulders. "What," he would ask, "could he do?"

In 1978 the showroom threw a party for the launch of one of its new cars, the Fiat Strada. That night Macklin was in fine form, dressing up tidily in his suit and tie and convincing his old friend Stirling Moss to join the party. It was almost like old times as the two laughed and joked with each other, knocking back glass after glass of complimentary wine and together becoming the life of the party. Afterwards they went out on the town with some of the other Fiat employees and partied away until the wee small hours. It was a throwback to over twenty years before, when they were at their height of their powers and had the world at their feet, when any responsibilities, aside from driving cars quickly, seemed trivial. Moss had gone on to achieve great things in the cockpit, and great wealth out of it. Macklin, on the other hand, had done neither. Back to reality the next morning, his head swimming from the free wine, Macklin couldn't have helped wondering just where he'd gone wrong.

The Strada launch was one of the last things Macklin did while living in London. That same year he moved in with a new girlfriend before selling his beloved yacht to a friend of Paddy's, who promptly took it sailing around the Mediterranean. In September, he – with his new girlfriend in tow – finally gave in to the lure of Spain; stumbling across a little farmhouse for sale outside Alicante, in the south of the country, he decided it was too good an opportunity to pass up. Before 1980 arrived he'd left Fiat, the boat and the UK. His days as a salesman – indeed, as a regular member of the workforce – were over for good.

Chapter 22

Twilight in Spain

The farmhouse wasn't in particularly good condition. Years of neglect had left it semi-dilapidated, its roof partly caving in, and generally in desperate need of a tidy-up. It was pretty, though, and the countryside around it was truly gorgeous. A glance out the front door revealed panoramic views of rolling vineyards and, on clear days, a view to the sparkling Mediterranean. Adding to the appeal was its relative isolation. Over the years, and especially since returning from New Zealand, Macklin had become increasingly disinterested in being around bustling cities and rowdy crowds and the dog-eat-dog lifestyle he felt they embodied. He was also still routinely recognised by motor racing fans, who tormented him by asking about Le Mans. He wanted to get far away, and a farmhouse in the middle of nowhere in Spain seemed the perfect place.

It took about a year for him to get organised enough to leave England after buying the farmhouse, but as soon as he did he went straight to work. Ever inventive, his attention had been captured by the energy crisis of the late 1970s, and he was determined to rebuild the house and make it as ecologically sustainable as he could, which he did by setting up solar panels and wind generators. He also got to work building a completely separate house at the bottom of the property, a Californian-style bungalow that he built into the side of a hill. It was completely self-sustaining, a triumph of engineering that he would later move into and live in for most of the rest of his life. Relatively basic, it consisted of one main room with a little kitchen off to the side and a small shower tucked away around a corner. He spent his days busily tinkering away on both the bungalow and the farmhouse, happily indulging his inventive streak.

The local wine also proved to be exceptionally cheap, and he would often spend long afternoons drinking himself into a stupor. Whether he ever became a full-blown alcoholic is debatable – his daughter, for one, thinks he was more a dipsomaniac than anything else – but he was certainly hooked by the bottle to at least some degree by this stage of his life. It was quite a change from when he was younger, him and Moss chatting-up women over glasses of Coke. Somewhere along the line, either during his breakup from Shelagh or after Le Mans, he developed a drinking habit that never entirely went away. His Spanish life of solitude only saw it grow worse.

In March 1980, Leslie Macklin died. It was, her son said, a "merciful release." She had been ill for a long time, and Lance and Nada had been paying £170 per week for her hospital care, putting considerable financial strain on both of them. Additionally, upon examining the finances they were mortified to discover that she had ended up broke. Leslie had never worked, yet had spent money as if she was a millionaire, blowing huge amounts on extravagances like exotic rugs, high class hotels, and servants. Now, after years of flinging money around, there was nothing left. If her son had been hoping for at least some financial benefit he was to be sorely disappointed.

In early January 1981 Gill came to visit, with the now ten-year-old Perry in tow. It was the first time Lance and Perry would properly meet, although they'd occasionally conversed by letter, and they were both slightly nervous. Luckily for Lance, Gill had proved to be as understanding and tolerant outside the marriage as she was inside it, not holding the trouble her ex-husband had caused against him. "My mother never spoke down about him," Perry said. "She never said a bad word about him, so I always looked up to him as a kid, I guess." When the three met at Lance's place in Alicante there was initially a bit of awkwardness. "It was a little bit overwhelming for just a few minutes," Perry recalled. "Here was this guy who I knew was my father, but what do you say as a ten-year-old kid to somebody you don't really know?" Soon, though, they warmed to each other and settled in, Gill and Perry spending a week at the farmhouse and revelling in the fresh Spanish air. The visitors could tell there wasn't much money about, but he seemed happy nonetheless. "It was a pretty simple existence," Perry said, "but he was happy there. He was very kind, a real gentleman."

Perry later went on to inherit many of Lance's skills – as well as his physical features – and, just like his father, became a highly talented skier. Ten years after their first meeting Perry was again back in Europe, this time as part of the New Zealand ski team for a European skiing championship. During a break in the competition he hopped on a train to Alicante to go see his father. He was nearly broke, only having enough money for the train ticket, a bag of oranges, a jar of Nutella and a loaf of bread, although his father promised he'd have some money ready when he arrived at the house in Alicante. After struggling to make his way there – he was nearly kicked off his bus on the way to the farmhouse for not having a ticket, only being saved by a sympathetic local who paid for him – Perry arrived to find Lance even more broke than he was. Nevertheless, the two spent a pleasant week together, spending their evenings talking about skiing and motor cycling (which Lance, incidentally, thought a terrible idea), Lance spinning tales from his long-ago racing days. Perry later became an airline pilot, leading an organised life in complete contrast to Lance's own rambling existence.

Although the two only met a few times Lance was always quietly proud of his son, often inquiring after him in letters to Gill, and sending little pieces of fatherly advice. "Don't worry, Perry, about your size (sic)," a typical letter went. "You will probably end up about my build, which is ideal for motor racing, pot-holing, in fact just about everything except basketball, but who wants to play basketball?" He was chuffed when Perry was admitted into the prestigious Dilworth School in Auckland, advising his son to study hard and make the most of such a fantastic opportunity. His advice was always pragmatic and sensible, qualities that Lance himself hadn't been particularly noted for. It was a classic case of do as I say, not as I do.

1981 turned out to be a rough year. Things started off badly when he came down with a severe infection in his right eye, forcing him to spend a week in hospital and nearly robbing him of his sight. It wasn't the first time he'd had problems with his eyes, for he had already been battling glaucoma for several years. Late the previous year, Paddy had even sent him a bag filled with marijuana seeds with a note saying that smoking marijuana would help with his eye problems. "In the USA they have proved that POT is good for glaucoma, so he thought that I should get on it!" a bemused Lance wrote to Gill. Still, it took him months to recover from his eye infection, and even longer before his vision returned to normal.

Then, just before Christmas, he endured the most traumatic experience he'd had in years. Carolyn Foot, an old friend from England, had made a rare appearance at the farmhouse. One night after dinner she'd gone upstairs while Macklin set to work on the dishes. He was in the middle of scraping off a pot when he heard a tremendous crash behind him. Spinning around, his eyes immediately rested on his friend lying on the floor at the foot of the stairs, not moving, and with a steady stream of blood beginning to trickle out of her ears and mouth. His mind raced as he rushed over and laid her on her side, relieved to find that she, at least, still had a faint heartbeat. Sprinting out the door, he jumped in his car and headed to the local doctor's house. Finding nobody at home, he then floored it to his neighbour's house where he called an ambulance. Medics soon turned up at his house and, finding Foot in critical condition, rushed her to the nearest hospital.

Her condition turned out to be so bad that the hospital couldn't give her the care she needed, and so, within minutes she was in yet another ambulance – with Macklin, who was fighting off the cold wearing only a thin cotton shirt, holding her IV drip in place – on the way to Valencia. The trip took two and a half hours, the whole time Macklin watching the life ebb out of his old friend. Only three hours earlier they'd been sitting together, laughing and drinking in front of the fireplace in his home, and now she was lying prone in front of him, fighting for her life. Arriving in Valencia, she went straight into an intensive care unit where she finally stabilised. She had fractured her skull, and although she would make it through the night she would never fully recover, spending the rest of her life in a semi-vegetative state. Macklin was distraught.

The years slowly ticked by as he sank further and further into isolation, his solitary existence occasionally punctuated by the odd outside event that caught his attention. Paddy and Miranda were now fully grown. Miranda had married into a wealthy family and led a busy social life, one that allowed her to fulfil her love of riding horses that she'd first developed back in New Zealand. Paddy was leading a much more bohemian existence – consisting of travelling, communal living, plenty of music festivals and, occasionally, drugs – although he eventually cleaned up and bought himself a tidy little Folkboat, announcing to his father that he intended to sail the small yacht single-handedly around the world. "Of course, he is quite mad," Lance wrote to Gill with an almost perceptible shake of the head, "although as his father I am the one person who cannot tell him so."

In 1981 he broke up with the girlfriend he'd brought with him to

Spain, buying-up her share in the farmhouse and leaving him even more broke than usual. It wasn't a huge change. By this stage he was quite used to having no money.

He spent his days tinkering around the house, his mind occupied by working on one project or another. He gained a much-needed income stream by moving into his now-renovated bungalow, and renting out the main house to a young Spanish couple. Paddy visited occasionally, and was surprised to find his father had taken a keen interest in deep philosophy, particularly the Russian philosopher/spiritual teacher George Gurdjieff. "I had a big connection with him over Gurdjieff, there's no doubt about that," Paddy said. "We talked to each other in a different way once we found out about that. He was into him all his life, although he later came back to him after reading him at Eton, which I was astounded by. He was only 16, and by that stage the books weren't even that old." Lance also fell in love with Richard Dawkins' 1986 book *The Blind Watchmaker* and its argument for natural selection. "He was quite anti-conventional religion," Paddy said. "He saw religion as the source of trouble." When Paddy came to visit, the two would stay up talking late into the night, not about motor racing but about philosophy.

The two also bonded over sailing. When Paddy had bought his Folkboat, Lance, who was living on The Frigate Bird in Twickenham at the time, had come on-board for a few short trips up and down the English coast. On one of the trips Lance, who had a lifelong disdain for smoking, riled Paddy by making his son go into the boat's cramped cockpit to light up a cigarette. "We'd come back from the pub half-pissed," Paddy recalled, "and I lit up (a smoke). He asked me to not to, so I said 'Dad, it's my boat, I can smoke if I want to,' but he said 'No, I don't like it, go smoke in the cockpit.' Which I did actually, the old sod."

Lance had been an excellent sailor in his youth, of course, and his technical know-how proved invaluable for his son. "We stayed more and more in touch when I started sailing," Paddy said. "That was a complete bond between us. Because we grew up on his yacht we knew about the basics of being on boats, so that was sort of inside us. We knew how to tie knots behind our backs at night with our eyes closed. He taught us all that. He really was a phenomenal seaman." In 1988, Lance was ecstatic when Paddy made his first solo crossing of the Atlantic in his tiny Folkboat. He later revealed to his son that, before he'd left for New Zealand, he had put a deposit down on a Folkboat of his own, intent on sailing his young family all the way down to the bottom of the world. Fortunately for all concerned, his plan fell through. "God, it would have been cramped," Paddy said. "You can barely even get four on a Folkboat. Bloody hell." Still, the far-fetched idea showed how much he loved to sail, as well as his undying love of the ocean. "He was always fascinated by long distance sailors," Paddy said. "He had a yearning to do it himself." Lance never would, but Paddy, years later, would fulfil his father's ambition in a big way.

– – – – –

In 1986 tragedy struck again, this time in an even more traumatic way than Carolyn Foot's accident a few years earlier. Though Macklin was living a hermit-like existence he still, even in his late '60s, managed to have an active love life. At some point he'd fallen in love with a Frenchwoman called Christiane, who was about 15 years his junior and lived in Paris. They didn't see each other too often, due, presumably, to the distance factor and Macklin's lack of funds, and during one of their spells apart he was upset to learn that she'd developed cancer. He drove up to Paris to see her, and received a huge shock. "She was a young and healthy 50-year-old," he wrote, "but all of a sudden she was a pathetic little ... bald headed old lady." She had completely changed since he'd last seen her three months earlier, her recently-healthy body now ravaged by cancer. Though she was undergoing constant chemotherapy treatment her doctors gave her a month off, upon which she jumped in Macklin's car and took off to her small house on the coast of Brittany to spend what little time she had left together. There, looking out over the shimmering, deep blue water they spent every moment at each other's side, Macklin accompanying his ailing girlfriend in her garden as she planted shrubs she knew she would never see grow.

One morning Macklin was in the kitchen making coffee when Christiane slowly shuffled in. He asked her how she felt. "Terrible," she replied, before promptly passing out. Macklin rushed over and grabbed her just before she hit the floor, gently lowering her down before calling her sister and asking for advice. He then called an ambulance which rushed her, with Macklin at her side, to hospital in Paris. He stayed by her bedside throughout the night and into the next day, only leaving at 6pm when Christiane's sister arrived to take over. Exhausted, he wearily headed back to a flat Christiane owned in Paris, which, he sadly noticed, suddenly felt very empty. Sometime around midnight he was woken up by the phone ringing. It turned out to be Christiane's son calling from the United States to see if there had been any updates. Macklin replied there hadn't been and hung up, only for the phone to ring again five minutes later. This time it was his girlfriend's sister. Christiane, she said between tears, had died twenty minutes earlier. "It must be many years since I shed a tear," he wrote soon afterwards. "In fact I always reckoned that nothing could make me cry, but on this occasion I wept like a child." He was devastated. Though he was invited to the funeral he politely declined to go, excusing himself by saying he had an eye appointment that day down in Alicante. It's hard not to think that, really, it may have simply been too much for him to bear.

Christiane's death made him reflective. Not long after the traumatic experience he wrote in a letter that he'd come to regret his lifetime of womanising. "I think that in life we have to accept the fact that 'nobody' is perfect, but at least if we find someone with whom we are able to be happy with, then it is better to abide with them rather than going on indefinitely hoping to find some new adventure," he wrote, sadly.

– – – – –

In 1989 Macklin turned 70, which, to him, came as something of a surprise. Not only had he made it through the war and a hideously dangerous racing career, but he was now far and away the longest-living male Macklin of the 20th century. The others generally hadn't made it past 50. His celebrations were tempered by the disappointing discovery that his pension wasn't going to be as much as he had hoped, due to a flippant decision he'd made as a young man nearly 50 years earlier. Back at the peak of the war in 1941, he'd opted out of contributing to his pension for an additional five shillings a week. It had made sense at the time – with his friends dropping off left and right he had no great hope that he'd even survive a few more months, let alone until the age of 65 – but his youthful short-sightedness came back to sting him when it was time to pick up the pension further down the track. His eye still caused him trouble, and his overall health was beginning to fail, which was no great surprise given his age and the total lack of care he'd taken of himself. On the bright side, though, he'd managed to pick up another girlfriend who lived just down the road, a typically younger woman who he spent much of his time with. She lived in a villa, and, as much as he loved his little bungalow, he often abandoned it for his girlfriend's place, stretching out on a soft, comfortable couch and spending his days glued to motor racing on TV. Though he hadn't followed Formula One racing particularly closely for years, his love for the sport remained.

As well as tinkering with his inventions he occasionally found other ways to keep himself busy, even turning his hand to writing and knocking out a brief family history that mainly focused – admiringly – on his father. His financial situation remained less-than ideal, despite renting out the farmhouse and his Spartan living style. He'd been hoping to hold onto the house in order to pass it on to his children, but a debilitating lack of money forced him to sell. Cleverly, he negotiated terms allowing him to continue living in the bungalow at the foot of the property. Feeling lonely, he acquired a dog to keep him company. "I remember when I was young my parents always used to complain (quite rightly) that I treated the house as a hotel, just coming in to sleep and for meals" he wrote. "Well 'Changy,' that's his name, behaves just like that." This time it was his turn to be the disapproving parent, even if it was only to a dog.

The children visited from time to time, including Perry, who visited Lance for the second time. "I think, after talking to him about it, that he is going through the same problems that I went through when I was trying to get into the Olympic Games in 1948," Lance wrote after Perry's visit. He had all the skill of the top skiers, he added, but his small stature and physique had proved to be a stumbling block, useful in cars and horses but not so much on the slopes. "The endurance just wasn't there for a top downhill race," Lance wrote. "By half way my legs felt like jelly."

Chapter 23

"Nobody would be interested in that"

By the late 1990s, the decline in Macklin's health had accelerated considerably. He was no longer as active, although he did still make the occasional trip to the UK and France to see old friends and family, people he always kept touch with via letter. Back home in Alicante he had begun to receive a steady stream of fan mail, which he found bewildering. "[It is] mostly due to the fact that the time I was driving is now history and people seem interested in those 'golden years,'" he wrote. "It is a little bit tiresome but I suppose I shouldn't complain." Signed pictures of him would later appear for sale for tidy sums of money – often a couple of hundred pounds a photo – which he could have done with later in his life, although he apparently never had the idea of signing and selling pictures himself. "He wasn't money motivated at all," Paddy said. "He was always broke. He was empathetic, egalitarian and generous to a fault, hence he never had any money. But it just didn't bother him."

His mental facilities began deteriorating quickly, making him less and less able to take care of himself. The final straw came 1997, when Miranda turned up to the bungalow and found him no longer able to effectively fend for himself. She brought him back to England to stay with relatives, at first with Sally and Michael Harrison for a while in their home outside Canterbury. There he would spend hours sitting in front of the radio listening to the BBC, suffering from delusions as he continued to decline. "Why are they talking about me on the radio?" he would ask his confused hosts, before ringing up the station and questioning a hapless station attendant on the other end of the line. He thought they were talking about Le Mans.

At this stage in his life, his mind rapidly going, nearly the only thing that remained was the memory of his terrible accident nearly 50 years earlier. In his last interview, given to motoring journalist Martin Buckley in 2002, he appears confused and lost in another world until asked about his role in the aftermath of the Albert Camus Facel Vega crash. Hearing the word 'crash,' his mind suddenly flips back on. "Are you talking," he asks, mistakenly, "about Le Mans?" Throughout his life he may have avoided talking about that dark Saturday in 1955 but the memory was always there, buried away in the deepest recesses of his mind, right up until the very end.

At one point he rebelled against his family and insisted on heading back to Spain. They eventually gave in, but his excursion didn't last very long, as he quickly found he couldn't look after himself. He soon returned to England. He moved in with Miranda, then, after a while, was put in a rest home in the quaint town of Tenterden, in Kent. He no longer knew where he was. When he first moved in he wasn't happy, barricading himself in his room and flinging his clothes out the window in what was almost a psychotic episode, but he soon began to calm down and quickly fell in love with the place. Though it could easily have been a sad situation, at this late stage in his life it wasn't. He was under the illusion he was living in a hotel – perhaps, in his mind, the George V – and he would spend his days sitting in his chair while watching friends and acquaintances from the distant past wander around. His life was a constant trip back in time. The staff adored him, too, for his exceptional, Eton-taught manners always remained, and he insisted on standing when women walked into the room, and politely walked them out when they left. His memory may have disappeared, but he never lost his charm.

On August 29, 2002, just four days before his 83rd birthday, Lance Macklin died peacefully in his sleep. He left behind few material goods and almost no money, having lived his last 15 or so years as a pauper. Letters of condolence flooded in for his family, and he was remembered throughout the motorsport community as one of the nearly-men of British motorsport. Of course, most of the obituaries focused on Le Mans, which he would have hated. "It used to quite upset him that people never wanted to talk about other things he'd done in his life," Miranda said. "They only wanted to talk about Le Mans. I think that was a really big sorrow in his life, that he became famous because of that, or, rather, that's what he became renowned for." "He was completely un-egotistical," Paddy said. "He didn't like being recognised, he put up with it rather than enjoyed it. He was the antithesis of the fame culture, the complete opposite." In later years Miranda would occasionally try to convince her father to write an autobiography, like so many other drivers from the period – often with far less interesting life stories – did. "Oh," he'd say, dismissively. "Nobody would be interested in that."

Epilogue

On February 6, 2011, Paddy Macklin, wind-whipped and exhausted, hauled his battered yacht Tessa around Cape Horn. That morning he'd been woken by falling out of his bunk, a huge wave breaking over the boat and nearly tipping it on its side. It was a state of affairs he'd become used to as he tried to become the first person to single-handedly circumnavigate the world non-stop in a 27-foot boat, just like he'd told his father he would do all those years earlier. A stop in New Zealand had dashed the non-stop aspect but he continued on, ploughing through the huge, black Southern Ocean during the darkest depths of winter. He'd become the adventurer he'd always said he would. His father would have been amazed.

That morning, after he'd rounded the Horn, he went below deck to grab something he'd carried all the way from England. He came back on deck with a small jar of his father's ashes, a jar he'd kept for years waiting for this very moment. Both he and his sister, laughing, later said that Lance would have preferred to be scattered in the warm, calm equatorial waters rather than the writhing, freezing mass of the Atlantic, but there was a good reason for this particular place. Paddy wanted to do it in honour of his father's Second World War excursions in the Atlantic, of the long nights on the MGBs and MTBs that he never talked about. He was always at home on the sea, and this, Paddy felt, was where at least part of him belonged.

He opened the jar and went to scatter the ashes, only to find that weeks of life at sea had solidified them. It didn't matter. He held his father's ashes one last time, before kissing the top of the jar and saying, quietly, "Bless you, dad." Paddy threw the jar over the side and watched as it hit the water with a small splash. It bobbed slowly through the green, choppy Atlantic water, heading gradually away from the yacht and growing smaller and smaller until it was nothing more than a tiny speck on the long, grey Atlantic horizon.

Also from Veloce Publishing –

A unique collection of rare original colour photographs of Grand Prix and sports cars, taken between 1954 and 1959 at races and hillclimbs in England & Ireland.

Now available as a paperback, this book is an absolute must for Revivalists and all lovers of classic motorsport.

ISBN: 978-1-787112-49-0
Paperback · 22.5x22.5cm · 160 pages
· 200 pictures

A defining era in motorsport is documented in words and intimate photographs, both black and white and colour, from the mid-1950s through the 1960s, when motor racing was still accessible to all, and the 1970s when overt sponsorship and television changed the sport for ever.

ISBN: 978-1-787115-23-1
Paperback · 22.5x22.5cm · 208 pages
· 300 pictures

Also from Veloce Publishing –

The biography of a larger-than-life character in the world of motoring, especially among classic car collectors. David Scott-Moncrieff, aka 'Bunty,' claimed to be the Number 1 in the Rolls-Royce second-hand car trade. He was a colourful personality, an experienced car expert, a charming entertainer and a passionate vintage race car addict.

ISBN: 978-1-787113-48-0
Paperback · 21x14.8cm · 216 pages · 81 pictures

For more information and price details, visit our website at www.veloce.co.uk · email: info@veloce.co.uk · Tel: +44(0)1305 260068

The Official Biography
of **John Chatham**

'Mr Big Healey'

Norman Burr: Foreword by Simon Taylor

Now in Paperback! The authorised biography of one of the best-liked bad boys in British motorsport, John Chatham – driver, racer, repairer, rebuilder, tuner, trader and lover of Austin-Healeys. With 150 photographs, many previously unpublished, this is an important and entertaining account of one of motorsport's biggest characters.

ISBN: 978-1-787115-35-4
Paperback • 25x20.7cm • 160 pages • 150 pictures

*For more information and price details, visit our website at www.veloce.co.uk
• email: info@veloce.co.uk • Tel: +44(0)1305 260068*

Index